This engagingly written book does just what it promises: It gets you to think, and think more carefully, about the practical decisions in your life.

Virginia Postrel
Author of *The Substance of Style* and *The Future and Its Enemies*

If you think economics is only for bookworms and whiz kids, think again. As Henderson and Hooper show, with story after colorful story, economic reasoning can help you understand everyday life—and improve the quality of your own life as well.

James C. Miller III
Chairman, CapAnalysis Group
Former Director, Office of Management and Budget

David Henderson and Charley Hooper help the reader understand the power of decision analysis techniques through the use of practical examples—translating theory into practices we can employ in our daily lives. Unlike many business books that state a single concept and beat it to death, *Making Great Decisions* builds one useful tool on top of another. The result: a uniquely entertaining and informative experience for the reader.

Gayle Mills
Senior Vice President, Business Development
Abgenix, Inc.

What could be more relevant to our humanity than learning to think more effectively? Henderson and Hooper take you on a delightful tour, showing how you can make better decisions. This book introduces readers to the sophisticated field of decision analysis used by savvy business people for years, but without the obstacle of heavy mathematics.

Sam W. Tagart, Jr.
Retired, Project Manager
Electric Power Research Institute

Henderson and Hooper not only explain decision making and risk management clearly, but also connect it with everyday life. *Making Great Decisions* is a mix of insights and controversy that will guarantee interesting reading.

Dan Spiegelman
Senior Vice President, Chief Financial Officer
CV Therapeutics, Inc.

Making Great Decisions in Business and Life

Making Great Decisions in Business and Life

David R. Henderson
Charles L. Hooper

Chicago Park, California
www.ChicagoParkPress.com

First edition. Second printing.

This book is printed on acid-free paper.

Published by Chicago Park Press
P.O. Box 542, Chicago Park, California 95712
www.ChicagoParkPress.com

Library of Congress Control Number: 2005903574
ISBN 0-9768541-0-4

To Rena and Lisa

CONTENTS

Chapter 1

THINKING WORKS

*I think there is only one quality worse than
hardness of heart, and that is softness of head.*
— Theodore Roosevelt

The Case of the Stanford Limousine

My (Charles') brother Douglas Hooper has photographed
hundreds of weddings in the San Francisco Bay Area. One of them
was at Stanford's Faculty Club in the summer of 1999. The
ceremony was complete and the reception was progressing nicely.
The mariachi band had gotten everyone in a celebratory mood,
and the disk jockey took charge of the dance music. The wedding
couple's 225 guests were enjoying themselves, lost in
conversation, food, and drink at this upscale, prestigious
university restaurant. Douglas was preparing to photograph the
remaining elements of the reception—the cake cutting, bouquet
throwing, and garter toss—when the wedding couple, looking
harried, approached him. They explained that they had to leave at
precisely 5:00 PM, a time that was quickly approaching. And leave
they did.

The mystery of their sudden departure was soon revealed. They had left at precisely 5:00 to avoid paying their limousine driver's customary fine of one dollar a minute for tardy passengers.

Think about it. After planning for a year, inviting hundreds of people, and spending many thousands of dollars, the happy couple cut short the event they will remember their whole lives to avoid paying a fine of $1 a minute.

Let's put that dollar-a-minute into perspective. Assume that, on average, the 225 attendees spent $200 for clothing, travel, gifts, and lodging—a total of $45,000. Assume, also, that the bride and groom spent $30,000 (probably more) for rental of the Stanford Faculty Club, food, drinks, music, and everything else. Then the total cost of the wedding was $75,000. Including the ceremony, the event lasted just over five hours, for a cost of $15,000 per hour. Had the bride and groom stayed the extra hour, from 5:00 to 6:00, the cost would have been an additional $60, or one two hundred and fiftieth $(1/250^{th})$ as much. Even ignoring what everyone else spent, the additional $60 would have been only one one hundredth $(1/100^{th})$ as much per hour as what the bride and groom had already spent. What were they thinking?! Perhaps they *weren't* thinking.

If they had stopped to consider the situation differently—if someone had asked them if they would like to extend their party for a mere $60—no doubt they would have happily agreed. They could have even passed around a hat and collected 27 cents from each guest. If their wedding guests were typical, the newlyweds would have been fighting off uncles and aunts shoving fistfuls of money at them and demanding to pay the whole amount.

Our central theme is that a little clear thinking goes a long way. This book will help you make great decisions in your business and in your life. In most of the situations you'll ever face, whether in your personal or business life, if you use some basic tools to clear your head, you'll do better than if you don't. This book is your toolbox.

What motivated us to write this book is that, over the years, both of us have regularly come across people in organizations—often bright people with MBAs or other graduate degrees—who don't think they have the time, energy, or skills to make good decisions. They have many clues but don't know how to put them together. They regularly face situations that they could analyze with some of the tools they learned in their courses, but they don't realize that. We don't hold ourselves apart from this group. See David's story in the box below.

DUH!

As a 26-year-old assistant professor at the University of Rochester's Graduate School of Management (now the Simon School), I (David) was telling a student about an apartment complex in Los Angeles whose rents were way too low. The absentee property owners, a group of doctors in Philadelphia, weren't paying attention. Some UCLA graduate school friends and I were thinking of making them an offer, I said, but we didn't know how much it was worth. "Why don't you figure it out?" asked Mark Zachmann, the Ph.D. student. "I have no idea how to do that," I answered. "Yes, you do," he replied. "You figure out the stream of net income, use a reasonable interest rate, and compute the present value." "Oh, yeah," I said sheepishly, suddenly realizing that the economics Jack Hirshleifer had taught me at UCLA had a very practical component.

To succeed in business, or in any organization, you need a range of skills: political skills, language skills, knowledge of how to dress, and knowledge of your industry, just to name a few. This is what you need to keep the train moving, so to speak.

However, a large part of running or working in a business is not simply keeping the train on the track; sometimes you need to switch to a new track or turn the train around. Momentum alone might keep your train moving, but changes in direction require explicit decision-making. Whether you're in computers, cars, or non-profits, you face many decisions. And good decisions require good thinking.

3

So what does it mean to make a decision? The ultimate goal when you think is to have clear understanding that leads to action. Understanding for the sake of understanding is great. But this book is about **understanding that allows you to solve a particular problem.** While understanding for education is the source of much of our learning, the danger in it is the lack of a clear endpoint or goal. That may be fine while you're a college student and can take the time for protracted inquiry. But when you're a business executive, you face immediate problems and waiting isn't an option. **You want to do just the right amount and right kind of analysis to quickly achieve the understanding you need to make a decision.**

MESSY PROBLEMS

Many subjects in school are presented with a clear problem and a clear answer. In trigonometry class, we knew the solution was trigonometric, while in algebra the solution was algebraic. This approach didn't give many of us skills at framing messy problems. Our abilities broke down when the problem wasn't clear, had significant complexity or uncertainty, or just was too squishy. Once in the "real world," if we couldn't solve a problem analytically, perhaps we'd resort to judgment out of desperation. Judgment and analysis were thus seen as different or opposite ways to solve problems, not as complementary parts of a complete solution. When we solve problems in real life, we need to figure out which tools apply to the problem. And that's something that few of our college or graduate school courses have taught us. It's one of the main skills this book teaches.

The tools we offer are taken from three areas: economics, decision science, and common sense. We have found that our respective disciplines—economics for David and economics and decision science for Charles—are full of incredible insights. But here's the problem: in both disciplines, few of those insights are communicated effectively and, therefore, don't make it into the "real world." In both, the key bottom lines are hidden in complicated graphs and even more complicated mathematical proofs that the virtuosos typically celebrate at the expense of what they proved. Nevertheless, the insights and core ideas are there— they just have to be teased out.

Both of us are passionate about communicating the core ideas from our disciplines because we both have witnessed the power of those ideas in running our businesses and helping us live our lives. But economics and decision science are not enough. That leads us to the third discipline: common sense—which, by the way, is not all that common. We've found that many things get in the way of common sense. In this book, we have melded the most important insights from economics, decision science, and common sense—insights that, once you understand them, will enhance the quality of your decisions. Follow them consistently, and, as a bonus, you can improve your friendships and other relationships.

Here, in a nutshell, are the insights:

⇨ Use powerful techniques to help think clearly (Chapter 2)
⇨ Think about what is really valuable to you (Chapter 3)
⇨ For something to change, something else must have changed. Ask what changed. (Chapter 4)
⇨ Know what you want before you choose (Chapter 5)
⇨ Watch out for biases—and we all have them (Chapter 6)
⇨ Realize what's important (Chapter 7)
⇨ Think about what is available to you, and then create better alternatives (Chapter 8)
⇨ Consciously choose the best alternative (Chapter 9)
⇨ Accept risk and learn how to take account of it (Chapter 10)
⇨ Exploit life's inequalities, and in doing so, learn to appreciate non-linearity, balance, and proportionality (Chapter 11)
⇨ Get the right amount of information for any situation by first determining the value of information (Chapter 12)
⇨ Think simple (Chapter 13)
⇨ Discover arbitrage opportunities—shifting resources from uses that are less valuable to those that are more valuable—that help yourself and others, too (Chapter 14)
⇨ Do the right thing (Chapter 15)

Back to our penny-pinching newlyweds. What should they have done? They should have considered other alternatives (Chapter 8), and they should have looked at what was really important (Chapter 7). Here are several more stories to give you a feel for how to apply these insights to everyday decisions.

Ronnie Lott's Finger

Ronnie Lott was a fearsome hall-of-fame safety for the champion San Francisco 49ers football team. In the December 22, 1985 game, as Lott tried to tackle the Dallas Cowboys' powerful running back, Timmy Newsome, something went terribly wrong. Lott's finger caught on his chest, allowing Newsome's helmet to smash it awkwardly. "My chest acted like an anvil upon impact, and my pinkie splattered onto my jersey. All I saw was blood and a mashed finger."[1]

Later, the extent of the injury became evident: part of the bone was missing and the painful wound refused to heal. "The bone at the tip of the finger and the bone at the first joint would not fuse in the area of the nail bed. Clearly I couldn't play football with my pinkie in this shape," explained Lott.

Lott and his doctor, Dr. Vincent Pellegrini, discussed his options. First, there was retirement. The second possibility was waiting and hoping—something that had not worked yet. A third alternative was to remove some bone from Lott's wrist and graft it into his finger with the help of a pin, but the problem was that it would take a long time to heal and could easily break again. None of the options looked good.

Dr. Pellegrini explored one last, radical, seemingly barbaric alternative: they could amputate the end of the finger. Although it was not an easy decision, Lott decided to do the unthinkable. "Practically speaking, amputation was the only way I could be sure of playing in the 1986 season, and every other season after that, without the finger bothering me."

The surgery was a success, and, while embarrassed by his shortened finger, Lott lengthened his celebrated professional football career by nine years. Lott and Dr. Pellegrini explored all available alternatives to select the one that best met Lott's objectives and values. We discuss alternatives further in Chapter 8.

Saving My Father's Life

In 1988, my (DRH's) cousin Doug called from Canada to tell me that my father was in the hospital. Doug's tone made me wonder if he was telling me something in code, but I couldn't figure out what. I then called the doctor, who told me that my father had taken an overdose of sleeping pills. He didn't say whether it had been accidental or deliberate, but something made me think it was deliberate. So I asked him directly if my father had tried to commit suicide. After beating around the bush for a while, the doctor admitted that he had. My next call was to buy a plane ticket to go see my father.

On the way to Winnipeg, I had time to collect my thoughts and, I realized, I didn't know *why* he had tried to commit suicide. I had spoken to him on the phone less than two weeks earlier, and he had seemed to be doing well, or at least doing as well as he ever did. What had changed? Why had he suddenly made a decision so at odds with what I had thought to be true about his psyche? I realized that *that* is what I needed to understand. Simply understanding why my father had tried to kill himself would be a good starting goal and, in fact, would be a necessary achievement if I wanted to tackle the more ambitious goal of talking him out of it.

When I asked my father why he had tried to kill himself, he told me that he had some pains in his leg that wouldn't go away and that he was miserable. He was a very active man—aged 78 at the time—and he still rode his bicycle 20 to 30 miles in a day. With physical activity like that no longer possible, he would understandably get much less pleasure out of life. I asked my father whether he would want to kill himself if he knew that a surgery could fix the pain in his legs. "Of course not," he answered, "but what assurance do I have that the pain will go away?" "I don't know," I answered, "but *that* is the question we need to get answered."

So I talked to the doctor and learned that there was a good chance that surgery could improve his condition. "Good," I answered, "then let's get that done." But there was a problem. My father's condition was not serious enough to put him at the front of the queue, and in Canada's socialized medicine system, there was always a queue. Given my father's age and the "non-seriousness" of his condition, he might well wait months or years for his surgery.

Even this piece of information was news to my father. He had not even asked the doctor if there was such a surgery available, but had simply assumed that there wasn't. Just the prospect of being able to get surgery, even if it meant waiting months, lightened my father's attitude. But not that much. Once he started thinking about it, he decided he was unwilling to bear months of pain while waiting.

But I realized that we could do better. There was no need to wait months when we could pay for the surgery across the border in Grand Forks or Fargo.

"But wouldn't it be expensive?" he asked. I answered that it would, that I could imagine it costing $20,000 in 1988 dollars. But I pointed out that his house was paid for, that he had over $50,000 in savings, and that his various pensions in total exceeded his annual expenditures. "But I want to leave you and April [my sister] something in my will," he answered. "You'll still be able to leave us something. It'll just be less," I answered. "Besides, I would rather give up my 50-percent share to have you live a few more years."

My father was convinced. However, he, like most of us humans, had trouble with new thoughts, however clear, that challenged his previous conclusions. When I came back to the hospital after lunch, he had backslid. So we went through the reasoning again, and he got it. Then when I came to visit him after dinner Saturday evening, he had backslid but not as much. Then Sunday morning, he backslid even less. By Sunday afternoon, he haltingly laid out the logical sequence to me: "I'll see if I can get the surgery quickly. If not, you can come up in the next week or two and take me down to Fargo for surgery. And I can afford it." After dinner, he laid it out beautifully, with no hesitation. Sunday evening, when I drove into Winnipeg to stay at a hotel before leaving for Monterey early the next morning, I felt incredibly satisfied and proud of myself. I had gone there with a less ambitious goal—understanding why my father had done what he had done—and had left there achieving a much more ambitious goal—giving my father a clear way of thinking about how to preserve his future. That evening I went to see the movie "Stand and Deliver," about the dedicated school teacher who teaches calculus to inner-city students. It was a wonderful movie to see after having taught my father, a master math teacher, something about looking for new solutions and creating better alternatives, a subject that is explored more in Chapter 8. The other techniques I used were asking what changed—the pain in his legs (see Chapter 4), and thinking about what was really valuable (Chapter 3). [In case you're wondering, the next week his leg got worse, putting him at the top of the list, and he got the surgery in Canada. He lived another 9 years and our relationship was much closer after that. He died of natural causes at age 87.]

The Case of the Corporate Printers

Turn now to a successful biotechnology company. Because the company had bought an unplanned proliferation of brands and models of computer printers, it established a task force to narrow the number and establish some standards. The dozen-person task force met over many months until an agreement was reached.

Separately, a manager from the same company analyzed a major licensing deal for a $100-million-a-year product. After a few hours of analysis, he ran off to present his findings to the top management committee. The committee members reached an agreement and the product was licensed.

The printer task force spent more than ten times the hours as the management committee on licensing. Adjusting for the differences in costs between the two classes of employees, pricey senior management versus cheaper information technology analysts, the printer analysis still cost the company significantly more than the licensing analysis. Given the level of investment, you would conclude that the printer decision was more important to this company, wouldn't you? Yet, in fact, the printer decision was less than one hundredth as important.

The amount of analysis put toward a problem should be proportional to the importance of the problem. This company had not learned the *One-Percent Rule*, which we explain in Chapter 12.

The Expensive $65 Muffler

There's no product that can't be made cheaper by some manufacturer. Those people who buy based only on price are his victims. — Anonymous

For some products, purchasers seem to repeat the mantra "cheaper is better." Why buy a computer for $800 when you can get one for $600? Why pay for a cellular phone when you can get one for free? A number of years ago, I (CLH) had two mufflers installed by two different companies. One charged me $65 and the other $155. Which was the better purchase?

The $65 company made me wait for two hours before they even started. It took them another two hours to finish, so by then I had already killed half a day. One reason they took so long was their utter incompetence. It was all I could do to keep from grabbing the welding torch and finishing the job myself—or running for cover as these Abbott and Costello impersonators torched the underside of my truck. While it took four hours to install the muffler, it took less than an hour to uninstall it; it broke off as I drove over a bump in the road.

The next day, I tried the second muffler company, Kwik-Way Muffler in Santa Clara, California. I was in and out quickly, and, although my wallet was $155 lighter, five years later the muffler still worked perfectly. The bottom line: I got over 10,000 times as much useful service for the $155 as I did for the $65. Even taking into account the higher cost, my second purchase was still more than 4,000 times better.

If muffler shops can offer such dramatically different value, what about all the other products and services people price-compare so aggressively? Consider the local bicycle shop that charges $5 more for a helmet than one purchased through a catalog, but spends 15 minutes helping you fit it properly to your child's head. When you pay Craig, the bike god at Saratoga Bike Shop, or Jason at Tour of Nevada City, you sometimes pay more, but you get the services of someone with enormous understanding and experience. The Harborview Injury Prevention and Research Center in Seattle reports that riders with poorly fitting helmets are almost twice as likely to suffer head injuries in a crash.[2] Wouldn't you pay $5 to have your child's (or your own) helmet fitted correctly?

If you consider initial costs only, you buy the cheapest computer, the cheapest muffler, and the cheapest helmet. And you often end up paying more. You need to consider the overall experience. In business, the overall experience is measured in profits. The trick is to consider costs, especially initial costs, as only part of the equation. Add in revenues and maintenance costs and you have the profit picture.

Costs truly are important, but only for two reasons. First, you don't want to pay too much. Second, you don't want to spend money before you have it, which is a cash-flow problem. But at the end of the day, profits are what you deposit in the bank. If given the choice between profits of $200,000 and $100,000, you should pick $200,000, even if this path has higher costs. We need to think about profits and our ultimate value from every situation, as we explain in Chapters 3 and 7.

Turning Lead Into Gold

My (DRH's) friend, Pat Parker, tells of the time he had his arbitrage epiphany. As a seventeen-year-old, he was sailing his small boat in the Long Island Sound off Larchmont in 1948, three years after World War II had ended. Suddenly he realized that his boat had something on it that other people really wanted, something they'd pay a lot of money for. Having grown up in a mining family where metal prices were regularly discussed, he was well aware that since the World War II price controls had been lifted, the price of lead had skyrocketed. And here he was, a teenager sailing on a boat with a lead keel. He pulled his $1,000 boat out of the water, unbolted the lead keel and reinstalled an iron keel. He then sold the lead keel for more than the boat's price and the boat for about $1,000, informing the new buyer that the keel was iron. Now it was obvious what to do; he bought another boat. The script was the same. He would buy a larger boat, remove the lead keel and mount an iron keel. He'd sell the lead for scrap, repair the boat, and sell it for about what he bought it for. In this way, the seventeen-year-old made a significant fortune until the market came to recognize the facts. He earned about $20,000 that summer (about $160,000 in 2005 dollars).

Interestingly, by taking advantage of this arbitrage opportunity, Pat helped increase the supply of lead. That's what arbitrage does—it shifts resources from uses that are less valuable to uses that are more valuable. "Buy low, sell high" is a formula for both getting rich and improving efficiency. Pat found lead that was being used for low-valued uses and transferred it to people who wanted it for higher-valued uses. In this way, he helped himself and others, too. In Chapter 14, we show how to spot arbitrage opportunities where you otherwise might miss them.

The Dishonest Mortgage Application

One day, an associate passed a piece of paper in front of me (CLH) and asked me to sign it. It was a mortgage application stating his employment history, assets, and sources of income. I signed it hurriedly without reading it. However, my better sense and curiosity took over, and when I glanced at the important sections of the form, some incorrect statements jumped out at me.

When I pointed out the "errors," my associate explained that he could not get a preferred loan if his true situation were known. Worse, he was not just shopping; he had already bought an expensive house and was now trying to close the purchase. He was stuck, but now I was in a bind, also. Although I shouldn't have, I handed him the signed paper, but not without first expressing my displeasure. After all, this man had put my reputation at risk in an underhanded way. My associate replied, "Everyone does it." "I don't," I thought.

As the days passed, I started to see my associate in a different light. "If he was willing to lie to a mortgage company for personal gain, would he lie to me, too?" From then on, I trusted him a little less and scrutinized everything in our business relationship, which ended not long after that. I also vowed that I would never again allow myself to be pressured into signing a false statement. Years later the same situation arose and I kept my vow.

One of the problems with dishonest behavior is that others see it and wonder if they will be the next targets. Chapter 15 shows why, if you want to do well for yourself, you are better off being honest and ethical.

The Cornfield of Life

I (CLH) went to my boss at a large corporation and told her that I was having trouble completing all the projects I'd been assigned. When I asked which ones should take priority, she replied matter-of-factly that they were all important and that I needed to finish them all on time. In other words, "Tough!" I was supposed to either work longer hours or work smarter. The phrase "work smarter, not harder" has been repeatedly ridiculed in the Dilbert comic strip and elsewhere, not because it is a bad idea, but because it is thrown like a brick lifesaver to drowning employees. To tell someone to work smarter is like telling him or her to be happier, healthier, and richer. It's not much help to merely repeat the objective; what people need is a plan for *achieving* the objective.

Our aim in this book is to show you how to achieve your objectives. It is written to help those in business and those in the business of life—i.e., everyone—to work smarter. What we offer is both simple and powerful: a better way to look at problems so that the solutions are easier to find. We offer a way of supplementing your clear thinking by summarizing powerful techniques we've discovered.

Have you ever driven through corn country? From a distance, all you see are corn stalks and more corn stalks in a jumbled mess. Then suddenly, when you get closer, your perspective changes and you can see down the rows and realize that the corn was planted perfectly in straight lines. Your perception of the crop changes from a messy jumble to a clear picture simply because you're in the right spot. **This book gives you perspective on the cornfield of life.** So many problems seem like hopeless jumbles, but then, when you start using the techniques we discuss here, they start to look as straightforward as the straightest line in an Iowa cornfield.

Why We Mix Business with Personal

I (DRH) learned early in my teaching career that one of the most effective ways of teaching economic principles was to connect it to events and experiences in my students' lives. Actually, I learned this as a Ph.D. student of noted UCLA economist Armen Alchian. One of his many lessons stands out in my memory. Alchian taught us a subtle principle about relative prices and consumer demand by relating it to the issue of why the average orange sold in Florida is of lower quality than the average orange sold in New York. After transportation costs are included in the price of both good and bad oranges in New York, good oranges appear to be a relatively better deal than they are in Florida. This leads New York consumers to buy more good oranges, which, in turn, signals retailers to supply them. Whenever we graduate students wanted a shorthand to refer to this subtlety of consumer demand, we called it "the oranges principle." Interestingly, when my friend and former editor at *Fortune*, Dan Seligman, was writing an article on gambling, he came across an empirical regularity: people who traveled a long distance to get to Las Vegas lost, on average, more money than people who traveled a short distance. Dan, the most sophisticated student of economics I've ever met in the world of economic journalism, asked me if economists have a name for the principle that leads to that result. "Yes," I answered proudly. "At UCLA, we called it the oranges principle."

Bit by bit, I tried to teach the way Alchian taught. If my students had run businesses, I would have tried to connect economics with their experiences in those businesses. Of course, few of my 18- to 21-year-old students at Santa Clara University, where I first got good at teaching undergrads, had run businesses. But many had been employees and all had been consumers. So I connected the economics with those kinds of experiences. Then, once the students got it, I would relate it to some other story in the larger business world or economy, so that they could see the connection between their experiences and the bigger picture, and see how the underlying economic principle or concept was the same. Once this happened, the students had a grasp of the concept that they were unlikely to lose. I think that explains a conversation I had years later with my former colleague Hersh Shefrin, an economist still at Santa Clara who wrote the excellent finance book *Beyond Greed and Fear* (Harvard Business School Press, 2000).

Hersh told me that he occasionally ran into alumni of Santa Clara who remembered me and thought well of me. "That's not that unusual," he said. "A lot of professors around here teach well and make some connection with the students. Here's what's unusual: your students remembered specific things they learned."

One of my Santa Clara students who immediately got the concepts and the connections between his experiences and the bigger world was my co-author, Charles Hooper. Charley saw almost immediately the power of that way of thinking, teaching, and writing. That's why we're writing this book the way we are. That's why we will jump from a consumer story about a back-yard barbecue to a business story about a $100 million decision. The principles are the same. The stories are wide-ranging. So let yourself be drawn in. Read the story about the Hatfields and McCoys and we guarantee you'll stay out of a few fights in your life that otherwise would have drawn you in. Read about climbing Mount Everest and we guarantee that you'll make better decisions about sunk costs. And above all, while you're reading this book and learning the techniques, try not to have *too* much fun. This *is* serious stuff, after all.

Chapter 2

THINK CLEAR.

Think on the Margin

*The way to go from rags to riches is to start by
decent set of rags.* — Leonard and Thelma Spinr

Consider situation one: Would you rather tr
for a year without water or without diamonds? Th
obvious. Without water, you would be dead before the
the first month. We have never owned a diamond in
except perhaps the one on the stylus of our record playe.
we can confidently say that survival is pretty easy without

Consider situation two: If you could win one
following two prizes in a contest, which would you pick—a b.
diamonds or 50 gallons of water? The answer here, too, is obvi
You would select the diamonds because they are worth so mu
more.

We've already agreed that you cannot live without water,
and yet you pick the diamonds. Is this suicidal? No. In situation
one, choosing diamonds means you try to live without *all* water
for a year. In situation two, choosing diamonds means that you
add to your existing wealth, which includes, perhaps, a diamond
or two *and* enough money to buy as much water as you need. If
I've already got more water than I can drink, why would I want
another 50 gallons? When I select the prize I want, I know that I
am adding to my current wealth, not starting from scratch.
Additionally, even if I start from zero, I can immediately sell one
of the diamonds to buy plenty of drinking water and still have the
rest of the bag to buy other things. In other words, the diamonds
are equal to 50 gallons of water and so very much more. The
diamonds are a better choice. This is an example of thinking on
the margin. We all do this clearly when choosing between water
and diamonds. But we often fail to do it in other situations.

Many people make bad decisions by making the situation
much grander than it is, lumping together things that are relevant

hose that are irrelevant. For example, if the issue at hand is
her or not to hire another cashier in a grocery store, they
ate the average productivity of all cashiers and evaluate their
ion against that yardstick. This is poor decision-making.

The approach for good decision-making, which is so
verful that almost all of economic analysis since about 1870
ts on it[3], is to think on the margin. **Thinking on the margin
eans thinking about the next increment only.** Do I want one
ore cupcake? Do I want to hire an extra employee? Should I buy
hree more delivery trucks? Do I want more water or more
diamonds? The opposite is thinking about averages. We all do this
occasionally, but we rarely make decisions about averages. A
person thinking about averages may decide not to hire a new
employee because doing so may reduce the average productivity
of all his employees. A person thinking on the margin will hire
that new employee if the additional revenues this worker creates
exceed the additional costs of hiring him or her.

When you think on the margin and act accordingly, often
the *average* return does go down, but the total net return goes up.
Whether your average costs go up or down is irrelevant. If you get
a better overall outcome, who cares how your average costs
change?

Consider a dry-cleaning company with 30 employees, a
total wage bill of $600,000, total revenues of $800,000, and profits
(ignoring other costs) of $200,000. On average, each employee
produces $26,667 and costs $20,000, leaving a net profit per
employee of $6,667. A thirty-first employee is added and increases
revenues to $825,000 and wage costs to $620,000. Now the average
employee will generate a profit of only $6,613. This may appear to
be a step in the wrong direction because profit per employee has
fallen. But it's actually a step in the right direction. Total profits,
not average profits, are what go in the bank. In this case, total
profits are now $205,000, a full $5,000 more than before. And
thinking on the margin, by comparing the cost of the last
employee with the marginal revenue she generates for the
company, leads you to the right answer.

Abraham Maslow's famous "needs hierarchy" theory is
classic thinking on the margin. Maslow, a clinical psychologist in
the 1940s, conjectured that, as people grow and develop, they

move up a ladder of needs, from more basic to more advanced.[4] If we have nothing, what do we want most? Maslow said that we want basic physiological needs such as food, water, and sex. Without food and water you pretty quickly die. Now that you have these, what do you want? Notice that we are thinking on the margin. We don't continue worrying about our basic physiological needs because they're covered. Now, according to Maslow, we want safety. Once we have that, we want to belong. As we keep climbing the ladder, we want to establish our esteem and then reach self-actualization, which is the pinnacle of human development.

If we slide back down the ladder, our top priorities change. Take someone focused on improving his self-esteem, put him in a sinking boat, and see if he wants to sit quietly while we lavish him with praise.[5] No. As the stern of the boat slips under the water, this person will have one and only one thought: safety. Maslow is really saying that we think on the margin. In other words, given what we already have, we think about what we want next.

Thinking on the margin also means rejecting the all-or-nothing thinking that is so common. At a conference I (DRH) attended at the Hoover Institution in the late 1990s, I was impressed by the thoughtful comments of Pete Wilson, the former governor of California. During one of the breaks, I told him I was impressed and that, in fact, he appeared to be such a clear thinker that he might want to spend considerable time working on public policy analysis. He smilingly took the compliment and then quipped, "I would do more of this kind of stuff except my wife thinks I'm allergic to making money." I replied, "I'm guessing that you could make a fair bit of money by being on three or four boards that meet four times a year and still have lots of time left over for this kind of work. It isn't all or nothing; it's more or less." Wilson grinned and said, "Actually, that is what I'm trying to do." I told you he's smart. Most people who are highly effective in their lives, we've observed, think on the margin, even if they don't always articulate it.

He who waits to do a great deal of good at once will never do anything. — Samuel Johnson

Finally, thinking on the margin is very important for helping you through large projects. Someone once said, "A 3,000 mile walk begins with a single step." If you think of big projects as a series of steps, you can avoid the feeling of paralysis that many of us get. I (DRH) remember when I was spending week after week avoiding work on my Ph.D. dissertation, something I absolutely needed to do if I was to get my Ph.D. So desperate was I that I went to see a therapist. He asked me how long I wanted to work on my dissertation every day.

> *David*: At least four hours and more like six.
> *Therapist*: How long are you working on it now on an average day?
> *David*: On an average day, zero.
> *Therapist*: Then here's what I want you to do starting tomorrow morning. Sit down and work on it for two hours.
> *David*: Two hours? That's no good. At that rate, I won't be finished nearly in time.
> *Therapist*: But you're asking how to get from here to there. Right now you're not working on it at all. Two is greater than zero.

His method worked, and I gradually raised my number of hours from two on a bad day to as many as ten on a good day. He helped me see the problem "on the margin," and it worked for me. I had been approaching my work in a way that exaggerated its difficulty. Yard by yard can be just too hard, while inch by inch is a cinch. So I did it inch by inch. Fifteen months later, I had my Ph.D.

Most of our readers are not trying to earn a Ph.D. But we're sure that almost all of our readers, and a large percentage of the population, do want to become relatively wealthy. Few people we know want to spend the last years of their lives living on Social Security. And thinking on the margin is a powerful tool to help you become wealthy. Let us explain.

One of the most common questions I (DRH) get when I meet someone who finds out I'm an economist is "How do I get rich?" Sometimes people ask "How can I get rich quick?" To that question I answer, "I don't know, but I can tell you how to get rich slowly." Indeed, some economist friends of mine, Richard McKenzie and Dwight Lee, wrote a whole book on the subject, *Getting Rich in America: 8 Simple Rules for Building a Fortune and a*

Satisfying Life, in which they, essentially, applied two things: thinking on the margin and the power of compound interest. People who want to get rich quickly are already thinking the wrong way, because to get rich quickly you have to either have an incredible breakthrough in your career, buy the next Microsoft stock early, or win the lottery. But if you're content to get rich slowly—which for the great majority of us is the only way to get rich—you need simply to save a substantial fraction (10 to 20 percent) of your earnings regularly, invest these earnings in a stock index fund such as Vanguard's Total Stock Market Index Fund (VTSMX), which, between its inception in 1992 and 2004, averaged an annual rate of return of over 10 percent, and keep doing that year after year, starting ideally before you are 35. A fund that has been around longer is Vanguard's Wellington Fund, which has had an average annual rate of return of 8.3% since July 1929, interestingly, just three months *before* the great stock market crash. If you invest $2,000 a year and earn an 8 percent real (i.e., inflation-adjusted) rate of return, after 40 years, you will have $477,882. Indeed, when I read McKenzie's and Lee's book, I realized that I had been following all 8 of their rules, starting at age 31, and I'm happy to report that by age 50, I had become a millionaire.

I Must?

Another way many of us think unclearly is by going through life with a list of made-up obligations. We wake up in the morning with a long list of "must do" items. After a while, our feet start dragging and we feel a heavy burden on our shoulders. But we "must" press on. Such phony obligations get in the way of clear thinking.

There is very little in the world that we actually must do. Let's face it, unless we are in jail or otherwise detained, we have complete freedom about how to spend our day. The reason we don't just pack up and go sit on the beach every day is that our actions lead to outcomes—and many of our "have to's" give us the outcomes we want. Going to work, for example, provides camaraderie and a feeling of importance, as well as the money to buy the things we need and want. The "I must" person tells himself that he must go to work. The clear-thinking person says, "If I work at this job for another year, I'll be able to buy a house. I could quit my job today, but if I want that house a lot, I'd better show up for work on Monday morning."

The "I must" attitude increases our burdens and lessens our humanity. When we have goals in mind, we should reframe the issue from "I must" to "I want." I *want* to go to work so that I can feed my kids, buy a car, buy a house, or change the world. If my goals don't seem to justify the effort, then maybe I should rethink my goals and my overall strategy. When we act with clarity of mind, we cease being a fake prisoner and realize our true freedom. For more on this, see David Kelley's powerful essay "*I Don't Have to.*"[6]

A Good Reason is Not Good Enough

As we choose among alternatives (possible choices), reasons factor into our decisions. For most of our choices, there is not just one, but many reasons; some are important, while some are less significant. To use reasons properly, we would have to consider *all* the reasons and factor them by their importance. But even a casual examination of human behavior shows that the reasons we give for our choices are often as much a *result* of our choices as they are a factor in making them.

Years ago, I (CLH) was on a first date with a young woman I had met at a bar the weekend before. I seemed to have made a good impression in the bar while we were drinking, talking, and dancing. I must have seemed less exciting to her in the quiet light of day. On our way to the restaurant, she informed me that she had to get up early the next morning to go water skiing with some friends. Because of this, she said, she would need to get home early. She clearly had decided she wasn't very interested in me and gave this reason as justification for cutting the date short. Although the need for sleep appeared to drive her decision, in truth, she had decided that sleep would be better than a mediocre date. If she had been having a great time, she probably would have stayed out late and worried about sleep later. She gave me a reason because of her choice not to spend much time with me, but she stated it as if the reason led to her choice.

This kind of thing happens all the time. My (CLH's) wife Lisa used to tell men, back when she was single, that she had plans and couldn't go out on Friday night. In reality, her plans were to have a quiet evening at home with her cats and a good book. We are conditioned to think of reasons and use them for our justification when we really should focus on our alternatives, as Lisa did, and decide to stay home because it is the preferable alternative.

For a classic case of letting good reasons lead you to bad decisions, consider the long, bloody feud between the Hatfields and the McCoys. "Four Hatfields were killed in West Virginia in a continuation of their feud with the McCoys," read *The Union* newspaper in March 1902.[7] A year later, the same newspaper reported that, "...Fred and Floyd McCoy of the infamous Hatfield-McCoy feud had a pitched battle with officers. Several men killed on both sides."[8] Both the Hatfields and the McCoys had good reasons to continue their feud and you can imagine their thinking process. "The Hatfields shot my pa. I'm gonna kill them." "The McCoys have been harassing us for years. It's time we taught them a lesson once and for all." However, good reasons are not enough. **A good reason is not a good reason to act.**

In the larger sense, the Hatfields and the McCoys were making a decision: continue the feud or end the feud. While the two families appeared to have good *reasons* for continuing the feud, an overall view would argue for termination. By ending it, both families could have prevented the high cost of the feud, in terms of lost work and death and destruction. The Hatfields and the McCoys were really just pursuing a policy of "I must." They must have felt that there was no option but to avenge violence with violence. And that is what they did. The feud ended eventually, but not until two state governors, the National Guard, and the U.S. Supreme Court were called in. But, by then, both families were so decimated by bloodshed and incarceration that their ruffian days were over anyway.[9]

Those of us looking in from the outside see the vicious cycle that no normal person would want. Many of us think of reasons for our actions when we really should be making the best possible decisions. Below is the Hatfield-McCoy decision laid out in a decision tree, a common format for thinking about choices. We introduce decision trees here, even though this problem is relatively straightforward, to foster a useful way of thinking about the structure of decisions. This will help later in the book, and in real life, when the problems become more complicated. The square on the far left signifies a decision we have to make. The decision alternatives are shown as "Continue Feud" and "Stop Fighting and Enter Peace Talks." The decision to continue the feud will have an outcome of more fighting and deaths with probability p1, which equals one, or 100 percent. "More Fighting" is the outcome and the probability p1 is displayed near the circle. In this case, there is only one possible outcome, which is why there is only one branch leaving the circle and that branch has a probability of 100 percent.

If the alternative "Stop Fighting and Enter Peace Talks" is chosen, life isn't always simple, and so we note that the decision to stop fighting may or may not result in peace. The two possibilities are shown as "Successful Peace Agreement" with a probability of p2 and "Fail" with a probability of p3. Note that the probabilities for each decision alternative must add to 100 percent (i.e., all possibilities are taken into account), which is why p1 is 100 percent and p2 + p3 = 100 percent. After the focus is lifted from reasons, the question becomes: Will my life be better with "Continue Feud" or "Stop Fighting?" That is the issue at hand.

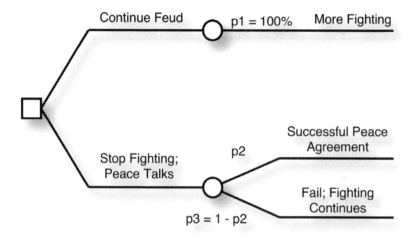

The decision tree above perhaps oversimplifies the issue because each side really hopes that by continuing the feud it will eradicate the other side and "win." We ignored this possibility in the decision tree above. If we include the possibility of winning or losing the feud, we end up with the following decision tree.

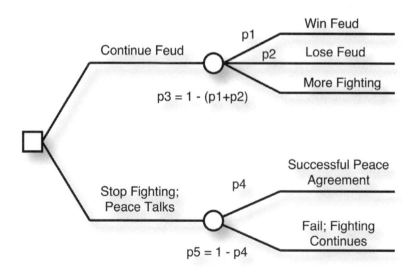

Neither family may have realized that probability p1 is likely to be small. When has a feud between two families ever been won? It is hard to even imagine what sequence of events would cause a feud to be declared "won." Would the Hatfields say to the McCoys, "Gee, we guess you won. What would you like us to do? We could pay you some penalty or we could just move away." That's highly unlikely. The only realistic way we can see to win a feud is to kill all the members of the other side, but to do that would require more aggressive and concentrated fighting than either side practiced. If probability p1 is low, so is p2, for exactly the same reasons. Therefore, by choosing Continue Feud, each family pretty much guaranteed continued fighting. Even if probability p4, the probability of a successful peace agreement, is small, choosing Stop Fighting offers the only real hope for a better future. And even if the peace talks fail, the families are back where they started. In other words, peace talks carry little downside risk.

Making Distinctions

Using distinctions is one of the easiest ways to dramatically increase our clarity of thinking. We can blow away the smoke surrounding an issue and actually see the problem for what it is.

Speaking of smoke, cigarette smoking is a contentious subject. Part of the issue is the addictive nature of cigarettes. Various groups debate whether and to what extent cigarettes are addictive; some say they are and some say they aren't. A number of things are at stake in our society: more and more governmental control of cigarettes; more taxes; more restrictions; more lawsuits; and the quality of our overall public health. Because these are important implications, the process of scientific fact finding is greatly complicated and compromised. In some situations, this pressure leads the side with the less defensible position to make silly or dishonest statements. It also creates a smokescreen, so to speak, because one or both sides might not want the truth known. Both sides might actually agree if they could get over their minor quibbling. They seem to follow the maxim that where you stand on an issue depends on what you stand to gain.

When people think only about the final outcome, an honest exchange of facts is much less likely to take place. A participant in this exchange may reason that she doesn't want more government control of cigarettes, either because she believes in freedom or because she worries that increased government control would cause other problems; so she claims that cigarettes are not really addictive. "Based on the facts I have seen, cigarettes are certainly less addictive than some other substances, but they definitely have addictive characteristics. If I admit this, however, I may contribute to the banning of cigarettes," she may reason. However, if we use distinctions, we find that it is entirely reasonable to admit that cigarettes are somewhat addictive without advocating more government control. We use distinctions to separate the two issues to get to the root of the problem. The addictiveness of something can be separated from the usual response, which is to have the government control it more thoroughly or to ban it completely.

Many in the media like to put people into black and white camps, while the thinking person realizes that issues are generally subtler. Consider some controversial subjects. You may have strong feelings about each issue, but can you see the other side's position? If so, there may be some resolution to the issue that pleases both sides. Using distinctions helps peel away the layers to get to the core, from which a solution may emerge.

You may, for example, support the arts but disapprove of the National Endowment for the Arts (NEA). In other words, you can financially and otherwise support the arts and appreciate others who do so, yet not want the arts to be influenced by the NEA and funded with tax dollars. In the very same way, you can despise foreign dictators yet not support preemptively attacking them. Many of us make a distinction between what people say they will do and what they will actually do. We've learned, often the hard way, that there is such a distinction. Lastly, you can love your children yet still require them to do things they dislike.

Even forgiveness is a distinction. To forgive, you must make a distinction between the person and his action. Perhaps your carpool partner didn't pick you up after work yesterday. You may hate what the person did but still not hate the person. You have probably heard the phrase, "Hate the sin, love the sinner." This is a great example of a distinction. Your feelings are certainly important, but distinctions allow you to separate your feelings of hurt from your decision to forgive.

Forgiveness is an act of the will, and the will can function regardless of the temperature of the heart.
— Corrie Ten Boom

Distinctions are one of the most powerful tools an analyst can use because they help us peel away the layers to get at the essence of the problem. This may allow us to slip around an issue that is actually more contentious and would take significantly longer to address. Distinctions are a great time and effort-saving technique that help us think clearly.

Try to use distinctions with this example of Robert E. Lee and his views of freedom and slavery. Robert E. Lee was a prominent general fighting for the South in the U.S. Civil War. The South was fighting for independence from the Union and one of southerners' primary concerns was the North's opposition to slavery, especially after the election of Abraham Lincoln to the presidency. Can we infer from these facts that Lee accepted or even approved of slavery? Was freedom important to Lee? We can try to unravel this mystery with additional information and the application of distinctions.

Many people don't try very hard to unravel such mysteries. They just see the South as the "bad" side fighting the "good" North. Because Lee fought for the South, he must have been bad and because the war resolved the issue of slavery, Lee must have been fighting to maintain slavery. The truth is a lot more interesting.

Robert E. Lee has been ranked with Napoleon as one of the greatest generals in human history. Lee was the son of Henry "Light Horse Harry" Lee, a Revolutionary War General and friend of George Washington. Henry Lee gave the famous eulogy at Washington's funeral: "First in war, first in peace and first in the hearts of his countrymen." Many people may find it surprising to learn that Robert E. Lee believed slavery to be a great moral wrong, never owned a slave himself, and insisted that his wife—George Washington's granddaughter—get rid of her slaves soon after their marriage. Lee graduated second in his class at West Point and went on to great success in the Mexican War. He carried with him Washington's pocket watch and spyglass. In 1861, after the southern states seceded, President Lincoln offered Lee command of the armies of the United States. Lee declined because his conscience wouldn't allow him to fight for the "wrong" side.[10]

We need to make a distinction between the outcome—slavery in the U.S. or not—and the process of getting there. Lee wanted an end to slavery, but he wanted the states to have that right and responsibility. To him, the greatest threat to freedom was an overly strong federal government. Lee thought it important to follow the correct process to achieve the desired long-term end. (This argument is similar to that of Emma Goldman in Chapter 15.) According to professor J. Rufus Fears, "[t]wo great issues not resolved by the Constitutional Convention or the Bill of Rights were slavery and whether the ultimate loyalty of a citizen was to his state or the federal government. The resolution of these issues came only on the battlefields of the American Civil War."[11]

The Civil War was fought over conflicting ideas of freedom. Lee hated slavery but he strongly believed, as he thought Washington himself had believed, that the states were the ultimate check against a tyrannical federal government. With that power checked, the states could each address the issue of slavery and attain freedom for everyone. Abraham Lincoln and the North were initially just trying to hold the fractured Union together. As a later objective, they desired an end to the abominable institution of slavery, both as an issue of basic human freedom and as a tactic of war against the South.

Both Lee and Lincoln were fighting for freedom and believed that they alone were following the principles of the American Revolution and the Declaration of Independence. They simply had different ideas of the best way to facilitate liberty. Years later, president Theodore Roosevelt said that the two Americans who in his opinion best followed their moral consciences in the pursuit of liberty were none other than George Washington and Robert E. Lee.[12]

The Lessons Learned

Thinking on the margin is one of the best ways to clarify our thinking because it reduces the scope of the problem and wipes away extraneous clutter, allowing us to focus on the task in front of us. People, especially economists, have used this powerful technique consciously and successfully for over a century—and implicitly for much longer. Making distinctions, too, helps us see the real problem clearly and, in addition, can help us resolve differences in debates.

We explored the "I must" trap that many of us fall into and explained how we can free ourselves by focusing on goals rather than on obligations. If you really don't like aspects of your life, change them. But those that you do accept, accept for good reasons—reasons such as buying a house or advancing your career or working for a worthy cause.

Speaking of reasons, we discussed how the reasons we use to explain our choices are often actually a result of our choices and are not always factors in making them. Our focus should shift from reasons to the different outcomes of our choices. When we select among alternatives, we should consider the prospect of the final outcomes, and not just a reason or two. The Hatfields and the McCoys made this mistake, but we can learn from their painful lesson.

We introduced decision trees as a useful and powerful way of structuring problems with alternatives (possible choices), uncertainties, and outcomes. Frequently, the most difficult part of any problem is the structuring, or framing. Once that is accomplished, the solution starts to take shape. If the Hatfields and McCoys had done this task, they probably would have seen that peace talks would have been a wonderful investment.

Chapter 3

THINK VALUE

Top Economist's Headache

A Nobel prize-winning economist was to be guest of honor at a large dinner party at a university. A professor from the university picked up the economist at his hotel. On the way out the door, the economist mentioned that he had a headache, so they stopped into the hotel store to buy some aspirin. "$4.95 a bottle!" the Nobel laureate complained, "I can get this for $2.50 in my town." "Let's go find a regular drug store," he demanded. Because they were already running late, the professor said, "It's your lucky day. I'll pay." This professor could see that the real cost of the elusive $2.50 bottle of aspirin was far higher than the cost of the $4.95 bottle in front of them because of the extra search time involved. The professor was happy to spend the extra money to ensure that he got what he valued more: a relaxed economist giving a good talk and some time to socialize beforehand. Does the irony in this story jump out at you? It is, of course, the Nobel prize-winning economist who should have offered such a solution. He should have seen that, given his situation, the $4.95 bottle, available then and there, was much more valuable than the $2.50 bottle across town.[13]

Tickle Me Scarcity

The Tickle Me Elmo doll came out during the Christmas of 1996. Tickle this $21 doll's belly and it would laugh. It was very popular—so popular in fact, that stores kept running out of inventory. The humorous, friendly Elmo entered the hot, collectibles market. One radio station auctioned an Elmo for $550 and, it was rumored, some Elmos sold for much more.

This is crazy. What happened and how can this be explained? The amount demanded at the $21 price far exceeded the amount supplied, causing buyers to compete with each other, driving the prices up to match the willingness of the highest bidders to pay outrageous amounts. This same process happens often in other markets, yet usually over longer timeframes; Elmo allowed us to see it happen in fast motion. An example of a slower market is lakefront properties. People want to live next to the lake, but the supply of waterfront properties is limited. As more and more people decide to locate to the area, the value for these desirable properties rises to match the value placed upon them by the highest bidders. The highest bidders set the price, while lower bidders either watch from the sidelines or jump back in with even higher bids.

Investors thought that Elmo was a collector's item that would hold its incredibly high value over time. Investors are frequently looking for scarcity because scarcity keeps prices high. The problem with Tickle Me Elmo dolls was that the scarcity was artificial. Given enough time, Fisher-Price, the maker of the Tickle Me Elmo doll, could manufacture enough dolls to supply whatever demand people have. For example, if everyone on the planet wanted two, it could make 12 billion dolls, and if the dolls were relatively indistinguishable from each other, the price was *guaranteed to decline*. Tickle Me Elmo dolls were guaranteed to be a bad investment if purchased during a period of artificial scarcity. Many other investments offer the same dismal future, although it may take longer for the scarcity to pass. True collectibles, on the other hand, often hold their value over time because their supply is truly limited. No more 1969 Jaguar E-Types are being made, for example, and no more Renoirs are being painted. Bottom line: buy Elmo dolls to entertain your niece, not to supercharge your investment portfolio.

What Constitutes a Good Deal?

What constitutes a good deal?

Grace: I got a great deal. I saved $5,000 on my new four-
wheel-drive vehicle.
Paula: But you don't drive off-road. You really should have
bought a sedan at full price. It would have been a
much better deal for you.

Whether a purchase is a good deal depends solely on the difference between the value to you and the cost to you, not how much you saved over the regular cost. Unless Grace was hoping to get into the arbitrage business—by immediately selling her new

4x4 to someone else, where she would probably fail anyway because others could buy the same new vehicle for the same low price—she should focus on the value to her. The tough, outdoorsy image that comes along with a 4x4 may be her priority. If so, she has chosen the right vehicle. Otherwise, an assessment of her needs would probably lead her to another type of vehicle that would be cheaper to purchase and operate, be easier to climb into, and offer better and safer handling and much better gas mileage. Think of it this way. Chances are you don't smoke cigarettes. If you see a great sale on cigarettes, should you start smoking?

We should keep value in mind whenever we buy things. Consider the following silly example. It's from a cartoon I (DRH) saw on the door of one of my favorite UCLA professors, Jack Hirshleifer.

Salesman: Want to buy an elephant for $800?
Customer: No.
Salesman: How about an elephant for $500?
Customer: No! What would I do with an elephant? Come on, I live in an apartment.
Salesman: You drive a hard bargain. How about two elephants for $500?
Customer: Make it $400 and you've got a deal.

Unless this customer can later sell these elephants for a nice profit, he is foolish to buy them. A low price does not guarantee a good deal; a good deal comes from buying something below its value to you (its value in use) or its value to others (its value in trade). If you know that someone else will buy it from you for a higher price in an arbitrage transaction, or if you value it more than the price, then it's a good deal. Otherwise, forget the elephants.

The Missing Postcard Stamps

Have you ever attempted to mail a postcard and looked in vain for a postcard stamp? You have a roll of regular letter stamps right in front of you, but you know that postcard stamps are cheaper, so you look for the postcard stamps, which you know are around somewhere. Perhaps they're in another drawer.

Imagine you do find your postcard stamps under the pile of things in your desk drawer. If you took five minutes to find your stamp, you implicitly valued your time at only $1.68 an hour, less than one-third of the minimum wage. You could have put a 37-cent stamp on the postcard, losing 14 cents but saving five minutes. Implicitly, you sold your time, your five minutes, to gain 14 cents. That hourly rate is $1.68. To some people, perhaps, that would be a good deal, but for the great majority of readers of this book, it is probably between ten percent and one percent of the value of your other opportunities. Stated differently, if you are someone who makes $200 per hour you should allocate only 2.5 seconds to find the missing stamps. To make it worse, perhaps there is some chance that the stamps are lost or gone. Perhaps your co-worker or spouse used them or moved them to a "better" location. In this case, you could look until the next Post Office rate increase and never find those pesky stamps. Even if there is a 75-percent probability that you will find the stamps eventually, you should look for only 1.89 seconds. Time's up. Here's the decision tree.

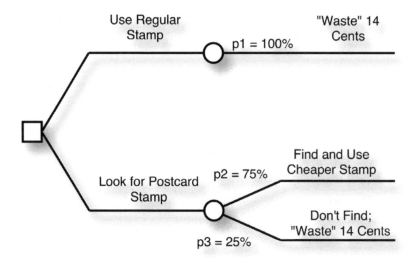

We recognize that this is a rather trivial example, but we are using this problem to teach important concepts—concepts that may save you a little here and there, but a great deal elsewhere. Back to our stamps. We solved this problem by setting the value of the Use Regular Stamp and Look for Postcard Stamp alternatives equal. Use Regular Stamp costs 14 cents because you are wasting a more expensive stamp on the postcard, and so Look for Postcard Stamp should cost 14 cents, too. Look for Postcard Stamp has a 25 percent chance of wasting 14 cents if the lower-priced stamps are not found, for a subtotal of 3.5 cents ($0.14 times 0.25). Therefore, we want to see how many seconds of your time we could buy with the remaining 10.5 cents. At $200 per hour, 10.5 cents is 1.89 seconds ($0.105 divided by $200 times 3,600 to convert from hours to seconds). You should look *at most* for 1.89 seconds, which isn't very long. You should just give up, put the higher-priced stamp on the postcard, and move on with life.

Opportunity Costs

One Saturday night, I (CLH) stayed home with my family. I love doing that, but this time I was even happier than usual. I had been invited to a bachelor party and had been tempted to go. But weighing that against my alternative of staying home, I had decided that I would rather stay home on that particular night.

My "opportunity cost," what I was giving up to stay home, was the value I put on the pleasure of attending the bachelor party. What if the bachelor party would have been a lot of fun? Then I was giving up a lot to be with my family.

So, why was I unusually happy staying home? Because after I had decided to stay home, I learned that the bachelor party was postponed. My cost of staying home, therefore, immediately fell.

Opportunity costs are the costs you incur by not doing something else. You went to the movies on Sunday, but you could have played volleyball or soccer or gone to the beach. To be precise, your opportunity cost is the value of the highest-valued opportunity you give up. If you valued volleyball over soccer and being at the beach, then your opportunity cost of going to the movies is the value you put on playing volleyball. Opportunity costs are pervasive. A date with Don means you can't go out with Samir or Jacob. If you would have preferred Jacob to Samir, then your opportunity cost of going with Don is the value you put on going with Jacob.

Opportunity costs are one of the few areas in life where really successful people have it worse than average people. It must really annoy the latest Hollywood heartthrob to think of the ten lovely ladies he could have dated. It must bug well-heeled vacationers to think of the fun they are missing in Monte Carlo because they went to Paris instead. Pity the woeful driver in his Porsche 911 Carrera, wondering how his Ferrari 360 Spider with its top down would have handled the mountain road to the beach on that particularly beautiful day.

Opportunity costs limit our profiting from situations by raising our costs—kind of like increased expectations. Because we know that profit equals revenue minus cost, considering our opportunity costs helps us pick the best investment of our time. Opportunity costs should figure into most of the decisions we make in life. For instance, we would love to attend any number of conferences. Some are free and some are relatively cheap. Even if the out-of-pocket cost is only $100, their primary cost to us is not the check we write, but the time we take to attend. If we can earn $2,000 a day through consulting, the cost to us of attending the conference is $2,100. The conference organizers could triple the price to $300 and it would only slightly affect our willingness to attend.

Similar reasoning applies to tuition increases at state universities. Imagine that a state university charges annual tuition of $4,000 and is considering raising it by $400. This is a ten-percent increase, which seems large, but the main cost of attending a state college is the opportunity cost of the student's time, not the tuition. If a student could have worked at a full-time job for $10 an hour rather than attend college, the opportunity cost of attending college for eight months is over $13,000. So, ignoring the cost of books, the overall cost of college before the tuition increase is $13,000 plus $4,000, or $17,000. When the tuition increases by $400, the real cost increase to the student is a mere 2.4 percent.

Not surprisingly, therefore, when state schools do raise their tuitions, they don't lose many students, even though many may complain. And complain they do, because most students gloss over their opportunity cost and see the extra $400 as a big chunk of their budget.

Opportunity costs also explain some of our purchasing behavior. Have you ever tried to sell a product when a similar product was being given away for free? Private schools are a good example. Your private school had better be really good because down the street the government is offering a similar product for "free." It's paid for by taxpayers, of course, and is, in fact, very expensive, but it is priced to you, the customer, at zero. But, you say, a good education is worth at least $5,000 a year. Perhaps we can agree on that. But, if the private school is priced at $5,000, then it's competitive with the government school only if it is worth at least $5,000 **more** than the government-provided education. Say the government-provided education is worth only $2,000. Then, for you to be willing to pay $5,000 for the private education, it must be worth at least $7,000 to you. To use another example, drinking water from the tap is almost free, and so the price of bottled water is based on its relative, not its absolute, value.

Opportunity costs are really just a way of saying that there are other good alternatives that could have been chosen. Being aware of these alternatives beforehand reduces the possibility of picking a bad one in a vacuum. In other words, an alternative may look good in isolation, but not compared to other, better ones.

A friend calls and asks you if you want to go see the latest "Star Wars" movie. You've liked most of the "Star Wars" movies, and you're only cleaning your kitchen, and so you agree. With this type of analysis, you determine that the new alternative, the movie, is better than the existing alternative, cleaning the kitchen. Ten minutes after you leave on this beautiful spring day, another friend calls and gets your voice-mail. When you get home you hear his message, "Hi, this is John and Barnabas. We just wanted to see if you are up for some kayaking today on the American River. If you get this message, call us back or meet us there at 1:00. Ciao." You love kayaking. You live for kayaking. Had you made a list of possible ways to spend your time today, you would have put kayaking with John and Barnabas at the top of your list. The cost of going to the movie was not just the cost of the ticket and popcorn, but the cost of your alternative activities. In this regard, the movie was better than cleaning the kitchen, but not better than your other opportunities. As singer Kenny Rogers says, "Don't be afraid to give up the good to go for the great."

A focus on opportunity costs can be enlightening in another way. A major pharmaceutical company's opportunity costs were so high that it nearly ignored a clinical trial that would have returned $500 million for a cost of only $10 million. This company's successful product was near the end of its patent-protected life, after which it would be decimated by generic competition. Instead of simply letting it die, this company could conduct trials in pediatric patients and, if successful, receive a six-month patent extension. Management wasn't sure whether to spend the $10 million because of all the other, exciting opportunities they had. Of course, this was an opportunity that this company positively shouldn't have passed up, but it showed the management team the value of their other opportunities and how high the investment hurdle had gotten. If your company can even think of passing up a $10 million investment that will return $500 million, you've got a problem and should increase your total level of investment. In other words, if you can afford to be so picky, you invested too little. The world loves ten- to 20-percent returns on investments. Investors from far and wide would salivate over a venture returning 4,900 percent. If you ever find your company in such an enviable position, you should secure more outside investment or borrow money to allow your company to capitalize on such juicy investments. When I (CLH) helped this company work through this problem, they were leaning toward not bothering with this opportunity, but later decided to conduct the trial. My analysis helped them see the issue more clearly.

Sunk Costs

Sunk costs are the nemesis of many decision-makers. Say you want to climb Mount Everest and you prepare by training and saving money for years. You also try to get a permit from the bureaucratic Chinese government, something that proves harder than you anticipated. After repeated attempts, you think of giving up, but refuse because of all the time, money, and energy you've invested in this venture. Your determination is admirable: many of the greatest accomplishments in history have been achieved by those who refused to give up, even as their situation became more difficult. That's one side of the coin. The other side is the forward-looking side, the side that takes the perspective that today is the first day of the rest of your life. If you started fresh in the world on this particular day, with all the skills and resources you have, what would you most like to experience and accomplish? If the answer is to climb Mount Everest, then you should continue on your path. If the answer is anything else, then climbing Everest is an inferior choice and you should change direction. In other words, all the time and effort you put into training, getting permits, and everything else is in the past ("sunk") and is largely irrelevant. If your answer is that you really don't want to climb Everest and that your only reason for persisting is that all the effort you've already invested would otherwise be wasted, forget it: it's already wasted.

Consider the plight of an entrepreneur trying to start a coin shop in Kulpsville, Pennsylvania. For two years, he loses money. He knows that the market for coins in Kulpsville is just too poor to sustain a business, but he persists and, consequently, loses even more money. A friend questions what he is doing, asking him, "Are you crazy or just plain nuts?" "Well, I've already put so much money into this shop, I can't walk away now," he replies. His friend considers the situation and says, "So you aren't going to stop investing in the coin store until you are completely broke?" Five years from now, would the storeowner wish he'd kept losing money at the coin shop or moved onto another opportunity?

Many people, when considering walking away from ventures such as the coin shop or the Everest climb, reason that if they quit now, their previous investments will be lost. We have been taught that quitters never win and winners never quit. But think about it for a minute. The coin shop owner has *already* lost his initial investment just as the Everest climber has *already* lost those years of his life. Who will be termed the winner: the coin shop owner who goes broke or the man that jettisons his coin shop to do something that actually generates a profit? Likewise, the potential climber who spends all of his time, money and energy on getting permission to climb Everest, only to attempt the climb without his heart in it, or the person who moves on to other, more rewarding, challenges? The winner and loser label can be applied today and tomorrow. The coin shop owner is already a loser today. That is a historical fact that no one can change. The only question is whether he will win or lose tomorrow. Quitting a losing venture will free up his time and resources, enabling him to start a winning venture. Those who quit losing ventures improve their lives, while those who refuse to quit ensure continued failure. Decisions are forward-looking, and the path to the best future is the only relevant question. At this point, would you rather have a failed past and a failed future, or a failed past and a successful future? Those are the only two alternatives open to you.

Consider a different situation. Would you go camping in a bad rainstorm purely because you'd already made plans and paid the reservation fee? The decision tree below shows that the reservation fee shows up on both branches: go camping in the rain and stay home or do something else. Whatever costs or benefits are present on both branches cancel out.

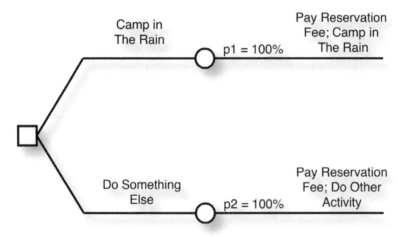

To solve a decision tree, we compare the two alternatives. Is camping in the rain better than doing something else? Simple algebra allows us to drop the reservation fee because it is present on both sides of the equation. Therefore, in this case it is irrelevant. What follows is the simplified decision tree.

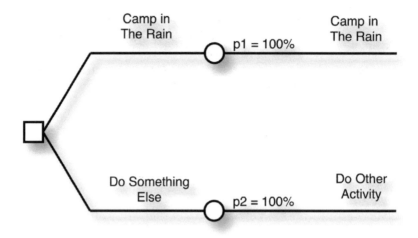

Take an introductory economics course and the odds are high that the professor, at some point in the course, will tell you that sunk costs are irrelevant to rational behavior. Rarely, though, do economics professors distinguish between two distinctly wrong ways of making sunk costs relevant. One is to throw good money—or time or whatever—after what has already been invested, even with dim prospects. A friend once told me (DRH) that although he had a lousy marriage and had spent the last umpteen years trying to make it work, he was just not willing to walk away from it. When I questioned him further, he admitted that he didn't really think the marriage would ever work. But still he wanted to stick with it. This is like the coin shop example and is the more common way of trying to make sunk costs float. A way to sum up this mistake is that the person refuses to abandon a course that he should abandon because of the investment or expenditure that he's already made. This first type of sunk cost can be called the "He's dead, Jim" sunk cost. That's the famous line from the original "Star Trek" television series whenever Bones, the ship's doctor, examined a recently deceased crew member during a tense scene, while Captain Jim Kirk watched intently from the side. These costs are dead, and even the amazing Bones can't revive them. We simply need to admit it and move on.

But that's not the only way to mess up with sunk costs. The other way is less common but just as counterproductive: pretending that the sunk costs are not sunk and are in the future.

About 15 years ago, I (DRH) was visiting an economist friend and helping him work on his house. He decided to get some weather stripping for a window, and so we hopped into his car and went to the local hardware store. He found what he wanted, but was disappointed that the price was $10 rather than the $6 he expected. Our conversation went like this:

Jack: Let's go. I'm not willing to pay $10. I'll find another hardware store some other time.

David: Wait a minute, Jack. This makes no sense. You showed by your behavior that the weather stripping was worth at least $10 to you.

Jack: How?

David: You got in your car and drove ten minutes to the hardware store, which makes the round trip 20 minutes. If your time is worth at least $12 an hour, and I'm sure it is, then you bore $4 in time costs to make the round trip to the hardware store. So that $4 in time that you were willing to pay, plus the $6 in out-of-pocket expenditure you were willing to pay, adds up to $10, the price they're charging. Now that you're here at the hardware store, the cost of getting here is sunk, and the cost of getting back to your house is sunk unless you plan to live in the hardware store. So you should ignore those costs and buy the weather stripping.

Jack agreed with my analysis but refused to buy the weather stripping, even though he later had to make another trip and incur yet another $4 travel expense. The only way that he wouldn't have had to pay at least $10 would have been to wait until he was running other errands and just happened to pass by the hardware store that sold the weather stripping for $6.

Have you ever made this kind of mistake with sunk costs when you go to a bank, post office, or store to do some business but, when you get there, see a line? You may decide to come back some other time when the line is likely to be shorter. Even if you're right in predicting that the line will be shorter some other time, your decision is generally wrong. Why? Because you've borne all the costs of getting there and, if you decide to come back later, you'll bear similar costs again. If you take account of those costs, you'll typically conclude that time spent in line now will be less than the time you would spend getting back later in the day.

So your best decision is to stay in line. And another good decision, now that you know this, is to carry a book or magazine so that you can use your time in line productively. Again, if you leave and come back later, the only way to avoid the cost of the return trip is to piggyback with another trip that you would run anyway.

When I (DRH) was in tenth grade, I discovered Bartlett's *Familiar Quotations* in our otherwise-skimpy high school library. Because it was a reference book, we weren't allowed to check it out, and so I stayed after school one day working my way through the whole thing and writing down great quotations. I still count this as probably the most productive two hours I spent in my 11 years at school. I still find myself, almost 40 years later, quoting lines I learned that day. One of the most prolific "quotemakers" was the famous 18th-century British author Samuel Johnson (whom we quote in another context in Chapter 2).

One of the lines I wrote down that day expresses the right way to go against this second kind of sunk-cost error. Asked if a play was worth seeing, Johnson replied, "Worth seeing? Yes. But not worth going to see." What he was getting at is that once you've paid for the tickets, hired the carriage, and spent the time to get to the play, the relevant cost to consider is simply the opportunity cost of your time. Johnson was saying that the value of seeing the play exceeded this cost. That's why it was worth seeing. But, he was also saying, if you could have known in advance the quality of the play, it would not have been worth buying the tickets, dressing up, hiring the sitter, and taking the trip to the theater. A number of my students have summed up this quote as follows: "Wait 'til it comes out on video."

Interestingly, both ways of mistakenly considering sunk costs came out in the Congressional debate about the B-1 bomber back in the late 1980s. The proponents claimed that to abandon the B-1 bomber now would waste the billions in R&D that had already gone into it. But, of course, these costs are sunk and essentially irrelevant. Some of the opponents said that the money already spent on the B-1 bomber, added to the expenditures anticipated for the future, made the B-1 not worth building. But they were mistakenly counting these costs as if they were yet to be borne. Given that much of the cost had already been incurred, even these critics might have been forced to conclude that the B-1 was worth more than its *future* anticipated costs and, therefore, should be developed.

The first type of sunk cost described above is, as noted, the "He's dead, Jim" variety. We aren't getting our B-1 bomber money back, so let's admit it. The second type of sunk costs can be called the "Night of the Living Dead" costs, because even after they are dead and buried, they come back to haunt us during the middle of the night. Even after the B-1 bomber money was spent, these people treated it as if it was still alive, discretionary, and relevant for cost/benefit analysis.

We said a few paragraphs back that sunk costs are irrelevant to rational behavior. This is not quite correct. Sunk costs do affect us. We can learn from the costs we have incurred and the process of incurring these costs changes us and puts us in new circumstances with new opportunities. We believe that this is the primary reason people incorporate sunk costs into their decision-making process. For instance, I (CLH) worked at NASA as a scientific programmer for seven years. I eventually went back to graduate school to study subjects that I considered more interesting and important. But did I acknowledge and accept my "sunk cost" and start from scratch? No. I leveraged my engineering background by selecting a department at Stanford where my skills were an asset. Decisions should always be forward-looking. The way I did this was to ask myself what career to pick *given* that I had a strong engineering and economics background.

Interestingly, sunk costs, decision analysis (see "Decision Analysis by Dirty Harry" in Chapter 9), and thinking on the margin (see Chapter 2) are all related and take advantage of the same perspective. Given that my past costs are sunk, what is the best course of action now? Thinking on the margin gets at the same result because the focus is on the next increment. The next increment ignores what has happened in the past and is purely forward-looking. Decision analysis is always forward-looking. All three techniques uncover the same insights. They use different words and approaches, but all demand that we think about what will happen next, and that precludes looking backwards (sunk costs) or including things that are already settled (thinking on the margin).

Value is Subjective

Many people believe that value is intrinsic in an object. But it's not. One of the most important economic insights of the late 19th century, an insight which was responsible for much of the progress in economics in the next century, was the idea that the values of items are subjective and depend on the valuer as much as on the item.[14] Value is not a function of an object per se; rather, it's a function of how someone views an object. The value a person places on an object tells us more about the person than about the object.

Consider water. If I turn on my tap I can get a gallon of water for about a penny. Yet, in another situation, I would pay $100 for a gallon of water if I were thirsty and hot enough—perhaps after a long hike in Death Valley. In a third situation, I would have paid $100 to get rid of the water that flooded my basement the night I (CLH) came home from work to find that my sump pump had seized. Water is water is water, but how it affects me and, therefore, the value I place on it, is highly dependent on the context. Context matters. At one time I don't think much about water; at another time I don't have enough and become desperate; at still a third time, I have too much and just want to get rid of it.

What is often missed is that the value of all marketable things springs from human demand, preferences, fashions, and uses. In short, what we are able and willing to pay (along with sellers' alternatives) drives the price. Because we all change, values change too. Don't be surprised if that antique desk you paid $5,000 for is worth as much as $20,000 or as little as $1,000 next year. Unless, of course, it is in my basement the next time it floods. Then you'll have to pay someone $50 to haul it away.

We see this mistake in the way people think about recycling. Recycling has come to be thought of as some kind of Holy Grail, something that you should do regardless of circumstances. But why did we want to recycle in the first place? Wasn't it because we were trying to save resources and also reduce pollution? The problem is that recycling itself often wastes resources. One of the most important resources left out of the calculation of whether or not to recycle is the value of time that you spend separating the items and hauling them out in separate bins to the curb. If the value of your time is worth more than the value of the recycled materials, society loses money each time you recycle. In this case, recycling is just too wasteful. Since we rarely know the market value of recycled materials and the true cost of discarding our trash, many of us recycle out of habit, peer pressure, or the simple hope that we are doing the right thing.

I (CLH) have a friend who has taken reuse to the extreme and is suffering accordingly. He has been diligently extracting old nails from scrap wood for reuse in his house construction projects. Don't underestimate the effort involved in this process, which requires finding boards with nails, pulling the old nails, straightening them before they can be rehammered by hand, and then dealing with the ones that are so weak or rusted that they crumple from the ordeal. In his efforts to save the Earth, he is reducing his enjoyable time on Earth. Given this realization and his objectives, isn't there a better use of his time?

Is the Value of Human Life Infinite?

Years ago, Ford Motor Company sold a car named the Pinto. Perhaps you owned one, or your parents drove one, or you had a friend who owned an ugly brown one, as I (CLH) did. (David's friend drove an ugly blue one.) What made this car notorious was not its poor handling and anemic acceleration. This car had a "feature" whereby, in a rear-end collision, bolts could be thrust into the gas tank, causing the car to become a jumbo-sized Molotov cocktail.[15]

People burned and people died. People also sued Ford for millions of dollars. During the process of discovery of evidence, an internal Ford memo reached interested outside eyes. People discovered that Ford knew of the problem and, worse, knew how to fix it. The fix was neither complicated nor expensive; a simple $11 rubber covering on the bolts would have prevented the gas tank from puncturing. The internal memorandum suggested against installing the fix because it did not make financial sense. Given Ford's calculations, it was not worth it, from a cost versus benefit standpoint. This made the public even more upset than the knowledge that Ford knew about the problem. Ford was seen as doing something horrendous—putting a value on a human life in its analysis. Based on Ford's estimated value of human life and its estimated probability of fires, it concluded that the $11 part was too expensive.[16] This might sound absurd, because surely a human life is worth more than $11. Even the Ford decision-makers would agree with that, but the problem was that they would spend $11 each on millions of Pintos to avoid an estimated 360 deaths and serious injuries. The vast majority of Pintos—over 99.9 percent of them—would not be involved in the kind of accident mentioned.

Something similar happened more recently with General Motors. A Los Angeles jury awarded six people badly burned in a collision $107 million in compensatory damages and $4.8 billion in punitive damages for injuries suffered in their 1979 Chevrolet Malibu. A 1973 study that projected the cost to General Motors of settling claims for injuries and deaths was instrumental in the jury's decision for such a large settlement. "We figured that if they had no regard for the lives of people in their cars, they should be held liable for it," jury foreman Coleman Thornton said after the verdict.[17]

GM's internal memorandum stated that, while "a human fatality is really beyond value, subjectively," it would be cheaper to pay fuel-fire-related deaths at $200,000 each than prevent such deaths. To prevent the deaths would require paying $8.59 per vehicle, while paying claims was estimated to cost $2.40 per vehicle. It is not clear whether this memo was distributed and subsequently influenced any GM designs, but it was the smoking gun that the plaintiffs' lawyers needed. What is less clear is whether this $8.59 amount applied to this particular Chevy Malibu and whether it would have prevented a fire in this case, given the extreme force of the rear-end collision from the other (drunk) driver's high velocity.

Is human life really priceless? If the value of a human life *is* infinite, then we should never pursue a career because work is the exchange of our time for money. If our entire life has infinite value, then it stands to reason that each piece of it also has infinite value, as our lives are made of only about half a million hours. Infinity divided by half a million is still infinity, so we would have to charge our employers infinity dollars per hour. This would make for some interesting paychecks and W-2s. But this is not really what happens in the labor market; we humans certainly don't act as if we believe our lives are infinitely valuable.

This particular Los Angeles jury, while unhappy with GM, should be happy to hear about two other auto companies that operate in ways that are more consistent with their beliefs, and that, therefore, the jurors should support: **Ignorant Cars International** (ICI) and **Infinite Motors** (IM).

Ignorant Cars knows that it can be held liable if it is aware of some design flaw in its cars. So the company policy is not to look for flaws and to ignore them if they surface.

> *Engineer*: Hey, I just discovered a major problem with our new sedan.
> *Manager*: You know it is against company policy to discuss problems with our cars.
> *Engineer*: I know, but this is really bad. If you operate the CD player, the car's power brakes fail at the same time the wheels fall off.
> *Manager* (holding fingers in ears): La la la la la. I can't hear you. La la la la la. What did you say? La la la la la.

Would the Los Angeles jurors want to own and drive cars made by Ignorant Cars? Ignorance may be bliss, but it doesn't make safe cars. How can you fix problems if you refuse to acknowledge them?

Infinite Motors is much more safety conscious. It knows, as the Los Angeles jurors know, that life is infinitely valuable. Any attempt to actually assign a value to life is cold and calculating and degrading to everyone involved.

> *Engineer*: I just realized that it is theoretically possible that a tree could fall on one of our cars while it is parked. If the occupant is inside, and the tree is rather large, the occupant could be injured.
>
> *Manager*: How much will it take to redesign each car we sell?
>
> *Engineer*: Probably $800 per car, and it will delay the introduction of our new sedan by at least four months.
>
> *Manager*: You know that our policy is to fix each and every problem. Start a team working on this problem immediately.
>
> *Engineer*: I guess I don't have to ask, but what about the slight chance of a collision with a train. A fix will delay us by ten months and cost $10,000 per vehicle.
>
> *Manager*: Fix it.

Engineer: And how about the one in a trillion possibility of death due to solar flares? It will take $20,000 per vehicle and set us back a decade or two.
Manager: Fix it.
Engineer: How about...?
Manager: Fix it.
Engineer: How about...?
Manager: Don't even ask, just fix it!

Would the L.A. jurors want to own and drive cars made by Infinite Motors? The car would be delayed so long they would never get a chance. And if it did somehow manage to see the light at the end of the production line, it would cost millions, and so they wouldn't be able to afford it anyway.

Is this the end of the story? No. Assume for a minute that the L.A. jurors get their way and all car companies behaved like Infinite Motors. All development of cars for regular people, like us, will cease. Is that bad? Yes, it is. Remember the 1974 Ford Pinto and the 1979 Chevrolet Malibu? Those will be the cars that the L.A. jurors and you and I will own. All progress will cease and our existing cars will get older and older and more and more unsafe, kind of like the ones you see on the streets of Havana. This is certainly sub-optimal... Whom do I sue?

What would my life be like if I placed an infinite value on it? No other value would compare, and no risk would be worth the possibility of injury or death. I would buy the best bicycle helmet money can buy to walk to the garage to look at my bicycle. Ride it? Never! I would hire two paramedics to follow me everywhere, except to the bathroom, even though many accidents happen in the shower. I would limit my contact with germ-harboring humans and refuse to ride in a car, let alone other more dangerous contraptions such as kayaks and hang gliders. I would eat well, exercise, and watch a lot of television. I would read and work on my computer. But I would never dance, swim, play golf, fly, or drink beer. Of course, in reality, we do many of these things because we have a more modest assessment of our value.

Fortunately, ICI and IM have a competitor: **Reasonable Agent Vehicles** (RAV). Reasonable Agent knows that it acts as your agent. When designing the doors to your new sedan, it could have required you to climb in through the windows, "Dukes of

Hazzard" style. It did not. Instead, it put four nice doors on your sedan. It could have left off the trunk and saddled you with a 25-horsepower engine. It did neither, and you have the power you need to haul your groceries around town. By acting as our agent, RAV makes the thousands of little decisions that need to be made, but for which we are incapable of speaking up. If we like the decisions RAV made, we get to buy their car for a reasonable price right off the dealer's lot today.

What value of human life do they assume for us? Well, the right one, of course: definitely not infinite and definitely not zero.[18] [19]

In the extreme, people who advocate an infinite value to human life should be willing to forgo our entire national income to prevent just one single death. Stated differently, we should all become dirt poor to prevent just one death. But, of course, poverty is a contributing factor to death—poverty cuts more lives short than smoking, driving, murder, fires, and flying combined[20]—so ironically, many more people would die. We just can't win unless we acknowledge the situation as it is, not as we wish it to be. **Human life is simply worth too much to endanger it by considering it invaluable. Attributing anything but a reasonable value to human life causes us to endanger it.**

Part of the problem is that the people arguing for perfectly safe cars don't appreciate the tradeoffs involved. They see the possibility of a perfect world and ask, "Why not?" Well, the answer is that, yes, we can pick the best world, but there is no guarantee that the best world will be perfect. For more on this subject, see Reality Versus Fantasy in Chapter 8.

Micromorts and Real Life Safety Decisions

You may have noticed a subtle, but glaring problem with assigning a value to your life. Consider the following hypothetical situation. Shortly after you realize that your life is worth $10 million, a stranger approaches you with a check for $10 million. He would like to give you the check, give you just enough time to deposit it in your bank, and then, um, kill you. "Wait a minute," you think. "How will I ever enjoy this money if I'm dead?!" The short answer is that you won't. Your heirs might, but *you* are suffering the supreme cost and *they* get the benefits. If that's what you want, fine, but most people won't make that sacrifice. This is a hypothetical, but useful exercise to see that, while it is highly unlikely that a stranger would approach you with such an offer to buy your whole life, we can't ignore the thousands of day-to-day decisions we make to sell bits of our life. Stanford's Ronald Howard has invented the concept of a micromort. A micromort is a unit of cost that you bear for engaging in risky activities. **A micromort is a one in a million chance of death.**[21] So, while you may not sell your entire life for $10 million, you may sell a one in a million chance of death for $10. In that case, your micromorts cost $10 each.

Do you pay extra to buy a safer car? Do you buy the chainsaw with extra safety features? Do you drive or fly from Des Moines to Tampa Bay? Do you buy and wear a helmet while bicycling? These are real-life decisions, not like the $10-million check example above, and here is where micromorts are useful and enlightening. Consider buying a car. For each million lighter cars—those weighing less than 2,500 pounds—that are on the road, 109 people die each year. For each million heavier cars—those weighing 3,500 pounds—that are on the road, only 53 people die each year.[22] If we use an average of 10,000 miles per year per vehicle, then each mile driven in a smaller car costs the driver 0.0109 micromorts while each mile in a larger car costs 0.0053 micromorts. If you keep this car for 100,000 miles, then the smaller car has a safety cost of $10,900 (1,090 micromorts times $10 per micromort) while the larger car has a safety cost of only $5,300 (530 micromorts times $10 per micromort). The larger car undoubtedly costs more to purchase and operate, but given everything else equal—don't consider the smoother ride, the bigger trunk, or the worse gas mileage—it is worth $5,600 more purely due to its safety.

The next time you purchase a potentially dangerous product or service, see if you can apply micromorts to help you decide what's appropriate for you in your particular situation. After all, you wouldn't ever sell your whole life, but you risk your life each and every day, and that has a real cost. The micromort concept helps us quantify that cost.

The Value of Your Time

When we think of value, we should think of the most precious of resources: our time. What is your time worth? As we explored earlier, your life is not infinitely valuable, and so your time must have a finite value. How much it's worth exactly stumps a lot of people. Once you have the answer, though, you can resolve a lot of other questions. For example: should you hire a gardener to mow your lawn? Should you work overtime to make an extra $100? Should you recycle glass bottles?

Determining the value of your time is not simple, primarily because your time has many values depending on what you're doing. There is both a cost and a benefit when you spend an hour doing something. The benefit, or enjoyment, you receive from your labor is essentially something that only you can know through introspection and by studying your past behavior. How much do you enjoy or disdain mowing the lawn? How much do you enjoy shopping for clothes? How much would we have to pay you to clean a sewer or to trim the top branches of a 125-foot-tall Ponderosa Pine tree? How much would *you* pay to participate in the most enjoyable, rewarding, and meaningful activity you can imagine?

While the benefit side depends on the activity and is illuminated through introspection, the cost side is more easily determined based on the employment opportunities you reject. If you are a lawyer and charge $500 per hour, and you can work one more hour but choose not to, we can determine that the value of that one extra hour is more than $500 (really $300 after taxes). Even if you "waste" that extra hour watching television or reading the classified advertisements for that perfect four-wheel drive Land Cruiser you'll never buy, that one hour is worth more than an extra $300, or else you would have stayed at work.

Consequently, it will be better for you to hire a gardener to maintain your law office grounds than for you to do it yourself because gardeners charge much less than $300 per hour; your time is much more valuable than a typical gardener's. This is the classic "make versus buy" analysis. **If you can buy it cheaper than you can make it yourself, you should buy it.** Perhaps your business has been somewhat slow and you have a few free hours each week. Don't pick up those pruning shears and head for the shrubs. There has to be something you can do to boost your business: call clients, call associates, read a book, take a class, organize your office, or study some new cases. The gardener is still cheaper.

If you are salaried and work a fixed number of hours per week, the value of your time is harder to ascertain. A simple analysis would look at your average wage rate—your annual salary divided by the number of hours you work. Then, after computing this hourly wage, multiply it by one minus your marginal income tax rate. If your federal marginal tax rate is 25 percent and your state marginal tax rate is 7 percent, then your value of time is 0.68 times (68 percent of) your hourly wage. The cost for one additional hour should be equal to or greater than this net-of-tax rate, just as the spot market price is usually higher than the long-term contract price. But even if you are salaried, you are implicitly rejecting other income-producing employment during evenings and weekends.

Because time is so valuable, the value of your time should be an integral factor in your decisions. Should you drive or fly from Sacramento to San Diego? After you consider how much you like/dislike flying and driving, the rest is economic. Flying may be the smart choice for you because, while it costs perhaps $120 more in cash outlay, you save about 12 hours for a round trip. Is your time worth at least $10 an hour?[23]

Bottom line: your time is worth what you determine it to be based on what you are giving up and what you are doing. It is a matter of supply, demand, and preferences. Its value may be more than you are currently aware, but certainly less than infinity.

The Lessons Learned

This chapter deals with value and to think clearly we need to think about value. Value is the ultimate measure of worth or the ultimate reason for your efforts, and can be either financial or non-financial. By knowing what is valuable and why, you can make better decisions and act on them. In the first story, the top economist thought a few dollars were valuable. Luckily, his colleague realized that a few dollars were nothing compared to the prospect of a productive and enjoyable evening. It is, of course, the top economist who should have produced this insight. In the second story, many people thought, correctly, that Tickle Me Elmo dolls were valuable because of their scarcity. However, the scarcity was temporary and so were the high prices.

An honest assessment of value can help you determine what constitutes a good deal and whether you should spend time trying to save money, such as by looking for cheaper postcard stamps. That example was somewhat trivial, but the approach is the same whether you are saving pennies or the Parthenon.

One good way to determine value is to look at opportunity costs—the cost, through foregone enjoyment or financial return, that you incur by not pursuing other promising opportunities. When calculating costs, we need to be careful not to include sunk costs. They are sunk—already incurred—and should be irrelevant to our decision-making. This chapter discussed how value is in the eye of the beholder, which is why two people can assign such different assessments of value, whether to a desk or something as dear as human life. What is one of your most valuable possessions? Your life, of course. Does that make it infinitely valuable? You certainly don't act as if it is, partly because you don't protect it fervently and partly because you don't place infinite value on chunks of it—hours and days. The price you put on your hours and days is the value of your time, and it determines whether you work two jobs or jealously protect your precious evenings. We need to consider value to make good decisions and to act on them.

Chapter 4

ASK WHAT CHANGED

A body at rest will remain at rest and a body in motion will remain in motion unless acted upon by an outside force.
— Sir Isaac Newton's First Law of Motion

Have you ever had a conversation like this? You point out to a friend that the stock price of Hunky Chunky Potato Chip Company doubled in the last six months. Then your friend explains, "Yeah, that's because people love potato chips. Their love borders on addiction." Or you comment that far fewer people are attending Major League Baseball games this year, and your friend's explanation is that baseball is so boring.

Your friend explained nothing. If people love potato chips so much, didn't they love them last year too? Then why wasn't Hunky Chunky Potato Chip's stock just as high six months ago? If baseball is so boring, why were so many people attending last year? To explain a change in some variable, you have to point to something else that changed, not to something that stayed the same. What *did* change? Are people disgruntled over the baseball strike? Did ticket prices go up? Have people fallen in love with another sport? Something caused the change you're observing. The trick is to identify the key elements that changed and not the fundamental elements that didn't. We doubt that baseball has gotten less exciting or that people just recently discovered potato chips. It is entirely possible that the popularity of potato chips and baseball ebbs and flows, but then the variable that changed is the popularity itself.

The Malfunctioning Barbecue

Years ago I (CLH) installed a new part in my gas grill barbecue. The female and male gas lines didn't physically, permanently connect; they were designed so that one just slips inside the other with a remaining gap. The new parts didn't seem quite right. There wasn't much overlap. This concerned me, given the possibility of a gas leak in close proximity to a hot grill.

My concerns amounted to nothing. Everything worked for years until the evening the underside of the grill suddenly looked like a blowtorch. I immediately shut off the gas line. Days later I adjusted things and tried again, with the same result: the flames were under the grill instead of inside the grill, which is good neither for cooking hamburgers nor for living a long life. My conclusion: the parts had never been right, and now was my chance to buy the right parts.

The owner of the gas grill store listened patiently to my story and then asked if I had ever cleaned the parts. "Huh, what?" I replied, surprised. "Clean them?" "Did it work before?" he asked. "Uh, yes," I replied. He inserted a long, thin brush into the pieces and drew out a thick wad of spider webs and other gunk. For five years the gas grill "somehow" had worked, even though it had pieces that I suspected were too short. When it finally didn't work, I was sure that it was due to the length of the pieces and nothing else. But it had worked for five years! I forgot to ask myself what had changed. Something had obviously changed to make it stop working and it wasn't the length of the pieces. What could change with such a simple hose assembly? Now I know: Dirt, gunk, and spider webs.

The NASA Code

When I (CLH) worked at NASA Ames Research Center as a scientific programmer, my software group experienced the following situation so frequently that it became one of our inside jokes. Many of NASA's scientists wrote their own software for wind tunnel experiments and fluid dynamics simulations. They would often come into our office and ask us, as the software experts, why their code wasn't running. Their software program had been running properly, they would explain, but then it mysteriously stopped. They were looking for reasons and had come to us because they were out of possible explanations. It was as if they expected us to say that the VAX minicomputer or the Cray supercomputer just wasn't working today because somehow the circuits broke or the operating system went haywire.

But the reason was always the same: they would admit that they changed their code. "But I changed only one line of code," they would say, exasperated. As we well knew, their one change broke their code and was the smoking gun that we needed to fix the problem. These NASA scientists couldn't believe that their one innocent change caused the problem and, so, looked elsewhere. We knew that a computer designed and tested by hundreds of engineers and proven through years of faithful service was much less likely to cause their problem than one hastily written line of code buried within a highly interdependent software program.

Rising Gas Prices

In the summer of 1999, Californians were upset because gas prices had jumped 40 cents a gallon in the few months since March. It was natural for people to blame the world oil market, basically OPEC, and the greed of oil companies. Although it's true that the price of every 42-gallon barrel of oil had risen, it had increased by only about $3. At most, this could explain perhaps ten cents of the 40-cent increase per gallon. That left the remaining 30 cents to be blamed on the greed of oil executives, or so it seemed, until we consider that this gas price hike happened only in California and not in the rest of the country. Hmmm...

Here's what I (DRH) wrote in a 1999 article:

Why did California refiners suddenly get greedier in the last three months? Can't we assume that, whatever their level of greed, they've been that way for quite a while? So what changed in California that didn't change in the rest of the United States? The answer is the amount of gasoline produced in California.[24]

The amount of gasoline refined in California dropped seven percent during that period, mainly due to fires at two California refineries, one at the Tosco refinery in Avon on February 23 and the other at Chevron's Richmond refinery on March 25.[25] Interestingly, California's Air Resources Board had left the state gas market unprotected from production shocks such as these fires by requiring that all gasoline sold in California be a specific kind, different from that sold in neighboring states.[26] I wrote:

> Ordinarily, when the price of a commodity rises in one region and that commodity is easy to ship from another region, people called arbitrageurs make money by buying where it's low and selling where it's high. The arbitrageurs' increased shipments drive down the price in the high-price region. But that hasn't happened in California.[27]

The reason for the price increase was the fires. The reason the price increase was so severe was the regional nature of gasoline production in California. When people notice higher prices at the gas pump, they want to explain the change, but they frequently resort to explanations that rely on factors that haven't changed. Some of these factors may have made the change more severe, as with the California gas refining laws. Some of these factors were just "there" and didn't necessarily exacerbate the change, such as the greed of the gas companies, who are just as greedy elsewhere. We need to consider what really caused the change. Because if nothing changed, why did something change?

We Deliver, Maybe

I (CLH) have an office connected to my house. For the office address I gave to clients, I added a "Suite J," partly for fun, partly to mirror my old downtown office that was Suite L, and partly to keep my personal and business mail separate. Later, I realized this was silly, so I started phasing out the Suite J in my address. Then, one day, after almost three years of uninterrupted mail delivery, the Post Office marked some of my mail "Returned Undeliverable" and sent it back to the sender. I know this because I talked to a supplier who complained about a late payment for a bill I never got. I sent my office manager to talk to the people at the Post Office, who told him that Suite J is not part of our official office address and having it on our mail may cause it to be undeliverable. As you've probably noticed, this fails to explain how I got Suite J mail delivered for almost three years. Also, at least one of the missing pieces of mail did not have Suite J in the address because it was personal mail for a vehicle registration. So the Post Office failed to explain why, if nothing had changed, something had, indeed, changed.

A friend has a related Post Office story. Blair stopped his mail for two weeks when he went on vacation and then contacted the Post Office to resume his mail when he returned. After he had received his mail for a week or so, all delivery ceased. Perplexed, he went to the Post Office to inquire about the problem. Blair explained the sequence of events and said that he hadn't gotten any mail for days. The clerk looked at him inquisitively and asked, "Specifically, what mail hasn't been delivered?" Blair was dumbfounded. "I get a pile of mail each day. How am I supposed to know exactly what personal letter, magazine, catalog, bill, or junk mail didn't come today?!"

What had changed? A postal employee had somehow reinstated the hold on Blair's mail.

The Lessons Learned

Remember the story about David's father's attempted suicide in Chapter 1? David's first task was to determine why his father was upset enough to attempt a sleeping pill overdose. David's father had seemed fine less than two weeks earlier but now he was in the hospital. What had changed? The pain in his legs had started the whole process of depression and suicidal thoughts. Now the solution was clear: Try to eliminate the pain.

In our quest for understanding, knowing what drives any given situation is paramount. If we didn't have a problem before and now we do, something must have changed. And the first step toward fixing the problem is discovering what that something is. Whether it is a revised computer code or someone's incompetence, the first challenge is to open the curtain and see what is behind it.

In the potato chip stock example, knowing what was powering the sales growth could help you as an investor. Now might be a great time to buy, or a great time to sell—it depends on what is really happening. Investors who ask what changed and whether the change is permanent or not will have a distinct advantage.

If you learned the true reason for California's high gas prices, you could prevent similar problems at other times or in other places and save drivers billions of dollars. There is a lot of value in that information. (See Chapter 12 for more on the topic of information and its value.) Saving billions of dollars and making the economy more efficient is, of course, the very ideal of public policy analysis. The risk is to, instead, fall prey to the simplistic argument blaming greed because we have no reason to think that the level of greed has changed. How can the California state government do a better job without first truly learning from the gas price increases taking place? Based on our experience, we don't hold out much hope. As Newton warned, *that* body may stay at rest until an outside force requires *it* to change.

Chapter 5

KNOW WHAT YOU WANT BEFORE YOU CHOOSE

Give us clear vision, that we may know where to stand and what to stand for—because unless we stand for something, we shall fall for anything. — Peter Marshall

In his short story entitled "How I Edited an Agricultural Paper," Mark Twain tells of a time when he was hired as the editor of a newspaper with the express purpose of increasing circulation while the regular editor was on holiday. Twain does such a wonderful job that the regular editor cuts short his vacation and returns to the office angry—not happy, as one would expect, given the increased circulation. In a heated conversation, the editor tells Twain that he is incompetent and must leave. Twain responds, pointedly:

> I have fulfilled my contract as far as I was permitted to do it. I said I could make your paper of interest to all classes—and I have. And I said I could run your circulation up to twenty thousand copies, and if I had had two more weeks I'd have done it. And I'd have given you the best class of readers that ever an agricultural paper had – not a farmer in it, nor a solitary individual who could tell a watermelon-tree from a peach-vine to save his life. You are the loser by this rupture, not me, pie-plant. Adios.[28]

What had Twain done? In one article, he wrote, "Turnips should never be pulled; it injures them. It is much better to send a boy up and let him shake the tree." Everybody in town positively *had* to read the paper to see what zany thing Twain would write next. And it did get zanier. He said that the pumpkin was gaining favor as a berry that was preferred over the raspberry for feeding cows, but that the notion of the pumpkin as a shade tree was a failure. Twain said he would increase circulation dramatically and he did, creating quite a stir among the townsfolk in the process. He had never said *how* he would increase circulation. The regular editor's mistake was that he didn't specify exactly what he wanted. When the editor saw the disaster unfolding, he cut short his holiday to fire Twain.

If you don't know what you want, how can you get it? You may have it right now, for all you know. If your objectives aren't clear, you might not like what you end up with. Fortunately, we don't have to let this happen to us. We can learn from the mistakes of others and ensure that our objectives are clear. In other words, we should be clear what we want *before* we choose, which will help us focus our attention and make the right decisions. Like the Twain story above, the following stories span a wide range of experiences. While seemingly disparate, they all show the benefit of clear objectives and the peril of not knowing what is really desired.

The Customer is *Always* Right?

A story well known in marketing and customer service circles goes like this. An older lady entered Nordstrom's to return four car tires, saying that she didn't want them. Of course, Nordstrom's doesn't sell car tires; it doesn't sell *any* automotive parts or equipment. Nordstrom's is a prestigious retailer of fine women and men's clothes with great service and a great return policy. True to form, the quintessential Nordstrom's clerk happily took the tires and gave the lady a store credit.

It is generally accepted that to generate good profits, a business must have good customer service—in other words, profits are the ends and customer service is the means. This doesn't mean that all customers will always be thrilled, or should be thrilled, or that the customer is always right. What would you say to a customer who walks into your store and claims to have a $500 credit without any paperwork to substantiate it? After all, you are in business to sell products and services, not to give them away. There has to be a limit.

Keeping current customers happy is usually inexpensive when you consider their future stream of purchases and the cost of attracting new customers. At some point, however, even the lady with the tires has to be considered in the context of her likely future purchases. Is it really worth it?

Consider a difficult, high-maintenance customer standing at the front of the line and an unlucky, appeasing clerk doing her best to satisfy the customer. The other three customers in line get impatient and leave. This leaves the "customer-service-oriented company" with 25 percent as many customers. But it's worse than that: the company isn't left with a random pick from a set of four customers—it's stuck with the worst one, while the three better ones are long gone. This is ironic. With the objective of keeping customers happy in order to realize profits, this company has done neither. It has lost 75 percent of its customers and reduced potential profits.

My (CLH's) company, Objective Insights, derives 80 percent of its revenues from repeat business. Based on this number, you could rightfully say that we must be keeping our customers happy, and in addition, if we fell down in this area, our livelihood would suffer enormously. Should we then make sure that every customer is happy every time? No. Consider what happened with one unhappy customer.

We completed a sales forecasting and pricing analysis for a young company developing a new product consisting of an original delivery system for a corticosteroid. Corticosteroids in other formulations, such as ointments or creams, are not new; you may have used one in the past for such conditions as dermatitis or psoriasis. At the time, annual revenues in this market exceeded $630 million. If this new product was so good, this company reasoned, sales could exceed $200 million a year. But this product came in a new formulation that made it appropriate for only a small subset of the market. So instead of having the potential to sell $200 million a year, we determined that it would sell approximately—gulp!—$17 million. Understandably, this made for an awkward presentation to the CEO and management team. The CEO yelled at us for not presenting "creative ideas" to fix the problem. We replied that the narrow scope of our project was to tell them what was likely to happen given their present course, not to chart a new course. We certainly would have been happy to help them with creative strategies. Instead, we were kicked out of the boardroom so that the management team could arrest the calamity we had spawned. Goodbye client and goodbye future business.

The following year this product did launch. After a few years, the data were in. Neither of us were spot on—forecasts for new products rarely are—but the actual sales were well within the probabilistic range we presented. And our midpoint forecast value was only about 8 percent too low. In the forecasting business this is considered hitting the bull's-eye. The CEO's estimate, on the other hand, was about 1,000 percent too high.

Was the customer happy? Certainly not! Did we do the right thing? Yes, and we have done the same thing since. If we kowtow to a customer's unreasonable expectations, our reputation suffers and we cease providing a valuable service to all of our customers, even the unreasonable ones.

Sometimes it's just best to tell customers that they are wrong. My (CLH's) haircutter—who has the perfect name for someone in her profession, Caroline Northcutt—did just that. One day Caroline assessed a new customer who had just walked in. The customer had long hair that had been obviously abused with all sorts of perms and colorings and it revealed the last five colors it had been dyed. She asked Caroline to color it so that it would be a consistent color. "No, I can't. Your hair will break off if I try. I don't have enough insurance," Caroline informed the woman, who was quickly getting angry, and shortly afterwards walked out. Caroline later found that this woman had gone to three other stylists, all who claimed that they could dye the woman's hair. The customer let one try and, just as Caroline had said, her hair broke off close to her scalp. The customer was not happy with inch-long hair, but she still came back to Caroline to express her amazement. "You were right. You were the only one who told me the truth. I guess the other ones just wanted my money," she admitted. Can you guess the name of this customer's new stylist? Caroline, of course. This story has two lessons. One is that sometimes the customer really is wrong and needs to be so advised to prevent bigger problems. The other is that honesty often pays, and certainly did pay for Caroline, which is a topic we explore more thoroughly in Chapter 15.

The following story shows how one company lost while trying to keep customers happy.

A large pharmaceutical company produced a nasal inhaler containing 60 metered sprays, or "puffs," per bottle. Its direct competitors all had bottles containing 120 puffs. The company's market research showed that customers were unhappy with its "small" bottle size. Lost in all this was the reason for the smaller bottle size: this product could be used once a day, rather than twice a day, and still achieve the same efficacy. In other words, the 60-puff bottle gave just as much pharmaceutical potency as the 120-puff bottle and was easier to use. Had customers understood this, they would have realized that the 60-puff bottle was actually superior to the competitors' 120-puff bottles.

But the company decided not to directly address this huge benefit to the customer. The product manager, wanting to keep the customer happy, asked the manufacturing branch to produce a 120-dose bottle. Now came the job of pricing. Some in the company advocated a price twice the 60-dose bottle's price. In the end, though, the 120-dose bottle was priced just slightly higher than the 60-dose bottle, even though analysts inside the company warned that this pricing would give the customer an implicit price decrease and that the firm would have to sell 90 percent more puffs *just to break even*. The company put more promotional effort behind this product and did break even, but consider how much work went into just breaking even. The company fielded market research, developed a new package, spent time analyzing its decisions, introduced a new bottle size, and invested extra time and money to promote this product. All this to make only as much money as it could have made by not innovating at all.

The company got into this mess because its customers didn't understand that its product was better than the competitors'. QD dosing (once per day) is almost always significantly better than BID dosing (twice a day), and companies are now working on once-per-week and once-per-month formulations. In this example, the company had failed to convince its customers of the value of its medicine. The customer wasn't right (the bottle wasn't too small); rather, the customer wasn't informed. This is a case of the customers being wrong, not because of some fault or shortcoming of theirs, but because they hadn't received the right information. Both Nordstrom's and the pharmaceutical company are saying that the customer is always right, but that view isn't necessarily true, and acting that way can cause a company to fall short of its real goals.

The following is a story of a company that is succeeding by realizing that customers aren't always right and, further, that some customers are better than others.

Best Buy is the largest retailer of consumer electronics in the United States with sales revenues of over $24 billion. Best Buy's CEO, Brad Anderson, is, as we write, sorting his customers into "angels" and "devils." One such devil bragged about purchasing "only steeply discounted loss leaders, except when forcing Best Buy to match rock-bottom prices advertised elsewhere."[29] Other devils were found to buy merchandise and then return it, hoping to later buy it back with an "open box" discount. Best Buy would like to get rid of its devils, which it estimates account for 100 million of its 500 million customer visits. The angels, on the other end of the spectrum—another 100 million customer visits—account for the bulk of its profits. Notice that only 20 percent of Best Buy's customer visits account for the majority of its profits and only 20 percent account for its problems. For more on this common result, see Pareto's Law in Chapter 11.

Best Buy has implemented the angel-devil strategy in about 100 of its 670 stores. Anderson says that early results show that the pilot stores "are clobbering" the regular stores and that sales gains in these stores are double those of traditional stores.

Larry Selden, a professor at Columbia University's Graduate School of Business and a consultant to Best Buy, says that often the losses produced by devils wipe out the profits arising from angels. Best Buy has no obligation to serve customers who are actively trying to thwart it. By realizing that customers aren't always right and that some customers are better than others, Best Buy has become financially stronger.

Focusing on Costs

In many pharmaceutical companies, the manufacturing folks carefully manage inventory levels. Product inventories cost money, of course, so the company may give the manufacturing people annual bonuses for minimizing inventory levels and saving the company money. This makes sense. If a company spends $120 million a year manufacturing a product, spending tens of thousands of dollars on incentives is prudent if even a small fraction of the $120 million can be saved.

Most pharmaceutical raw materials have long shelf lives, so if they are not used this quarter or even this year, they can be used next quarter or next year. The real cost is one of timing, or the time-value of money. If the next $10 million batch can be delayed a month, a month's interest on $10 million can be saved. This is a lot of money—many thousands of dollars.

But consider the gain from holding extra inventory. This $10 million will be turned into $100 million at retail prices, for a ten to one return. If I hold too much inventory, I suffer the cost of the interest I lose. If I hold too little inventory, I suffer lost retail sales. Either way I have a loss, but the losses from not having any product to sell—known as stockouts—are much bigger. The loss from stockouts is even bigger if this drug is for chronic conditions that require long-term treatment. Once I lose customers, I may have broken the cycle and lost them for the rest of their lives. Worse yet, patients, pharmacists, and doctors may lose trust in my company's ability to deliver product on a regular basis and then shy away from our other products, causing collateral damage.

This is not farfetched. Stockouts happen, usually with disastrous outcomes. The *Wall Street Journal* reported in early 2000 that a shortage of some antibiotics was partly due to the "just-in-time delivery and razor-thin inventories of the pharmaceutical business."[30] In March 2001, hospitals in several areas of the country experienced critical shortages of some anesthetics.[31] While the ultimate cause of the shortages was still being investigated, part of the problem was that hospitals had kept smaller inventories as they moved towards just-in-time inventory systems.

Let's consider just how asymmetric the two kinds of losses are. Based on typical values for medicines, the cost of holding one too many bottles for one month is 7.97 cents. The cost of holding one too few bottles, and thus having a stockout, is a whopping $1,350, for a 16,930 to one cost ratio. This means that the manufacturing people could hold one extra bottle for 16,930 months, or 1,411 years, to match the cost of a one-bottle shortage for one month. Of course, there probably won't be any branded medicines or companies around for 1,411 years, so we might as well say that they should plan on *never* having a stockout.[32] Are these results surprising? They probably are, but we reached this startling conclusion by using typical values for typical medicines.

These companies are focusing on costs, but their primary focus should be on profits. Reducing costs is good unless it reduces revenues even more. This perspective may lead to similar conclusions outside the pharmaceutical industry. Cisco, Lucent, and Seagate, all technology companies, have the burden of crushing inventory expenses as the rapid pace of innovation depreciates existing stock. It might appear as if they need just-in-time inventory systems to survive, but another technology company, Koss Corp., a manufacturer of high-fidelity headphones, abandoned just-in-time inventories after back orders sometimes hit 70 percent of a month's volume.[33] While each situation may be unique, the rule still holds: companies should focus on profits, not expenses.

This is not always what companies do. Many companies and many departments within organizations spend a lot of effort reducing expenses. What we have shown here is that these organizations would make better overall decisions if they were clear on their primary objectives. As the editor in the Twain story discovered too late: achieving your secondary objective at the expense of your primary objective may give you indigestion instead of a restful vacation.

Getting There Efficiently

Knowing what you want can also help you solve problems more quickly and efficiently. When attacking problems, sometimes people collect too little or too much information because they don't have a clear objective in mind. But even with a clear objective, you still need to be careful. I (CLH) live on a private road and we recently changed our system from one where everyone pays the same amount for road maintenance to one that is "fairer." The initial equitable solution was to measure the distance from the main road to each family's driveway, compute their proportional use of the whole road, and then charge them accordingly. That way, someone who drives a mile on our road pays twice as much as someone who drives only half a mile.

This may seem straightforward, but if your objective is to develop a system that is completely fair, you could literally spend your entire life analyzing this situation and still not succeed. A fair solution really depends on measuring precisely how much each family contributes to road wear and damage. Measuring distances to each driveway is a good place to start, but if my neighbor has a behemoth sport-utility vehicle and I have a small motorcycle, she is definitely causing more wear. So, we could start with:

- ❑ Distance to driveways
- ❑ Weight of vehicles
- ❑ Frequency of trips
- ❑ Aggressiveness of drivers
- ❑ Number of drivers in each household
- ❑ Number and frequency of visiting friends
- ❑ Frequency of delivery trucks (some people get a lot of UPS, FedEx, and newspaper deliveries)

- ❑ Time of day and weather during trips (driving during the rain and snow probably causes more wear on the road)
- ❑ An understanding that the weather, and not driving, causes 70 percent of all road wear

Even if you could spend the rest of your life analyzing this problem, you shouldn't. The maintenance cost for our road is only $3,710 per year spread out over 50 families—a modest $74.20 per family. If, for some reason, I were required to find the ultimate fair solution, and I knew that it would take me a year of effort to do so, I would propose the following solution. I would pay for the whole road maintenance myself and spend the subsequent 99.99 percent of my year in gainful employment. Financially, it makes more sense. After all, too much analysis is wasteful and slows our decision-making progress. Our stated objective was to make the dues process fairer, not to swallow the time of the road association directors in a futile search for a perfectly fair system. This leads to a general rule: **we need to clarify our objectives to see how much thinking and analysis is appropriate**. (See Chapter 12 for more discussion on the value of information.)

In the previous story, the private road residents succeeded in avoiding excessive analysis. In the following example, as you will see, there is a cost of too little analysis. The trick is balance.

An accountant got a list of clients from an associate who was dying. The accountant later called a woman on the list who had used the associate to file her income taxes for years. The new accountant took over in the middle of the process and did his best to clean up some pretty sloppy work. In the process, he saved the woman $2,000 in taxes. Was she happy? No. She was used to paying her accountant $125 for filing her taxes and found his $375 fee exorbitant. The next year, she gave him another chance but said, "Keep your charges down." Is this reasonable?

For an additional investment of $250 (the difference between $375 and $125), she received a return of $2,000, or eight times what she invested. She should have been ecstatic for finding such a thorough CPA. Instead of concerning herself with minimizing the accounting fees she pays, she should have concentrated on minimizing the sum total of the fees and the taxes. With this clearer overall objective, she would have been happy investing progressively more in accounting fees if each additional investment produced at least as much tax savings. Here is how a clear-thinking person would approach this stepwise problem:

❏ Investment One = $125. This is the cost of getting your taxes completed by a CPA. It is the base cost for getting your taxes accurately filed on time. After this much effort, your total tax bill stands at $12,000.

❏ Investment Two = $250. This is the next increment in accounting effort, allowing the CPA to look for further savings. With this investment, your tax bill drops by $2,000 to $10,000. This is a great investment, returning 700 percent (a net return of $1,750 divided by the cost $250). This is where we find this particular client right now.

❏ Investment Three = $125. The third investment drops the tax bill another $200 to $9,800. While this investment is less successful than Investment Two, it is still a good investment, with a 60-percent return.

❏ Investment Four = $125. The fourth investment reduces the tax bill another $100 to $9,700. This is not a good investment. You should request that the CPA stop all further work on your tax return, pay your $625 accountant fee (note that we can't undo the fourth step) and pay your $9,700 tax bill.

In total, you will have spent $625 but saved $2,300 on your taxes. This is an excellent investment. The solution for this situation would have been much more apparent had the client been clearer on her reasons for hiring a CPA. Was she trying to minimize her CPA's bill—that's easy: don't hire one—or her overall expense, including the payment to the IRS? She should have been clear on this before she gave the new CPA the job. Note that this is another application of thinking on the margin. Once you've completed the second investment, is it smart to proceed to the third? For a more complete discussion of thinking on the margin, see Chapter 2.

Look at the Big Picture—Is Something More Important?

You've probably heard about doctors who eat horribly and smoke, or financial advisors who have no financial assets. They are professionals who fail to follow their own advice.

I (CLH) have my own similar story. In my profession, I use analysis to help my clients make good business decisions. I help them see their problems clearly, so they can act confidently. And, as you may have guessed, I used analysis in my own business to make a bad decision—an awful decision, in fact. I hired an employee away from my best client. My analysis showed how much money I would make by properly using this currently underused employee. My client pointedly showed me how much money I *would not* make after losing 50 percent of my revenues as a result of being "fired" by him. Let me explain.

We took Roger to lunch, as we do with all new hires at Objective Insights. At the time, we saved the Los Gatos Brewing Company, a nice microbrewery and restaurant, for lunches like these and for when our clients visited. As we were sitting in the upscale surroundings eating our salads, I asked Roger how Scott, his previous boss, took his resignation. Roger said, "Oh, Scott is really pissed, and he said he may never work with Objective Insights again." Roger took another mouthful of salad, as if we had just discussed the weather or the route he took to work on his first day. I, on the other hand, saw the light go on, and then the whole world went dark as I slumped in my seat.

I couldn't believe it. We had analyzed this thoroughly, but only from our own perspective. We knew how many projects were needed to keep Roger busy and what to do if the work dried up. We thought of all the possibilities and all the contingencies. We did mathematical modeling on a computer and had many internal discussions and meetings with Roger to ensure his fit into our company culture. But we missed the big picture: none of us would have a job, especially Roger, if our biggest client fired us. I felt so stupid.

I could make excuses all day long, but excuses are worthless. I needed to come to grips with a mistake of legendary proportions. I had properly solved one of our problems, but I hadn't framed the *correct overall problem*: how to make my company most successful. I am embarrassed to repeat this story, but I learned something important: always look at the big picture. While hiring Roger was a wonderful decision in a narrow sense, it was, on a broader level, the worst thing I could have done. In one step, I both increased my costs and reduced my revenues. I should have considered and analyzed the possible response of all stakeholders, not just Roger and my company.

I apologized profusely to Scott and asked for ways to right my wrong. Scott calmed down after a few days, but our business with him declined dramatically. Just before the metaphorical buzzer at the end of the game, however, luck showed up to save the day. Unbeknownst to us, Scott had been recommending us highly to others in his company, and just a few days after this fiasco, a vice-president engaged us in a major project that kept all of us, including Roger, busy for over a year. We were lucky, not smart. Why not be both?

Some may say that the previous story shows the folly of analysis. Even when you do it, you may make mistakes, perhaps bad ones. But to completely avoid analysis is like studying a football game and concluding that, because running and passing didn't work for the losing team, a football team should neither run nor pass. That conclusion is absurd: running and passing worked for the winning team, didn't it? The key is to make sure that you're analyzing the right problem. Our narrow analysis of hiring Roger probably contributed to our lack of perspective, which can happen when you focus on trees and lose sight of the forest.

The trick here is to look at the big picture and see if something is more important, which is really just a different way of knowing what you want before you choose. Had we been clear about our objectives for hiring Roger, we would have considered our client's perspective and avoided a major mistake.

What is Your Objective?

To know what you want, first you have to spend some time thinking about it. Years ago a coworker asked me (CLH) which of two jobs his wife should take. I told him I couldn't recommend a job until I knew what her objectives were. He quickly realized that he didn't know either. How could he and I discuss jobs for his wife if we didn't know what she wanted? Without this knowledge, we would be merely projecting our values onto her, which wouldn't solve her problem at all—and if it did, it would be by sheer luck, not by good decision-making. It was to be her job, not ours, so we put our conversation on hold until he could ask her. Even when the decision *is* ours, and not our friend's wife's, we should pause just the same and figure out what we want *before* we choose.

Try this exercise in clear(er) thinking. Stop yourself when you are struggling with a decision and ask yourself what you want. What is your objective? You should be able to construct a one- to four-sentence response that a high-school student could understand. For example, "I want to find a job that will allow me to retire sooner. I need to believe in the company and its products. I'd like to have a good relationship with my immediate co-workers." Once you make this clear, you will be in a much better position to decide which of your alternatives best meets your objectives—or, as in the story above, to enlist some friends or coworkers to help you.

Is it an Expense or an Investment?

Is an expenditure an expense or an investment? This frequently stumps many of us. We should be clear which is which because we handle the two very differently. Consider the following example.

Depending on the current state of the economy, you may see headlines such as: "Company Job Cuts: Daimler Chrysler 26,000; Motorola 16,370; Lucent Technologies 16,000; Proctor & Gamble Co. 9,600."[34] The list goes on. Some of these companies' businesses were seriously declining, and they simply needed fewer employees. Others, however, stated that they wanted to reduce costs.

If reducing costs is really their objective, why not lay off *all* the employees? Employees *cost* money and laying them off *saves* money—definitely a good thing. Once again, though, we suspect that their real objective was not just to reduce costs, but to make the most money. To do this, they needed to maximize the difference between revenues and expenses.

This raises the issue of investments versus expenses. If you view all expenditures as expenses, it is natural to try to reduce them. But if you view them as *investments*, it is natural to consider their value. When you look at the big picture and see your objective as the maximization of profits subject to your cash flow constraints, you realize that you must invest to get a return, and do so with a deft balance of short-term cash flow and long-term profits. Investments usually don't pay off immediately. Imagine that you've started a restaurant. After months of work acquiring a building, setting up the dining room and the kitchen, hiring the right people, and developing a great menu, opening night arrives. Unfortunately, except for the friends and family you invited, only three paying customers show up. Realizing that you will never make any money with only three customers a night, you close your business the next day. Well, of course that's ridiculous. You need time to allow your investments to grow. You need to give your restaurant more time.

Go back to the issue of corporate layoffs: either the employees are profitable or they're not. If the employees generate a profit, firing them will reduce future profits. If the employees cost more than they are worth, then why were they employed originally? Recent research casts doubt on the merits of layoffs. According to Alan Blinder, former vice-chairman of the Federal Reserve Board, "The evidence that [downsizing] boosts productivity is very weak."[35] Blinder cites several studies that show that downsizing hurt companies more than it helped in the 1990s. Economists, consultants, and managers all have questioned the value of layoffs. "It has become ever more clear to management...that talent is a critical resource," says Donald Redlinger, who helped run AlliedSignal's human resources operation during much of the 1990s. "Going to layoffs on a knee-jerk basis would be a flawed strategy."[36] So, consider all those layoffs in the headlines. Possibly, these companies were simply being astute and were matching employees to workload. If this was the case, it's possible that employees who were profitable during boom times may not have been profitable during a bust. But if that's not the case, and if the companies had no cash flow problem threatening their immediate survival, they might have done better to hire *more* employees.

Here's another example of a bad decision caused by failing to distinguish correctly between expenses and investments. A well-known pharmaceutical company spent many hundreds of millions of dollars each year on basic research that the company knew would not return a dime for 15 to 20 years. This same company required its marketing programs to become profitable in one year. The company understood the long-term nature of its investment in pharmaceutical research, yet it viewed marketing programs as worthwhile expenses only if they paid for themselves within a year. See Looking for Arbitrage in Chapter 14 for an interesting potential solution to this problem.

When you make a relatively illiquid investment, such as going to school, buying real estate, or starting a restaurant, at first you become poorer. To be richer, first you must be poorer. The name of the game is profits, and very few profits are made without some kind of commitment of time and money. The trick is to make investments that you can afford from a cash-flow perspective and then give these investments time to reach fruition. Appreciating the distinction between expenses and investments will help you make better decisions for your company and for yourself.

My (CLH's) son Mitchell loves to help around the house. When we have a problem, he never hesitates; he just grabs a tool and starts to work. One night the toilet overflowed, and, as usual, Mitchell was right there, ready to help.

A simple question. Does my work get done faster or slower with Mitchell's help? Let's segue to the business world. An important project is going badly. Perhaps Motorola has lost its lead and has fallen behind in the design of cellular phones. Does Motorola's management fix this problem by keeping the team constant or by putting more or fewer people on the project? The answer is obvious from the framing of the question: they always put more people on the project in an attempt to make it go better and faster.

Back to my broken toilet. Did my work get done faster or slower with Mitchell's help? The answer, unfortunately, is slower.

Mitchell was three years old at the time. When he helped, I had to do twice as much work, and each thing I did took twice as long, so my work was slowed down by 75 percent.

Could this be happening at Motorola? It very well might be. Management needs to know whether additional workers will slow down or speed up a project. The implications for the success of the project are dramatic, as Frederich P. Brooks argues in his book *The Mythical Man-Month*. You can pick more cotton with more workers because you can partition the tasks. But computer programming may slow when workers are added because of the complex communication and interrelationships involved. The new programmers need to be initiated, a process that takes time away from senior programmers, and then communication increases roughly as the square of the number of workers because every programmer communicates with every other programmer. In this case, adding workers both increases costs and slows progress[37]—a lose-lose situation. This is the problem Mitchell and I encountered, one you'd prefer to avoid whether you're fixing a toilet or running a company.

The examples above show the problems with too many and too few employees. Here's another. Store managers often think that they save money by economizing on the number of clerks they hire. Indeed, they do save on their payroll, but often at the cost of their profits. Imagine that each checker in a grocery store earns $10 per hour. Assume that there are five customers in line and that the value of *their* time is also, on average, $10 an hour. In other words, they have other things they'd rather be doing. The five customers in line are "paying" a total of $50 an hour, while the checker earns only $10 an hour. Is this the way to attract or repel customers? In this case, society would be better off with more checkers, more evenly balancing the time-values of the checkers and that of the people standing in line—unless the store offers something even more valuable in return, such as very low prices. If opportunities like this exist, some other entrepreneur will try to find a way to exploit them, say by having more checkers and higher prices. The result is that the store with long lines may get short lines—because their customers have been competed away. What follows is a true story demonstrating this problem.

In 2001, I (CLH) flew home to California from Philadelphia and stood in a check-in line at the United counter for 45 minutes because 50 people were ahead of me. The real cause of the delay, however, was not the number of people in line. It was the fact that United Airlines had three people working the counter to check in the 50 regular passengers and the 25 or so first-class and premier passengers. And the woman who helped me shouldn't have even been there—she was working overtime! If we assume that each check-in clerk was earning $20 per hour and that the time of each person in line was worth $10 (like the people in the grocery line, they would have preferred to spend their time doing something else), United was paying $60 per hour, and we, as a group, were "paying" a whopping $750 per hour! To properly balance these costs, one that was paid directly and the other that was paid indirectly, United should have hired more clerks to speed up check-in.

Was I a captive customer? Yes, at that point I was, but my next dozen flights were on America West, which had much shorter check-in lines. Because the United and America West check-in lines were right next to each other, I could easily compare the two. The ticket prices were similar to United's, but the check-in was ten times as fast. So here is an example of a business that lost at least one customer due to a shortage of clerks. In United's defense, its employees are part of a powerful union and this may have hampered its ability to hire and schedule people for busy check-in periods such as those I experienced.

A similar insight is that it is better to make customers wait in line once rather than twice. The famous Golden Gate Bridge between San Francisco and Marin used to collect tolls in each direction, causing its customers to wait in long lines to pay both coming and going. In 1968, the toll was changed from 25 cents each way to 50 cents southbound (i.e., into San Francisco), with northbound passage free.[38] The Golden Gate Bridge was the first bridge in the world to offer such a seemingly obvious innovation.[39] Later, all the bridges in the Bay Area changed to collecting tolls in one direction only. This change allowed them to give better service, to cut their toll-collecting costs by 50 percent, and to collect the same revenues from the tolls that they doubled. Was this solution obvious? If so, why did it take 31 years for the Golden Gate Bridge to originate such an "obvious" solution?

Maximize the Ends, Not the Means

A biotechnology company was confused about what it wanted. This company considered dropping one of its top-selling drugs because of the high cost of manufacturing products that overlapped and competed with each other. The company's stated objectives were to reduce manufacturing cost and simplify the product line. Given a problem framed this way, the solution is easy: stop production of the drug to save money and reduce the number of products it offered. But this is not the proper way to frame this problem, and—as Charley's Roger/Scott fiasco shows—when you frame a problem incorrectly, you're likely to get an incorrect answer. Is this company in business to reduce its manufacturing costs and simplify its product line? No. If it were, the solution would be simple: drop all products and "succeed" wildly.

Success in business means developing products and services so valuable that profits flow for years and decades. Dropping products makes costs decline, which is good, but revenues also decline, which is bad. It's very bad if revenues fall more than costs because that means that profits decline. In this particular case, the company's own market research showed that discontinuing the drug would reduce revenues by $52 million per year, and we calculated that costs would decline by only $20 million, for a net loss of $32 million per year.

The objective should be to maximize profits, not to simplify the lives of the product managers. But because profits are often hard to predict and sometimes hard to conceptualize and measure, companies frequently focus on easier measures, such as revenues or costs. To increase profits, we want to maximize revenues and minimize costs (although we usually can't do both at once). But in our pursuit of these two goals, we need to remember that they are means to an end. And if we maximize these means independently, we may actually reduce the ends. Don't trade off means for ends. Don't focus on ways of getting there and lose sight of the end result. In other words, keep your primary objective in clear focus so that you will know what you want before you choose.

A woman in San Diego may have learned a similar lesson about keeping her primary objective in clear focus, but we might be giving her too much credit. She was pulled over while doing 61 MPH in a 45-zone. After being pulled over, she said, "I'm not sticking around." She grabbed the officer's citation book and sped off. Then she led the California Highway Patrol on a chase, throwing the citation book out the window on the way. "Here's your ticket book," she yelled out her window to the pursuing officer. What was her hurry? She was taking her 5-year-old son to school and didn't want to be late. Of course she was caught, but then she wouldn't get out of the car as ordered. Instead of getting out, she "puts a death grip on the steering wheel." She later apologized as she was driven off to jail.[40] What was her desired end? A fruitful education for her son. What was her means at the time? Driving her son to school promptly and safely. This means morphed into getting her son to school on time at all costs. Had she clearly thought this through, she would have realized that while being on time is important, it was more important to avoid a collision and/or a speeding ticket. It's hard to provide a good education to your son if you're in jail and your car is totaled.

Some companies, like many Internet companies at the end of 1999, have focused on market share as their objective. With established market share, they have credibility and leverage in the market, but without it, they may be ignored or risk being swallowed by a larger company. With some companies, market share is vital. Consider eBay. Its critical mass attracts more customers, which, in turn, attracts even more customers. If you can place your antique china closet on only one Internet auction site, why not select the one with ten times as many potential buyers? If you are looking for an old electric guitar, why not start shopping at eBay first?

But eBay is a fairly unusual case. In the more typical case, market share doesn't matter nearly as much. A person buying a stove that she expects to last for 10 years probably doesn't care much whether the stove's manufacturer supplies 4 percent or 40 percent of the market. Sometimes companies with large market shares are not very successful—General Motors, K-mart, and Sears being three examples. Companies are successful because they do a better job than others of selling valuable products and services to customers. According to Thomas Nagle and Reed Holden, authors of *The Strategy and Tactics of Pricing*:

> The ultimate objective of any strategic plan should not be to achieve or even sustain sales volume, but to build and sustain competitive advantage. Profitability, and in many cases, market share, will follow. Market share, rather than being the key to profitability, is, like profitability, simply another symptom of a fundamentally well-run company.[41]

In other words, since market share usually is a means rather than an end in itself, striving for market share may ultimately handicap a company. Profitability is a bit trickier because it is the best measure of the sustainable competitive advantage generated by successfully implementing a good strategic plan. Profitability is the tangible result of a competitive advantage, and so it is the easiest metric by which we judge the value, or desirability, of a competitive advantage. Your company could have a competitive advantage in financial services in Chico, California, and that may earn profits of $2 million per year. If instead, your company had a competitive advantage in financial services in the whole country, that could be worth $20 billion per year. This $20 billion profit is the metric by which we judge that bigger opportunity.

To be effective, you need to determine which are your ends and which are your means to those ends. Maximize the ends, but don't trade off means for ends. Don't focus on ways of getting there and lose sight of the end result, because the means may roughly, but not exactly, coincide with the ends.

Ford Motor Company seems to have learned this lesson. Rejecting the accepted strategy in the industry, Ford has cut capacity to focus on more profitable vehicles and markets. Ford still wants to sell lots of cars and trucks, but now it is focused on profits. "I've seen us in eras where we blindly chased [market] share and created all kinds of problems," says CEO William Clay Ford, Jr.[42] By practicing "revenue management," that is, monitoring prices and sales trends and adjusting tactics to maximize profits, and by saying "no" to bulk sales to rental car companies at low markups, Ford has lost market share but gained profits. From 2001 to 2004, Ford's U.S. market share dropped from approximately 22 percent to 19 percent, but quarterly net income went from minus $1.36 billion in 2001 to around positive $650 million for the four quarters ending in September 2004.[43]

Ford's experience shows that market share isn't essential for creating a profitable company. Perhaps Ford learned this from Toyota Motor Corporation. Toyota's U.S. market share is significantly lower than the combined share of the Big Three U.S. car companies, yet its market capitalization is more than that of the other three companies combined. Around the time that this was written, GM had 27.6 percent market share, while Ford had 19.6, DaimlerChrysler had 13.2, and Toyota had 11 percent. Market capitalization, the number of shares outstanding times the market price—the minimum you'd have to pay to buy the whole company—tells a different story. Toyota is worth $124.6 billion, while GM is worth only $21.8 billion, Ford is worth $26.2 billion, and DaimlerChrysler is worth $46.2 billion.[44] We realize that there is more to the worldwide automobile market than just the United States, but the U.S. market is the largest single market in the world. In that market, Toyota's market share is one fifth as large as the Big Three combined (11 versus 60.4 percent), but Toyota is still worth more than the Big Three combined ($124.6 versus $94.2 billion). If market share is so important, why is Toyota worth so much more? The answer is net income, that is, profit. Toyota's net income is about double that of the Big Three. Investors value profits over market share.

Market share can be a means to achieving profits, but means shouldn't take precedence over the ends. The automotive company that maximized the ends—Toyota—is more successful than the companies that maximized the means to the ends—the so-called Big Three. Profits can be put in the bank, but market share can't.

Oh Really? Revenues Are *That* Important?

A number of Objective Insights' clients focus on increasing their revenues. All else being equal, higher revenues will translate into higher profits. Yet, as we have discussed, profits are the end and revenues are the means. Profits are frequently hard to optimize, however, because they depend on fixed and variable costs and avoidable and unavoidable costs, some of which these companies don't readily disclose or perhaps even measure. The focus on revenues is the easy solution.

Unfortunately, many people forget that revenues are just the means and start focusing on maximizing revenues even if it means giving up profits. How often have you heard company managers, and even company owners, say things like: "Within three years, I want my company's annual revenues to rise from $5 million to $10 million." Oh, really? Consider the case where they're now making annual profits of $500,000 off $5 million in sales of existing products and services. After entering a new and expensive segment of the market, they enjoy $10 million in revenues, but, because of their astronomical expenses, have annual losses of $100,000. Would they really want that? They'd be better off sticking to what they are good at—their existing products.

You might think that company owners wouldn't make that kind of mistake, but we have found that they do. So these same people shouldn't be surprised when their employees follow this advice and take actions calculated to increase revenues at the expense of profits.

Consider the case of a pharmaceutical company's managed-care department which negotiates contracts with health maintenance organizations and pharmacy benefit management companies. The department is rewarded on the number of deals completed and on sales volume. Guess what? This group quickly figured out the incentives and acted accordingly, giving large discounts to get contracts and move lots of product. Is this the way to run a profitable company? No. The solution, as laid out by Thomas Nagle and Reed Holden, is to give incentives for selling *value* rather than volume. "Give sales people sales goals as before, but tell them that the sales goals are set at 'target' prices. If they sell at prices below or above the 'target,' the sales credit they earn will be adjusted by the profitability of the sale."[45] This makes the employees' incentives congruent with those of the organization, helping to boost profits. The previous examples help to elucidate the tension among revenues, expenses, and profits. Now consider the tradeoff between short-term and long-term results.

Short-Term Versus Long-Term Focus

Companies should focus on maximizing profits by creating a sustainable advantage in the market place. This advantage comes from offering better quality and better-value products and services than the competition. Do companies always do this? Certainly not. This sustainable advantage and profit perspective is a long-term focus, but many companies clearly focus on the short term. Is there any reason for a short-term focus other than an obsession with this quarter's earnings? Well, yes, there is. It's called cash flow. Cash flows are necessary to realize profits because profits are the end product of investments, and investments take time to mature. In essence, profits show desirability, while cash flows show feasibility. Cash flows enable profits to happen. The best idea in the world will die on the vine if cash flows are insufficient to allow it to reach fruition.

When we at Objective Insights make financial models for smaller, younger companies—for which cash flow is critical—we frequently use both profits and cash flow as key outputs. We calculate the probability of a cash flow crisis—i.e., having less than a certain amount of money at the nadir of the cash flow curve—as a key to the desirability of that particular decision path. In this way, we consider and balance both long-term and short-term objectives to help these companies decide with confidence.

The Lessons Learned

The editor who hired Mark Twain made a big mistake by not knowing what he wanted before he hired him. He eventually got what he *said* he wanted, increased circulation, but he didn't get what he *really* wanted, increased circulation coupled with the preservation of his paper's integrity. Twain had sacrificed the one to get the other, which is the source of the humor. The regular editor should have known what he wanted, and made that clear, before he hired Twain. Of course, we normally don't state the obvious—it's too obvious!

Those who preach to businesses frequently repeat the mantra that the customer is always right. All else being equal, we want happy customers, but companies shouldn't sacrifice more important objectives to achieve customer satisfaction because customer satisfaction is a means to an end, not an end in itself.

We have seen how we should never strive to achieve the means to the detriment of the ends, which is exactly what the pharmaceutical company did when managing its inventory levels so vigorously. In its quest to reduce manufacturing costs, it exposed itself to the significantly higher costs of stockouts. The biotechnology company was itching to make yet another ends/means mistake by discontinuing a successful product until we showed them the real cost—a hefty $32 million per year. And don't forget market share, which, like customer service, is usually a means, not an end in itself.

We have also seen how knowing what you want helps constrain the quantity of analysis. In the private road example, the tendency was to over-analyze, while in the tax accountant example, the tendency was to under-analyze. Both are bad, and if we know what we want beforehand, we can avoid the troublesome pair.

Charley's story about hiring Roger and angering Scott shows the need to look at the big picture and ask if something else is more important. Profits are always important, but younger companies may have a cash flow problem, too. They need to survive long enough to realize their profits. Both should be considered before making important decisions.

How do all these examples fit together? Knowing what you want is the first step in being effective in your life, and this needn't be any more difficult than constructing a one- to four-sentence statement to that effect. If you are clear about what you want before you choose, you can avoid the pitfalls described in this chapter. As Peter Marshall said in the opening quote, "unless we stand for something, we shall fall for anything." *Now*, not after you act, is the time to determine what you stand for.

Chapter 6

BIASES AFFECT THE BEST OF US

We have found that car salesmen are neither loved nor understood, as the following dialog demonstrates.

> *Lisa*: Car salesmen don't trust women. When I went car shopping with Charley, they just gave us the keys to go on a test drive. When I went alone, they always insisted on coming with me on the test drive. I would try to go on a test drive alone but they would say that it was "no trouble" for them to join me.
>
> *Bill*: I went shopping for cars alone and they never gave *me* the keys. I just figured they never gave the keys to anyone. Perhaps they give the keys to couples but not individuals. Maybe couples are more likely to bring the car back in one piece.
>
> *Lisa*: Maybe...

Biases affect all parts of our lives. We form mental models of the world, but often our perceptions are distorted by our biases, and this affects our mental models. Lisa and Bill experienced similar situations, but reached very different conclusions: Bill concluded that salesmen always go on test drives with the customer while Lisa concluded that salesmen do not trust women. Based on very limited evidence, it appears that both Lisa and Bill may have formed incorrect models and, therefore, incorrect conclusions. The lower your opinion of members of a certain group, the likelier you are to be biased against them. Because neither Bill nor Lisa especially cared for car salesmen, they didn't put much effort into understanding or respecting their behavior.

Consider a mid-30's Iranian man by the name of Mohammed Karimi. As this book was being written, and as you probably know well, Iran and the United States were at such odds that they hadn't had any diplomatic relations for 24 years. What is the U.S.'s gripe? State Department spokesman Adam Ereli summed it up by saying that "...Iran is one of the foremost sponsors of terrorism worldwide."[46]

Is Mohammed Karimi a violent terrorist or at least a potential terrorist? Is he a fanatical religious fundamentalist ranting about the corrupt West? Based on the information you now have, how favorably do you feel about Karimi? Our guess is that some of you aren't feeling particularly warm toward him. But here is the rest of the story.

Just a few days before the State Department's comments, Iran suffered a devastating earthquake, leveling three-quarters of the city of Bam and killing 35,000—one third of the population. We find the region's governor, none other than Karimi, at the cemetery where he is assessing the situation. "This is the Apocalypse. There is nothing but devastation and debris." The tragedy was especially personal for Karimi who lost both his wife and his daughter in the quake. He went on to describe what happened.

"'Last night before she went to sleep, she made me a drawing and kissed me four times,' he said of his daughter Nazenine, whose body he held in his arms. 'When I asked, 'Why four kisses?' she said, 'Maybe I won't see you again, Papa,' Karimi told an AP photographer, as tears streamed down his face."[47]

Did your impression of Karimi change after you read of his love for his family and his incredible suffering?

As we get closer to people and realize that they share many of our needs, wants, and values, we tend to care more about them. Political leaders, realizing this, sometimes try to create distance between groups so as to lessen the perceived humanity of the distant group. And once their humanity is lessened, as Adolf Hitler did with the Jews, Gypsies, and homosexuals, it is easier to hate and kill them.

Now that you have learned how Karimi loved his family, does that mean that he is a good person? Not necessarily. He could still be a terrorist. We don't have enough information to judge him, which is exactly our point. Biases also affect us in more mundane areas, as the next story shows.

The Crowded, Uncrowded Store

Customers may think that a store is usually crowded even if it is very rarely crowded. Why?

Assume that 75 percent of the time there is one customer in the store and 25 percent of the time there are ten customers. Say it's a small store and, therefore, if ten customers are present, the store is "crowded" and if only one is present, it's "empty." Objectively, therefore, the store is crowded only 25 percent of the time. A market researcher, however, doing a random sample of customers would "prove" that the store is crowded 77 percent of the time because ten out of 13 customer experiences were in a crowded store. Here's how we got this: three customers experienced an empty store, with one customer at a time for 30 minutes each (a total of 90 minutes), while ten customers experienced a crowded store for 30 minutes. Of the 13 total customer experiences, ten of them were in a crowded store. In fact, we know the store is crowded only 25 percent of the time if we sit in the store and observe that there are only three customers for the first 1.5 hours and ten for the next 0.5. Listening to the customers would give you their biased view. The customers are not stupid or unobservant; ten out of 13 truly saw a crowded store, but generalized inaccurately from their experiences.

Interestingly, the store manager is present in the store the whole time and sees that the store is crowded only 25 percent of the time. Perhaps that is why she is so reluctant to add more clerks. Interview her and you would hear her bemoan the fact that her store is "empty" 75 percent of the time. She may even be considering reducing her staff because the store is empty so frequently.

Biases can arise based on a perspective. Two different people see the same situation completely differently. The customers are correct in a per-visit sense (77 percent of visits are while the store is crowded), while the store manager is correct in a per-hour sense (25 percent of her time the store is busy). Both are right, yet both are also wrong. The customers are wrong because they used their per-visit information to generalize about the store's per-hour situation. The store manager is wrong because she took her per-hour information and ignored the customer's per-visit perspective when deciding how many clerks to employ.

The City Bus Mystery

"My city reports that, on average, a bus comes by my stop every five minutes, but I have measured an average wait of seven minutes for my last 30 bus rides. Is the city government lying?" Not necessarily. They could be telling the truth and your perception could be accurate also. Just as with the crowded store example, you may both be right!

Here's how. Bear with us for a little mathematical elaboration. You'll see that this issue is similar in spirit to the "stores are crowded" one mentioned above. Say that five buses come every two minutes (over a period of ten minutes) and then a sixth bus comes after 20 minutes. The city does the math and shows that six buses came in 30 minutes, for an average of five minutes each. But you see something different. Arriving at the bus stop during the first ten minutes of this 30-minute period would get you on one of the first five buses. In this case, you would wait, on average, one minute, because you arrive randomly within one of the two-minute gaps. The problem is that the chance you'll arrive in the first ten minutes of the 30-minute period is only ten in 30. But you have a 20 in 30 chance of arriving during the 20-minute period after the five buses have gone by. In that case, if you arrive randomly during that 20-minute period, you'll wait, on average, ten minutes. So your average wait, over many days, is 10/30 times one minute plus 20/30 times ten minutes, or seven minutes. Waiting for this last bus ruins your average wait time, even though the city officials can proudly say that the six buses came in 30 minutes, or an average of one every five minutes. The difference between your actual wait time and the city's average of five minutes gets more pronounced the more the first five buses are bunched together and the longer the period for that last, tardy bus. Isn't it amazing that both you and the city can draw such different conclusions about the same situation?[48]

Bias and Prejudice

Here's an example of a bias that most of us have experienced. "Whenever I'm driving in my car and my radio loses reception, I'm listening to a good song." This *is* how it seems. But when it happens with a bad song, you probably don't remember because you don't care. Moreover, don't you usually listen to good songs? Do you drive around listening to bad songs? If you didn't think it was a good song, you would flip stations, put in a tape or CD, or turn it off. It is our bias that causes us to remember only the interrupted good songs.

A coworker and I (CLH) were discussing various electronics and computer stores in our area. She said confidently and unequivocally, "I will never again shop at Fry's Electronics." I asked her why. "They discriminate against women," she answered adamantly. Intrigued, I asked how they discriminate. Her answer surprised me. "They ignore women shoppers and never assist them." Wow. I had exactly the same complaint against Fry's, but I have both X and Y chromosomes. It had never occurred to me that they were systematically helping male customers and ignoring the females. I had simply assumed that they were saving money by paring their service staff to the bare minimum.

She and I had exactly the same experience at Fry's and yet we drew completely different conclusions. She concluded that they were ignoring females, while I concluded that they ignored everyone. She identified herself as part of a group, and when she did not like the response she got at Fry's, she extrapolated it to the group. It never occurred to her that the real problem was almost certainly more innocent and more systemic: Fry's has great prices and selection, but their customer service is almost non-existent.

While women probably do encounter discrimination, so probably do men, and it is also probable that both women's and men's perceptions exaggerate discrimination because of their biases.

Now that we have broached the sensitive subject of bias and women, let us consider another controversy: women's representation in the U.S. health care system. Many people believe that women's health care issues are not treated as seriously as men's and that men get better treatment. With this belief as your starting point, imagine that you learn that the majority of pharmaceutical clinical trials test new drugs in men and not women. Your response may be something like this: "See, this just proves that women are second-class citizens when it comes to drugs. All the drug information we are gathering shows how to help men, not women. When we discover that the optimal dose is ten milligrams twice a day, that dose is for a man, not a woman. Who knows the best dose for a woman?"

Now keep the same starting belief in mind but change the facts around. You learn, instead, that more women than men are taking part in clinical trials for new drugs. Your response may be something like this: "See, men are so important in our society that we experiment with women to develop new drugs. Men are viewed as too important to be exposed to untested, possibly dangerous drugs. Women are viewed as guinea pigs."

To be fair, the first scenario is actually more plausible.[49] Before we get too far, we should point out here that women are much bigger consumers of health care than men and, consequently, women's issues do receive a lot of attention— though, of course, not in every situation. In reality, we find that both women and men receive deficient treatment, but for different diseases and for different reasons.[50]

Some, not all, "prejudice" observed in our society is a result of looking at the world with preexisting beliefs. Then, when things don't look right, it can be explained through these beliefs. Ironically, our prejudices lead us to see others' supposed prejudices. Just as when someone looks at me funny and I think nothing of it, a paranoid person may be sure that the stranger is either judging him or is up to something devious. Have you seen the movie *Anger Management*? Adam Sandler's character is dealing with some overreacting airline employees on a flight. Finally, a black air marshal comes over. He tells Sandler that he must calm down and stop raising his voice. Sandler, who had shown great restraint up until then, asks the marshal, "What's wrong with you people?" The marshal gets upset because "you people" sounds like a racial comment to him. Of course, Sandler would have said the same thing to a white air marshal, who probably would have taken less offense.

Nose Rings and Personal Appearance

When getting to know someone, we use whatever information we have about that person. After ten years we know someone pretty well, even though he may still surprise us occasionally. But if we know someone for only ten seconds, we know very little. Left grasping, we use whatever information we have, good or bad. A nose ring? Until I get to know you better, you are a composite of all nose ring-wearers to me. Is the word "Mercedes" monogrammed on your polo shirt? Until I get to know you better, you are a composite of all Mercedes-driving polo shirt-wearing middle-aged men (if you're a middle-aged man).

Is it any surprise that people dress for success? At Merck, I (CLH) wore a suit and tie every day. Business people meet a large number of people, many of whom they will never really get to know and some of whom may pay them lots of money. When I worked at NASA, we all knew each other and didn't need to impress each other. Is it any surprise, then, that we NASA employees wore casual, comfortable clothes? Life can be harsh. Life is harsher if your name just happens to be Osama bin Laden or Adolf Hitler or if you look like murderer Charles Manson. You may be sweet, but you are overcoming composites that existed long before you stepped into the room. Some biases are inevitable and difficult to overcome. So, what's the answer? In a business situation, dress in a way that reflects what you want to convey. And if you have the misfortune to be named Adolf Hitler, you'll probably have to work harder at letting people know the real you. Or simply change your name.

Overcoming Biases

Facing an unfair bias is not necessarily an insurmountable barrier. Biases are a challenge to be overcome, and many people find creative solutions. In 1942, when cultural biases against black people were much stronger than they are today, a young black man named John Johnson sought a $500 loan from a Chicago bank so he could start a magazine called *Negro Digest*. He was told, "Boy, we don't make any loans to colored people."

What to do? Most people would probably feel stymied—and bitter—and many of them would simply give up. It's one thing to be turned down on a good idea because you failed to persuade someone of its merit. In that case, you could change your approach. But what the hell do you do when you're turned down for a loan, not because you're a bad risk but because you're the wrong color? That's when this entrepreneur's creativity kicked in. He asked the loan officer who in town *did* make loans to colored people. When the loan officer recommended a small finance company, Johnson asked the loan officer to be his reference. Using his reference, Johnson got the loan and went on to found *Negro Digest*—and *Ebony* and *Jet*. By the late 1990s he was a billionaire.[51]

Coincidences

Many people allow themselves to be biased by the supposed importance of a coincidence. The bias is understandable but mistaken. Consider the following situations.

During a dinner conversation, my (CLH's) seven-year-old son, Mitch, told Lisa and me that he's glad we met, or else he wouldn't have been born. That's an interesting insight, especially for a seven-year-old. It reminded me of a Dr. Seuss passage.

If you'd never been born, well then what would you do?
If you'd never been born, well then what would you be?
Why, you might be a WASN'T!
A Wasn't has no fun at all. No, he doesn't.
A Wasn't just isn't. He just isn't present.
But you…You ARE YOU! And, now isn't that pleasant!
— Dr. Seuss

What were the odds that Mitch, or you, for that matter, would be born? For you to be born, your parents had to get married (we'll assume that marriage is a prerequisite for having a child) and have you. Assume for simplicity that once they married, they would have a baby—you. So the odds of their having you are 100 percent. But what are the odds that they would marry? Assume that each parent could have married, or set up a household with, any of 100 people. In other words, one parent was exposed, in school, work, and social settings, to 100 potential mates. You might object that the number is even higher; if so, it simply makes our point even stronger. These potential mates could have been better or worse (hopefully worse) than the mate they chose, but this doesn't matter. Of 100 potential mates each, your parents ended up with each other. Another way to say that is that the probability of each parent picking the one he or she chose is only one in 100, or one percent. Looked at from the perspective of both parents, the probability that they would choose each other is much lower, one in 10,000 (1/100 times 1/100). They could each have ended up with someone else.

Take it to the next step. For your parents to have been born, each pair of grandparents had to choose each other, which means, one in 10,000 for one pair of grandparents, times one in 10,000 for the other pair of grandparents, or one in 100 million. So the odds that you would have been born, just by going back two generations, were one in 100 million (the odds that your parents were born) times the odds that your parents got together (one in 10,000), which computes to one in one trillion. Mathematically, the probability was one in one trillion that you would be born. And here you are: the one in a trillion kid!

Here's the point. While it was very unlikely that *you* would be born, it was highly likely that some baby would be born. If you take eligible people back in 1920, some are going to choose each other and mate. If you take eligible people back in 1950, some are going to choose each other and mate. When their children grow up, they calculate the odds and see that, while the odds of their being born are tiny, the odds of *someone* being born are high. Of course, it is the someone who was born—you—who is able to calculate the odds. It is quite hard for the trillion minus one babies that could have been born, but were not, what Seuss calls the "wasn'ts," to calculate these odds.

Here is where coincidences can trip us up. There is only a very minute possibility that for any particular thing in your life, such as the middle names of your three closest friends, there will be a coincidence (for example, they are all the same). However, given the millions of bits of information in your life, the probability that there is a coincidence somewhere is very high. For instance, my (CLH's) brother Douglas knows three people born on April 4th who, for fun, regularly wear mismatched socks. The problem arises when such a coincidence affects our decision-making. We end up attributing much too much importance to it: "We were meant to be friends for life because we all have the same middle name."

A further example of putting way too much weight on coincidence is the seriousness with which many people took *The*

Bible Code, a book that came out in 1997. The author, Michael Drosnin, claimed that a secret code was hidden in the Bible and that he had found it. This code, he claimed, had predicted many things that had actually happened, including, most dramatically, the assassination of Yitzakh Rabin, the Prime Minister of Israel. Of course, Drosnin chose to point out these predictions after, rather than before, the predicted events. Drosnin found the hidden code by starting with a letter in the Bible and then skipping 49 letters in the Bible to the next letter and then 49 to the next, etc. Mathematicians and statisticians were quick to point out why Drosnin's finding was meaningless. With a modern computer, they pointed out, you can quickly sift through an electronic version of the Bible trying various fixed number of letters to skip, which, Drosnin admitted, was exactly what he had done. You can also start at any letter and, if that doesn't give you your result, start at the next one and so on. With literally hundreds of choices about the fixed number of letters to skip, and with literally hundreds of thousands of choices of letters to begin with, out of the mass of text that results, it's virtually certain that you will come up with actual names of famous historical figures and even with some true predictions about their fates. Of course, most of what you'll come up with is gobbledygook, combinations of letters that don't even make words.[52]

The real test would be, once you have chosen the letter to start with and the number of letters to skip, to see if other major characters have their names spelled out. Does Drosnin's method, starting from the letter he started from, and spacing 49 letters, show a character named Osama bin Laden along with the date September 11, 2001? We'll bet dollars to doughnuts that it doesn't.

Check Your Base

Many people make the mistake of not checking their base. The following example explains what me mean:

Person A: I was surprised that I met this really serious
  person from California. I thought everyone in
  California is relaxed and mellow.
Person B: There are 35 million people in California. Many
  of them are serious.

At a truly national event, such as a scientific conference or a square dancing convention with people from all over the country, you would have a much higher chance of finding a serious person from California than from another state, such as Iowa. This is true even if Iowans in general are more serious; there are just so many more people from California. Say one out of three Californians is serious and that double that fraction of Iowans, that is, two out of three Iowans, are serious. Given California's population of 35 million and Iowa's population of three million people, there are about 12 million serious Californians versus only two million serious Iowans. You are six times as likely to come across a serious Californian as a serious Iowan, even though Iowans are twice as likely to be serious. The real question is what you're doing at a square dancing convention looking for serious people. ☺

A child's riddle asks why white sheep eat so much more than black sheep. Check your base and the answer will be similar to the California/Iowa example above. The reason white sheep eat so much more than black sheep is that there are so many more white sheep.

I (CLH) live in a wooded, somewhat lightly populated area, so I shouldn't have been surprised to have a mountain lion in my own backyard. I wasn't surprised, but I was scared because my eight year-old son Mitchell was playing there by himself at the time. But the cougar was headed somewhere else and he left without incident. Had this large cat been the killer that many fear, my son would have been in deep trouble.

A few months later, my colleague took time off to walk his daughter to school after a mountain lion was sighted in his otherwise normal suburban neighborhood. These incidents caused me to question the issue of mountain lion safety.

How dangerous are mountain lions? The data tell an interesting story. Since 1980, there have been only 13 attacks in all of California (where I live) and three people have died as a result.[53] Compare this with attacks by dogs. Each year in California, about 100,000 dog attacks cause their victims to get medical attention.[54] This means that California residents are approximately 180,000 times as likely to be seriously attacked by a dog as by a mountain lion. But to really compare dogs and mountain lions, we need to check our base, because there are a lot more dogs than mountain lions. With so many more dogs running around, a reasonable person would expect more dog attacks. With about 8 million dogs and 5,000 mountain lions in California, we see that there are approximately 1,500 dogs for each mountain lion.[55] Once we check our base and correct for the numbers of dogs and mountain lions, we see that dogs are still more dangerous, and in fact, the risk of serious attack from an individual dog is about 120 times that of the risk from an individual mountain lion. Mountain lions present a daunting and ferocious image, but with so few attacks, they must have very little interest in attacking people.

These results may seem counterintuitive, but they make sense. I have lived and recreated most of my life in mountain lion territory and I've personally seen only one and my son saw another. Even my brother Stan, who has lived, worked, and played outdoors in the Santa Cruz Mountains for decades, has seen only four in his whole life. Compare this with dogs. I've been bitten a few times, threatened dozens of times, and scared to death a few more times. Perhaps the people who own dogs solely for protection need to consider the true threats, and checking their base is a good place to start.

Checking bases applies to a lot more than just mountain lions, sheep, and square dancing. A presidential commission formed in 2004 to review the "dead wrong" U.S. intelligence assessments of Saddam Hussein's chemical weapons programs found, among other things, one disturbingly simple blunder: intelligence analysts had failed to check their base. The analysts who were studying top-secret satellite photos of Iraq noticed a dramatic increase in photos of the type of tanker truck that Saddam had used in the past for chemical weapons manufacturing. They sounded the alarm because they believed they had a smoking gun. The problem? They weren't aware that intelligence satellites had more than doubled their surveillance of Iraq. In short, there were more pictures of Iraqi tanker trucks because there were more pictures of Iraq. They didn't check their base and, as a result, sounded a false alarm that contributed to a war that cost hundreds of billions of dollars and left many thousands dead.[56]

Market Share is *Always* Seventy Percent?

A biotechnology company was forecasting large sales for a new diabetes drug. All the numbers that were inputs into the sales forecast seemed fine to us, except for one: the team assumed a market share of 70 percent. When asked about this, the company official replied, "Our market share is always 70 percent." He was right, but the reason was that the company had always launched products into poorly served markets. A 70-percent market share generally means that you have the only good product in town and that all the other products are second-class products and must fight for the remaining 30 percentage points. That certainly wasn't going to be the case with the $7 billion worldwide diabetes market. If this company's market share will *always* be 70 percent, then it should enter the hypertension (blood pressure-reducing) and hypercholesterolemia (cholesterol-reducing) markets, with annual sales of $17.7 billion and $18.0 billion, respectively.[57] This company was letting its past experience bias it.

Regression to the Mean

Daniel Kahneman, who was later co-winner of the 2002 Nobel prize in economic science, was teaching flight instructors in Israel the psychology of training.

> Referring to studies of pigeon behavior, he was trying to make the point that reward is a more effective teaching tool than punishment. Suddenly one of his students shouted, "With respect, Sir, what you're saying is literally for the birds. . . . My experience contradicts it." The student explained that the trainees he praised for excellent performance almost always did worse on their next flight, while the ones he criticized for poor performance almost always improved.[58]

The student thought he was contradicting Kahneman, but he was unwittingly explaining yet another kind of bias: regression to the mean. Regression to the mean is the principle that, on average, you will be at your average. If you are really up one day, you will regress back to your average the following days. Another way of saying this is what goes up must come down a little and what goes down must come up a little. Most of the time the flight students flew at their average performance level, while sometimes they flew much better and other times much worse. If you happened to have caught them on their good day and praised them, chances are very good that the following day they would simply be average again. If you criticized the students on their poor days, you'd watch them return to their average the following day. This is the pattern the flight instructor saw:

Teaching Tool	Student Behavior Next Day
Praise	Performance Declines
Criticism	Performance Improves

Is it any wonder that he saw the benefit of criticism and the futility of praise? Yet it is simply a mathematical fact that your performance following your lifetime best performance is unlikely to be as good. This is called regression to the mean or average. The trainer's mistaken conclusion was caused by his biased point of view.

I (DRH) recently explained regression to the mean to my two brothers-in-law, who are both very bright. They both challenged it. Their counterexample was basketball star Michael Jordan. "When did he ever regress to the mean," asked one of my brothers-in-law? "He's always been above average." "Yes, he has," I replied, "but he hasn't always been above *his* average." When he scored 60 points during one game, I would have confidently bet that he wouldn't score as many in the next game.

Our country's tax system is graduated to take a higher percentage of your income the higher the income you make. What's behind this tax system, besides a good dose of envy, is the idea that people with high incomes can easily afford to pay a higher percentage of their income in taxes. But here's where regression to the mean is ignored. For many people, one year's high income is an aberration, not the norm. They might have sold real estate that had been in the family for twenty years. They might have gotten a long-term contract that paid them in chunks. They might have had a particularly good year in their business. The next few years will show them back at their mean, as the principle of regression to the mean acts on their income. A typical government employee, on the other hand, will have a very stable income that rises slowly but steadily. Over time, the person with variable income pays much more in taxes than the government employee with the same average lifetime income simply because the pattern of good and bad years causes him to pay much more in the good years and only a little less in the bad years.

The federal government used to have a partial solution for this problem: it was called income averaging. Under the law, you could use income averaging to pay taxes based on up to five years of income, but the Tax Reform Act of 1986 eliminated this provision of the tax code.

The Lessons Learned

Biases usually result from an incomplete view. Perhaps the observer was lazy and stopped looking further, or perhaps the observer witnessed something that was internally consistent and simply fit with his or her preexisting beliefs. The viewer may not even be technically wrong. It is as if the biased person is right about a tree but wrong about the forest.

Think about a major highway that you drive on regularly. Picture in your mind what it would be like to drive on this highway at night in the rain. Imagine the darkness, headlights, and splashing water. Now picture the same highway on a hot summer day during rush hour. Can you see the waves of heat rising off the sun-baked cars as their drivers sit, fuming? We form mental models that help us immeasurably. When deciding to drive on this particular highway, you may first picture the conditions. This helps you make decisions and prepare you for what is coming. Some have argued that this ability to form mental models and employ them for predictions is one of the defining characteristics of homo sapiens sapiens. It's one of the things that makes us human. However, it can also lead us astray.

The flight instructor was absolutely right about the sequence of events he witnessed. If he gave praise, performance would drop the next day. If he gave criticism, performance would improve the next day. The problem arose when he developed his mental model. Mental models, by necessity, require simplifying reality, so he ended up with the rule: criticism helps and praise hurts. Yet a bigger, and more accurate, view shows how this mental model is just plain wrong. It turns out that the flight instructor was measuring the wrong thing. What he did measure was performance today versus performance tomorrow. What he should have measured was performance tomorrow without the feedback and performance tomorrow with the feedback, which is obviously harder to do. How would a certain pilot have flown had he not criticized him? This is harder, but not impossible, and understanding regression to the mean is the first step. The flight instructor would just have to look closer and perhaps employ more data points to make a conclusion about criticism and praise. He would have to ask himself, "Given what I know about regression to the mean and given what I know about this certain pilot, did my criticism help or hurt?"

Biases grow from many fertile sources, and we've uncovered a number in this chapter. We may have to accept the presence of bias in the world, but we don't have to accept it in ourselves. We can prevent our own biases through respect for others and cold, hard mathematics. We can dig deeper and look beyond the surface explanation. We can use mental models to help us understand, for example, that a larger than average percentage of Iranians are dangerous, but still understand, as we can see from our own neighborhoods, that most people, including most Iranians, are good most of the time.

The crowded store example shows how two people can be right, but because of their perspectives, come to completely different conclusions. They are right in their observations, but their conclusions are wrong because they misapply their narrow observations to the larger situation.

This chapter also explained how coincidences can mislead us because we inflate their importance. Lastly, checking our base is one way to avoid incorrect conclusions as we saw in the California/Iowa example.

By addressing and correcting some of our biases, we can see the world more clearly and make better decisions in the process. If our biases are causing us to see the world incorrectly, we should discard them as we would distorted glasses.

Chapter 7

REALIZE WHAT'S IMPORTANT

There is nothing so useless as doing efficiently that which should not be done at all. — Peter F. Drucker

Sharpen your viewpoint on what's truly important—and keep everything else a blur. — Rachel Snyder

When my (CLH's) son Russ was nine years old, he wanted to tape together two plastic toy parachutists and throw them off the deck to see how they would fall. My first thought was that this was a waste of tape and that the parachutes would certainly become entangled and ruined. "How could he ruin his toys like this?" crowded my mind. Then it struck me that my son wasn't so much ruining toys as he was conducting experiments in physics. How much is it worth to me to have my son interested in science, inventive enough to design experiments and industrious enough to follow through? The value is very high, and certainly much higher than the value of the tape and ruined toys. Once I considered what was important, the solution became obvious, so I happily helped my son ruin his toys and learn physics while doing so.

The Ph.D. Insight

Years ago in Rochester, I (DRH) was working hard on my dissertation to attain my Ph.D. One advantage of a Ph.D. was that it would allow me to stay in the United States. I had grown up in Canada, but I wanted to live in "the States." I had selected a big project and the deadline looked difficult to meet. "Will I finish my dissertation?" I wondered many times and considered giving up. Why work so hard if, when the deadline came and I was not finished, I would be deported back to Canada?

After consulting with my friend Tom Nagle, I realized that I should continue working hard on my dissertation. Tom's reasoning, which became mine, was as follows: if I got to live in the United States, I would want to work as an economist, and even if I was deported to Canada, I would still want to work as an economist. Because I wanted to be an economist no matter where I lived, I decided to finish my dissertation—ideally on time, so that I could live in the United States. Here's the decision tree.

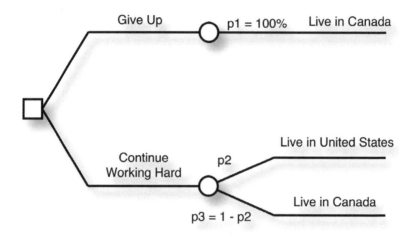

The decision was whether or not to continue working hard. If I decided to give up, the outcome was certain—the probability was 100 percent that I would have to return to Canada. If I chose to continue on my dissertation, there was some probability, p2, that I would succeed and, therefore, be allowed to stay in the U.S., while there was some probability, p3, which is 100 percent minus p2, that I would fail. Probabilities p2 and p3 must add to 100 percent because, together, they comprise all the possibilities once I go down the Continue Working Hard path. As we have defined the problem, either I stayed in the United States or went back to Canada. Living in America was important to me, but so was being an economist. That was my primary insight. My secondary insight was that I should keep working on my dissertation to have a chance of staying. Working on my dissertation would help me achieve both of my objectives: stay in America and become an economist. And I'm happy to report that I did achieve both.

The reason we need to use probabilities in this example is that, even though I controlled whether or not I tried to complete my dissertation on time, I couldn't know beforehand if I would succeed. This decision tree is also laid out chronologically; first I make my decision and then I find out if I succeed. Interestingly, unlike in fairy tales, the story doesn't simply end at the right hand side of the tree with the outcomes. Once I am an economist living in the U.S., I face a whole new set of decisions, alternatives, probabilities, and outcomes. So the outcomes of one tree become the starting point for other decision trees.

Can you see the distinction I used here? I had to make a distinction between earning my Ph.D. and where I ended up. As we saw in this example, both aspects of this decision argued for me to continue with my dissertation. If they didn't, at least by making the distinction I could begin to compare my objectives. We could have put this example in Chapter 2 under "Making Distinctions." It really should go in both places because both lessons are important. Distinctions are very good for clarity of thought and the framing of problems. Realizing what is important is another useful angle for solving this problem.

Lean Manufacturing

Ford Motor Company practices "lean manufacturing," an approach designed to increase quality and decrease costs, partly by having a streamlined, efficient, and responsive manufacturing process. Ford isn't the only manufacturer trying to streamline its operations. "Between 1990 and 2000, U.S. manufacturers' inventories dropped from those needed for 50 days of production to 40 days."[59] A big part of lean manufacturing is avoiding a build-up of inventory.

Ford also has a policy of paying parts suppliers for their shipping costs only if the delivery truck is full. This gives suppliers the incentive to send full trucks, and while it saves Ford some shipping costs, this works against Ford's bigger objective of getting the right number of parts at the right time.

> The auto maker can "save a penny on transportation cost, but it costs you a dollar with overall system inefficiency" by sabotaging the larger purpose of the lean method: receiving the right part at the right time.[60]

Ford should consider what is most important: saving a little on shipping costs or saving a lot through lean manufacturing. Faced with a conflict between these two objectives, Ford should consider what is truly important to avoid being "penny-wise and pound-foolish."

Employees Are Your Largest Cost

Imagine that one of your employees has a great idea to make the office more comfortable. Her idea could make the lighting brighter and better distributed or, perhaps, could make the temperature more agreeable. (Office dwellers often complain about offices that are too hot or too cold.) Her idea could be any of a hundred ideas to make the office a more appealing, attractive, and comfortable place to work. Unfortunately, this change will cost your company $1 a square foot a year. Is that too expensive? Shouldn't this employee focus on saving, rather than spending, money? Perhaps, but consider that employees cost the typical office 41 times as much as energy, repairs, and maintenance combined.[61] If we increase other costs by even a third, we need only increase productivity by less than one percent to compensate. If we increase productivity by just one percent, we get the same bottom-line benefit as eliminating the entire repair and maintenance or the entire energy bill. Here's how we got that result. If we completely eliminate the repair and maintenance bill, for instance, we save approximately one percent (0.0089) of total costs. We can get this same reduction by shaving one percent off total salaries (84 percent times 0.01 equals 0.0084, which is approximately equal to the 0.0089 above).

Costs of Running an Office

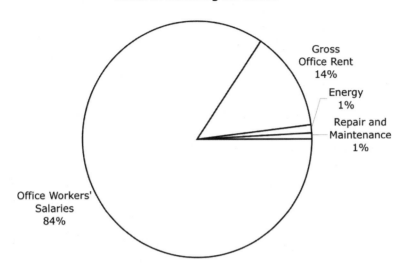

The question to ask as a manager is: if the employees stayed at work longer and were happier and more comfortable, would their productivity rise by one percent? When office workers' salaries comprise 84 percent of total office costs (including rent, energy, repairs, and maintenance), we should be less concerned with reducing the costs that enable the workers to be productive and more concerned with their productivity. Other costs should be compared to the value of the workers' labor.

The important metric isn't just employees' immediate productivity, but also their longevity and commitment. Smart employers will notice that it costs much less to keep existing employees happy than to find new ones. "Replacing an employee costs roughly 1.5 times a year's pay. Also, companies with highly committed employees tend to post sharply higher shareholder returns."[62]

First Find First-Order Effects

A decade ago I (CLH) had a conversation with a coworker about an upcoming football game between the Oakland Raiders—temporarily based in Los Angeles—and the Dallas Cowboys. He and I both shared an interest in the Raiders, but he loved to analyze football games in more detail than I thought was warranted.

> *Coworker*: The Raiders should win this game because their defense is good and this game will be played on wet Astroturf. Players won't be able to get good footing in the cold and wet. The Raiders' defense will capitalize on this.
>
> *Me*: The Raiders are 3-4 (three wins and four losses) and the Cowboys are 5-1. The Cowboys have won the last three match ups. The Raiders have a number of injured players. I think the Cowboys will win.

As many as 100 factors could determine the ultimate winner of an NFL game. He seemed to focus on the less important ones and ignore those most important. His points were valid, but were they significant? By the way, the Raiders did lose 28-13.[63] Although I didn't follow football as much as he did, I predicted better because I focused on what was important.

I (CLH) have had conversations with people in the pharmaceutical industry that go something like this:

> *Them*: This drug should do really well because we will have the full sales force pushing it.
>
> *Me*: Yes, but this product's efficacy is low and doctors will fear its possible side effects.

What do this and the Raiders conversation have in common? They were both with intelligent people who made valid points to support their conclusions. Unfortunately, while their points were valid, they were overridden by other, equally valid, but more important, points. The benefit the Raiders would get from wet Astroturf is a second-order effect, subsidiary to other more important first-order effects. A first-order effect was the weak Raiders team and the strong Cowboys team. Engineers and scientists know that first-order effects drive the day, and second-order effects come into play only when the first-order effects balance each other. In other words, to predict whether the Raiders will win or whether the new medicine will succeed, we should evaluate first-order effects before we consider second-order effects. *First consider what is important.*

The Soviets Make Nails

In the old Soviet Union, the government rewarded factory managers for production quantity, not quality. In addition to ignoring quality, factory managers ignored customer needs. The end result was more and more tractors produced, for instance, even though these tractors just sat unused. Managers of factories that produced nails optimized production by producing either fewer larger and heavier nails or more smaller nails.

> The fact that factories were judged by rough physical quotas rather than by their ability to satisfy customers— their customers were the state—had predictably bad results. If, to take a real case, a nail factory's output was measured by number, factories produced large numbers of small pin-like nails. If output was measured by weight, the nail factories shifted to fewer, very heavy nails.[64]

The lesson here is that the Soviets didn't, and, in fact, couldn't, meet the needs of individual citizens and so had to rely on crude quotas. Producing according to these crude quotas was much less efficient than addressing the real needs of the citizens. The Soviets couldn't align their production with the yardsticks that mattered. They couldn't see what was important.

Zero in on the Most Zeroes

A biotechnology company organized a half-day meeting to discuss its top seven business opportunities. The company spent the same amount of time on each product, even though Product A was expected to have annual revenues of $1 billion, and Product B was expected to have only $3 million in peak revenues. Every potential opportunity should get a fair hearing, but once the scale is known, the more significant products should get much more time. In this case, making effort more proportional to importance meant that the company should have spent just five or ten minutes on Product B and well over an hour on Product A.

As Martin Feldstein, my (DRH's) boss at the Council of Economic Advisers in the early 1980s, advised me when I became his health economist and he wanted me to use my time most effectively, "Put your effort on the parts of the budget that have the most zeroes."

Constrained Resources

A pizza restaurant wanted to grow and become more profitable, and so the owner decided to buy another delivery vehicle and hire another driver. She also put extra advertisements with coupons in the local newspaper. She skipped one important step. She should have considered why her business wasn't already larger. What was holding it back? It turns out that this business had a loyal clientele, good employees, and great pizzas. The current delivery vehicle even had some extra capacity. Here's the problem: the oven was too small. She was selling and delivering all the pizzas she could make. In the language of mathematical optimization, her pizza oven was a **constrained resource**. It is pointless to increase delivery capacity and customer demand when no additional pizzas can be made and sold. To expand her business, she needed to increase her constrained resource. She needed to figure out what was important.[65]

A few years ago, I (DRH) volunteered to serve hamburgers, hot dogs, and veggie burgers at a barbecue held at my daughter's high school. When it looked as if we were running out of any of the three items, one of the cooks would put more on the grill. At one point, the line got long, with about 12 people suddenly waiting for their meal. That was the symptom of the problem. The cooks quickly put more burgers on the grill. That was their solution. But I looked down and saw that I had about four each of hot dogs and veggie burgers. I realized that the cooks were implicitly assuming that everyone wanted hamburgers. But, I wondered, what if some of them were in line for hot dogs and veggie burgers? There was a simple solution that addressed the real problem: ask them. So I announced, in my booming voice, "Anyone who's in line for hot dogs or veggie burgers please come up here." Immediately, six people came up, cutting the apparent hamburger line in half. Interestingly, the server who had made the panicked request to the cook for more hamburgers was a high-level manager at a logistics firm. He didn't see any easy way around the problem.

PacBell (now SBC), the phone company in California, aggressively called potential customers of digital subscriber line (DSL) Internet connections. PacBell obviously wanted to grow its DSL business, but installation was over two months behind. PacBell was behaving as if its constrained resource was customer knowledge and awareness, when in fact it was installation capacity.

What is your primary constrained resource? When I (CLH) was fifteen, my brother Douglas and a few friends rode their bicycles from Santa Clara to Allegheny, 270 miles across California and up from 90 feet to 5,000 above sea level with a full load of camping gear. I didn't ride with them. Although I was tempted, I thought my bike, an old Clubman 10-speed, was simply not up to the task. I was bicycle-constrained. I did, however, have money in the bank, and I knew that I could have bought a decent bike and still have had about $20 left for the trip. It would have worked financially, but I would have been flat broke afterwards. Once I thought about it, I realized that I really was money-constrained. Not bold enough to spend every penny I had, I kept my old bike and flush bank account and joined the camping trip by driving up with my dad and my other brother.

My (CLH's) grandmother Cindy was 101 years old in 2002. Her mind was sharp and she had time and money, but her vision wasn't very good and her hearing was failing her. She could still get around—easily climbing stairs—but clearly she was health-constrained. Many of us have good hearing, good vision, and flush bank accounts. But something is always constrained, and, with many successful Americans, the constraint is time. There just aren't enough hours in the day to achieve what you want. If this is so, you should be less concerned with saving a few dollars than with saving a few minutes. If, for example, you must wait ten seconds for a retail clerk to give you a penny in change, you are being wise with your time if you simply leave the store without the change. A determination of which resource is constrained can help you make decisions regarding tradeoffs among resources.

If This is Fraud, I'm Guilty

Rosie DesParois was 87 years old and in horrible health. She was suffering from advanced breast and endometrial cancer, which doctors believed had spread to her liver. Because Mrs. DesParois wasn't expected to live long, she entered a hospice program in Plattsburgh, New York. The federal government's Medicare program provides hospice care to patients who have given up treatment and are expected to die within six months. The patients select a hospice program, stay in their own home, and receive palliative care, and then get reimbursed by Medicare for $88 per day. Hospice care is substantially cheaper than alternative care provided in hospitals or nursing homes. On the surface, everyone wins: Patients get good care in a familiar and convenient setting and Medicare saves substantial amounts of money.

The problem arises from the difficulty and ultimate fruitlessness of estimating how long any individual patient will live. Statistics tell us that some patients will live much longer or shorter than average. Herein lies the problem. The Centers for Medicare and Medicaid Services (CMS), formerly known as the Health Care Financing Administration (HCFA), which administers Medicare, was warned to crack down on hospice care because of concerns over fraud. Some patients were indeed living long past their six-month cutoff. This looked like fraud to the government auditors, and so they cracked down. "Under the bold title 'Medicare Fraud Investigations,' a company called United Government Services warned recipients that they were under scrutiny for cheating the government."[66] How were they cheating the government? By living too long. What nerve. Each could be liable for tens of thousands of dollars.

Ultimately, the solution chosen for some of the long-lived patients was to discontinue their hospice care. Many of these patients then quickly deteriorated and left their homes for care in hospitals and nursing homes. "As it turns out, the government's move backfired. Mrs. DesParois's nursing home charged Medicare about $150 a day, nearly twice the hospice's fee."[67] The government's action helped neither the taxpayer nor Mrs. DesParois, who was kicked out of the hospice program at age 91, lucid and devastated. The sick woman sold her house and entered a hospital, and then a nursing home. "Cancer spread to her pancreas and stomach. She developed gaping bedsores and was in agony. And on September 16, 1998, Mrs. DesParois died, away from her home and the hospice staff."[68] Apparently, the federal government had not considered what was really important.

Witch-Hunts and Probabilities

Witch-hunts are investigations and probes that are designed to root out "bad" people, whether witches, drug dealers, or terrorists, with the ultimate purpose of protecting innocent people. The problem is that witch-hunts normally snag more innocent than guilty people. And worse, due to the laws of mathematics, witch-hunts snag *mainly* the innocent.

Consider a witch-hunt that is implemented via a test given to everyone in a region populated with suspected witches. This test has a known accuracy of 98 percent. Assume that three million innocent people live in this region and that we suspect there are 100 evil and dangerous witches. To our surprise, our test finds not 100 witches, but 60,098 witches! Unfortunately, 60,000 of these "witches" are innocent people who just happened to produce a false positive reading on the test (60,000 equals 3 million times 0.02, which is 1.00 minus 0.98). Of the 100 true witches, 98 produced a true positive reading (98 equals 100 times 0.98), while we missed two witches who produced a false negative on the test and totally escaped our dragnet. In other words, 99.84 percent of the "witches" we uncovered weren't witches at all! In true witch-hunt fashion, we put all of our 60,000-plus "witches" through the ringer, but consider it a small "price to pay" for apprehending the 98 true witches. Witch-hunts, whether to find terrorists or drug dealers, often flag fewer of the guilty than the innocent because "witches" are the proverbial needles in the haystack.

Of course we made up the numbers in the previous example. Are there any real examples with real numbers that we can learn from? Unfortunately, the answer is yes.

During World War I, 250,000 volunteers formed the American Protective League (APL), a predecessor of the U.S. government's TIPS (Terrorism Information and Prevention System) program discussed in 2002. (In 1918, terrorists weren't the leading menace; German spies were.) These ordinary APL volunteers were very effective at getting information about American citizens and reporting suspicious behavior to the Justice Department. They cleverly found that they could "gain access to any house, on the grounds of checking their gas and electric service."[69] What was the result of their efforts? They reported well over a million "subversives," which resulted in some deportations for immigration violations and some number of men caught in the midst of marital affairs, but not a single conviction for espionage. Most of the people held in prison for weeks without any charges filed had simply been critics of the war or had made the mistake of eating sauerkraut or listening to Beethoven.

The problem with witch-hunts is that while they are supposed to protect innocent people by capturing witches, a huge part of their effect is to snag innocent people. Unless the tests are exquisitely accurate, and very few are, they'll snag many more innocent people than guilty. Keeping in mind what is important would have spared many innocent people who suffered from badly thought-out policies.

Witch-hunts are another example of means and ends (see Chapter 5). The desired end is the protection of innocent people. The means chosen is a hunt for witches. Does this means foster the desired end?

The Lessons Learned

Have you ever noticed that people aren't always consistent? Take education, for example. Parents may make a great effort to get their children accepted at college and then pay tens of thousands of dollars a year while their children attend a good university. But as many wise people will tell you, a heck of a lot of education happens outside the classroom. People probably learn their most important lessons in life at home, not in school.[70]

I resolved from an early age not to let school get in the way of my education. — Mark Twain

If parents place such weight on their child's education, shouldn't they assist this education even, or especially, outside the classroom? You'd think so, but sometimes we don't realize what is important. Unless we think about what's important, we'll find ourselves led astray in our search for solutions. Charley caught himself making this mistake. Luckily Charley realized that his son's education was more important than two plastic toy parachutists and some tape. His son was taking the initiative to think like a scientist. How fantastic is that?

Many examples in this book apply to more than just this chapter. The parachutes/education example also shows the value of distinctions (see Chapter 2). Parents rarely want their children to destroy toys, but if they make a distinction between the fate of the toy and the fate of the child, then they may decide differently. Another story that shows the application of distinctions is David's dissertation quandary. David learned that he wanted both to live in America and to be an economist. Working hard on his dissertation allowed him to kill two birds with one stone.

Wouldn't it be nice if everything was clearly laid out for us? Making good decisions in life would be so easy. Unfortunately, it is up to us to make distinctions and realize what's important. Ford Motor Company is in this boat and needs to consider how its two objectives conflict: lean manufacturing and efficient shipping. The other stories presented in this chapter all have the same theme: focusing on less-important objectives will lead you to the wrong conclusion. How could it be anything different? With limited time and attention, if we focus on the second-order drivers, we have that much less energy to look at the first-order drivers.

We are all limited in some way or another. Your constrained resource is your most important one. This is one of the biggest insights to arise from the field of optimization: If you have ten inputs, but only one is the constrained resource, you could increase the other nine and see absolutely zero benefit. If you want to increase your output, you must increase the constrained resource. It's that simple. Lastly, those who advocate witch-hunts should make a convincing argument, beforehand, that they will protect and not persecute many innocent people. An unwillingness to consider what is truly important is a huge handicap.

Chapter 8

CREATE BETTER ALTERNATIVES

Welcome all ideas and entertain them royally, for one of them may be king. — Mark Van Doren

About ten years ago, my wife, daughter, and I (DRH) were vacationing in Phoenix. After the first night in our hotel room, my wife and I both woke up with sore necks. The pillows were like rocks! We called around to find a nicer hotel, but found that we would have to pay at least an extra $40 a night for the next five nights for a better room. At the time, $200 was a lot of money to us. In thinking through a switch, we realized that we liked our room otherwise and that our real objection was its hard pillows. Then came the Eureka moment: why not buy our own high-quality pillows? Surely that would be cheaper than the cost—both in money and time—of switching hotels, even if we gave away the pillows afterwards. So we went to the local Sears, tried out a bunch of pillows, found the model we liked, and bought three of them for a total of $90. We saved money and time. As a bonus, the pillows were so soft that we squished them into our suitcases for future travel.

Here is how we uncovered this solution. Initially, we had two alternatives: stay in the cheap hotel (A) and move to an expensive hotel (B). It looked as though we just needed to decide between them. But we went one step further by considering ways to get most of what we wanted from both alternatives, to get both the economy and the comfort. Instead of thinking either/or, we thought of a hybrid alternative. Alternatives A and B were obvious from the beginning, but both presented major drawbacks. So, we invented our own hybrid C and got a better overall alternative. Look around and you'll see that many hybrid alternatives are possible. Of course, the new alternative must be feasible, as we'll consider later.

Was this solution obvious? We have told this story to some people and, after we explain that the pillows were too hard, they smile and say, "Buy new pillows!" But it isn't obvious to most people most of the time. Lance Armstrong is a seven-time Tour de France winner and in his book, *It's Not About The Bike,*[71] he complains about the food he was served and the hotels he stayed in while training and racing throughout Europe. "Some of the motels we stayed in made Motel 6 look pretty nice—there were crumbs on the bare floors and hairs in the bedsheets. To me, the meat was mysterious, the pasta was soggy, and the coffee tasted like brown water." Consider for a minute that Armstrong lives in a $2.5 million dollar "mansion on a river bank," drives a Porsche, and makes $2 million a year. Couldn't he "buy his own pillows?" Couldn't he, in other words, stay in a better hotel, eat at better restaurants, or give his cook extra money to buy better groceries? For perhaps an extra few thousand dollars he could be comfortable while he earns his millions. The solution certainly wasn't obvious to Armstrong.

Can You Sit in the Hallway?

A university department was looking to hire another professor. Although the need for a new person was clear, and the headcount had been approved, the hiring plans fell through—and you'll probably be amazed by the reason. This department had fully used all available offices and had nowhere to house a new professor. Or at least their office space *seemed* severely limited. By giving all staff members an office entitlement, the department had created an artificial shortage. Some professors did little of their office work at the school, yet they maintained full offices, basically using them as glorified storage spaces. Just as in the hotel problem, the department assumed that it had only two choices. Unfortunately, though, no one in the department even considered a third alternative.

That third alternative would have been to give staff members an office credit. They could have used the credit for office space at the school or exchanged it for money or other benefits. For instance, one professor does most of his work either teaching in the classroom or writing at a local Carl's Jr. restaurant and would have gladly exchanged his office for a reprieve from one international teaching trip per year. Additionally, some professors could choose to share an office. The net result: this department is going without the benefit of a $100,000 employee due to an artificial shortage of a much cheaper resource, office space, because the decision makers did not consider creative alternatives.

Closing the School

A few years ago, an Admiral in Washington, D.C. tried hard to close the Naval Postgraduate School (NPS), where I (DRH) work, and people at NPS fought successfully to keep it open. This fight consumed thousands of hours of people's valuable time, as well as numerous expensive roundtrip flights between Washington, D.C. and Monterey, California.

The impression we had at the school was that the Admiral, David Oliver, was a man with a mission—he seemed to want passionately to close the school. As far as I know, though, through all the months of debate and conflict, no one at the school asked Oliver point blank *why* he wanted to close the school. But shortly after that episode, my friend and colleague François Melese got a chance to do just that. François, an economics professor at the Defense Resources Management Institute, part of NPS, happened to sit beside Oliver at a dinner. A curious and direct person, François asked Oliver his reasons for wanting to close NPS. Oliver answered that it was important that Naval officers be exposed to civilians and that having the officers earn their graduate degrees at NPS meant they didn't get that exposure.

François was stunned. He thought for a few seconds and then said:

> That's interesting. It seems to me there are lots of different ways to expose Navy officers to civilians. Sprinkling them around the country, with a handful at each of a large number of civilian universities, is one way to do it. But another way would be to send them to conferences attended by civilians, and there are probably other options as well. Have you considered some of these other options?

Oliver stopped and replied, "No. I haven't."

We tell this story not to make fun of Oliver, but, rather, to point out what even very bright people often do. Think of all the airfares and hours that could have been saved had Oliver considered other ways of achieving his goal. That's the point of this book: a little clear thinking goes a long way, and there are rules for thinking clearly. In all three of the stories above, a little thinking was all that was needed to discover new and better alternatives. Of course, the new alternatives won't always be better. When you go exploring, you aren't guaranteed of finding anything good. But the best way to get good alternatives is to think of many.

The Online Payroll Service

Because Objective Insights is small, we find it easy and cheap to use a payroll service. We tell them how much each person gets paid, and they do the rest, from direct-deposited paychecks to taxes to W-2 statements. One of my colleagues wanted to switch from Paychex, the company we were using, to another payroll service, Payroll Online, because it would allow us to monitor our payroll better over the World Wide Web. After weeks of hassles, including filling out confusing forms, talking to both payroll companies, and getting trained on the new system, we realized that the switch would be harder than we'd anticipated.

Only then did someone think to ask the colleague what exactly he was after, what he would be able to do on the Web that he couldn't do now. It turned out that he wanted his payroll information sooner than he currently got it. We figured out a way to fax his payroll information to him as soon as it was available, and the problem went away, but only after we had wasted a lot of time and effort. Think how much better off we would have been had we asked him what his goal was and then considered alternative ways of reaching that goal. This story is also an example of knowing what you want before you choose. We discuss that topic in Chapter 5.

Positions and Interests

At Objective Insights, we had a hard time finding a good office manager to work 12 to 18 hours per week. This seemed to be a very difficult chunk of time for most people—either too small or too big. Still, we tried to fill the position. First there was Cathy, who proved to be a solid office manager; give her a task and she would deliver, with a bow neatly tied on top. The problem was that, contrary to our agreement, Cathy gradually started working more and more hours until she had herself a full-time job. After Cathy left for a real full-time job elsewhere, there was Lana, whose work was good—when she bothered to show up, that is. Her hours dwindled to nothing.

Next came Philip, who simply started scheduling fewer and shorter days at work. When I (CLH) reminded him of our agreement—12 to 18 hours per week—he replied that he no longer wanted to work that many hours. Philip was not lazy; he was just employed part-time at another company. Unfortunately, Philip was our bookkeeper as well as our office manager. If he left us, it would be relatively easy to hire a new office manager, but more of a challenge to train a new bookkeeper.

Philip saw no option but to leave Objective Insights. Really, he saw two alternatives: work more than he wanted or leave, neither of which he considered ideal. So, we constructed a third path: Philip could work eight hours a week and continue as our bookkeeper. We took the aspect he was most concerned about, his hours, and the part we were most concerned about, maintaining key bookkeeping functions, and patched them together to create an alternative that both sides preferred.

Negotiators use this same technique, but they use different words to describe it. They recommend that you negotiate about *interests*, not *positions*. In other words, instead of Philip saying, "I quit," (a position), he should say, "I do not want to work this many hours" (an interest). I could then state my interest in retaining Philip as a bookkeeper, and the solution begins to create itself.

> ## TERMINOLOGY
>
> An INTEREST is something you want—an objective, a preference, a goal.
> A POSITION is an alternative that you have selected to achieve that interest.

When negotiating this way, you should always start with what you *want*—your interest—and then consider how to get it—your position. Starting with a position limits your clarity and flexibility. Worse, in negotiations with others—with all the baggage of messy emotions, egos, and pride—statements of position can frequently end in deadlock. The two sides end up pushing their positions and lose sight of their interests. The solution is to unwind the positions into interests and then take the opportunity to build alternatives that best suit both parties, creating a win-win situation.[72]

Writing Off Yard Work

I (DRH) hate yard work. When my wife and I bought our house, we wanted a nice yard, but neither of us wanted to put time into it. Also, because we had used up our whole liquid wealth to make a ten-percent down payment, money was extremely tight. So, what to do? I realized that my problem was not one of coming up with hours to work in the yard; I could spare a few hours a week. The problem was that I felt about yard work the way many people think about going to the dentist. I needed a creative alternative.

What I needed to do was figure out how I could use those few extra hours a week to my advantage—but without ever having to get my hands dirty. I realized the answer. I could use this time doing something I loved—free-lance writing. With the after-tax amount I earned doing that, I could hire a gardener for more than an hour a week. Instead of getting stuck in my "I hate yard work" *position,* I let my *interest* guide me to create a beneficial alternative.

Interested in a Relaxing Vacation

Rosalyn and Sam make their living by renting houses to tenants. In the summer of 1999, they were planning a big vacation but were worried about a particularly troublesome tenant they were trying to evict. Aware of the time it takes to legally evict tenants, they imagined a disgruntled tenant leaving their rental house right in the middle of their vacation. Afraid of the consequences and concerned about their peace of mind, they offered the tenant $2,000 to leave immediately. With this creative alternative, the tenant was happy—and gone—and Rosalyn and Sam could relax and enjoy their vacation.

"But wait!" you may say. "The tenant was the one causing the problem. Why should Rosalyn and Sam pay that troublesome person $2,000?!" If you react that way, then you've fallen into the position "trap." Had our landlords insisted on sticking to a moral-high-ground *position*, then they would not have served their *interests*—enjoying their vacation without having to worry about the tenant's behavior while they were gone.

The Division of Labor

One thing that characterizes clever people, whether they are business people, inventors, writers, scientists, military leaders, parents, teachers, or negotiators, is their ability to think of new alternatives. Life is not a given set of options; you create the ones you want. This is not as hard as many people fear. You simply take the given alternatives apart and put them back together differently, keeping the aspects you like and discarding the others. Sometimes this thinking has already been done for us, so we aren't even aware that we're creating new alternatives.

Anyone who has studied economics is well aware of the principle of the division of labor. Adam Smith laid out the example of an 18th-Century pin maker, who, when he worked with others, was much more productive than when he worked alone. Smith describes how one pin maker could perhaps, "with his utmost industry, make one pin in a day, and certainly could not make twenty." Smith then describes a ten-man factory that he visited. These ten men divided their labor and employed a simple production line where,"(o)ne man draws out the wire, another straights it, a third cuts it, a fourth points it, a fifth grinds it at the top for receiving the head. . ." These ten men working in concert were each 240 to 4,800 times as productive.[73] What Adam Smith was really saying was that there was a fantastic alternative to pin makers working alone. By considering alternative arrangements and dividing their labor, these pin manufacturers increased their productivity by orders of magnitude.

Henry Ford is famous for developing the assembly line for automobile production. With the assembly line, he was able to pay workers much more than they were accustomed to earning and still reduce the cost of his Ford cars dramatically. These are the benefits of making workers substantially more productive.

The division of labor is certainly not perfect, but it clearly has been a boon for mankind. The idea, which is really just a creative alternative, is to recombine workers in such a way that they are many times more productive. The only limitation is the divisibility of the labor. Could William Shakespeare have written the nouns, while a coworker crafted the verbs to come up with *Romeo and Juliet*? No—this work, like many artistic endeavors, is simply nondivisible.

Reality Versus Fantasy

A note of caution is in order here. When we create new alternatives, we often need to unleash our imaginations, but we also need to make sure that the alternatives are realistic. The key with decision-making is to compare only those things that are available to us. Our alternatives need to be feasible, or else we are simply dreaming.

My (CLH's) son Mitch sobbed because we celebrated his sixth birthday on a Saturday, while his real birthday was the following Monday. He wanted the two to coincide so that his party would be on the exact day of his birth. "Mitch," I explained, "it's easier for your friends to come on a Saturday than on a Monday. If we had your party on Monday, some of your friends couldn't come." The problem was a choice between a Monday party without all his friends and a Saturday party with them. Mitch was normal in wanting the best of both worlds, but having all his friends attend a Monday party just wasn't feasible.

Mitch made a six-year-old's mistake. Surely, no adult would make the same mistake, right? Unfortunately, you may be surprised how frequently we see such thinking. What follows is but one example of choosing fantasy instead of reality. **Before you read on, let us warn you that we are about to challenge a commonly accepted belief.**

Some U.S. corporations contract out their work to companies in poor countries. These companies hire people, sometimes children, to work long hours at less than a dollar an hour. Many Americans find this practice reprehensible. The idea is so offensive to them, in fact, that they advocate boycotting companies that produce products under such conditions. To the extent that the boycotts are successful, companies respond either by moving their manufacturing elsewhere or by paying higher rates but employing fewer workers. In other words, jobs are lost. That's fine, you might say, the jobs were lousy anyway. Good riddance.

But think further. You're probably comparing those workers' jobs to yours or those of your teenagers—which is like comparing apples and oranges. No one is offering those third-world workers the kinds of jobs that Americans—even young, uneducated Americans—can get. There is only one job offer on the table, and that's the job they're in. So, what happens to these workers when the company either pulls out or raises wages but lays people off? It's simple: the displaced workers are worse off because they are unemployed or return to even worse jobs. From our good intentions often come bad outcomes.

The bottom line is that "[s]omeone who intentionally gets you fired is not your friend."[74] The workers themselves understand this. Candida Rosa Lopez, for example, a worker in a clothing factory in Nicaragua, had the following message for those who bought clothes that she produced under "sweatshop" conditions:

> Sometimes, at the end of the year, the factory doesn't have enough orders. Then we can't work as many hours, or make as much money. I wish more people would buy the clothes we make.[75]

Indeed, in January 2001, about 2,000 workers at a so-called sweatshop protested publicly in Nicaragua against the National Labor Committee, a U.S. organization that is pushing the anti-"sweatshop" agenda.[76] The workers understand what their real alternatives are and that the NLC is trying to take away their best choice. To help these workers, well-intentioned Americans should first do no harm, and should provide a better alternative (i.e., a better job), not eliminate their best alternative (i.e., get them fired).

You may be shocked by this different point of view. Perhaps you've never read anything that so challenges a cherished viewpoint. Good. That's what learning's about. If this makes it any easier, we can assure you that *all* economists we know of who have looked at the issue share our reasoning. Liberal Princeton economist Paul Krugman, for example, pointed out, in his defense of such jobs:

> The benefits of export-led economic growth to the mass of people in the newly industrializing economies are not a matter of conjecture. A country like Indonesia is still so poor that progress can be measured in terms of how much the average person gets to eat; since 1970, per capita intake has risen from less than 2,100 to more than 2,800 calories a day. A shocking one-third of young children are still malnourished—but in 1975, the fraction was more than half. Similar improvements can be seen throughout the Pacific Rim, and even in places like Bangladesh. These improvements have not taken place because well-meaning people in the West have done anything to help—foreign aid, never large, has lately shrunk to virtually nothing. Nor is it the result of the benign policies of national governments, which are as callous and corrupt as ever. It is the indirect and unintended result of the actions of soulless multinationals and rapacious local entrepreneurs, whose only concern was to take advantage of the profit opportunities offered by cheap labor.[77]

Take away the word "soulless" and we agree with Krugman. Journalists who have studied the issue also realize how much these jobs benefit the workers. In July 1996, for example, a *New York Times* news story datelined San Pedro Sula, Honduras reported that 40-cents-an-hour workers were happy with their jobs at apparel plants. One worker, Eber Orellana Vasquez, told the reporter, "Every time I go to visit the ranch, everyone wants to come back with me." He also pointed out that he had gained 30 pounds since working there, something that, in poor countries, is a good thing.[78] In June 2002, Nicholas D. Kristof of the *New York Times* reported:

> Indeed, talk to third world factory workers and the whole idea of 'sweatshops' seems a misnomer. It is farmers and brick-makers who really sweat under the broiling sun, while sweatshop workers merely glow.

Kristof pointed out that those in the so-called sweatshops had better jobs than their brethren in agricultural pursuits, a typical story in third-world countries.[79]

> The calls for international labor standards are very sincere, but they, I think, completely misunderstand the reality of a poor third world country like Cambodia. One needs to put the sweatshop jobs in perspective. The critique of the sweatshop jobs is basically right. They are pretty wretched jobs, but here in Cambodia, it is also clear that they are, for many poor workers, among the best opportunities they have. There are a lot of jobs that in third world countries are much, much worse. I visited some construction workers near the Bosoc River, and they all said that they would love to have factory jobs, partly, in fact, it was ironic, they said that in a factory job they wouldn't sweat as much. I also visited the dump in downtown Nom Pen, and this is just a scene from hell. You have not only adults, but little children walking through the filth, scavenging anything. Those people that I talked to in the dump, they said they would love to get some kind of factory job. And so I think what Americans don't perhaps understand is that in a country like Cambodia, the exploitation of workers in sweatshops is a real problem, but the primary problem in places like this is not that there are too many workers being exploited in sweatshops, it's that there are not enough. And a country like Cambodia would be infinitely better off if it had

more factories using the cheap labor here and giving people a lift out of the unbelievably harsh conditions in the villages and even in the urban slums.[80]

Take away the term "exploitation" and we agree with Kristof. In a voluntary trade, neither side exploits the other: both gain, or else they wouldn't do it. So, we see here that many of the people who fight against sweatshops, while well intentioned, are not choosing a realistic alternative.

Many people get tripped up in their own lives by comparing reality with an unattainable ideal. But few things, if any, are perfect. Still, some people believe that life should be perfect and become upset over anything less. Like Mitch, they are being unrealistic. *Your* life will be happier if you don't fool yourself by comparing real alternatives with completely unrealistic ones. We decision-makers need to consider only feasible alternatives, so we aren't left disappointed.

The perfect is the enemy of the good. Some of us are perfectionists, and some of us have worked with perfectionists. We know that always striving for perfection has a cost. Assume, for the sake of discussion, that perfection costs twice as much to achieve as "just good enough." Then it stands to reason that perfectionists can attack only half as many problems. Of course perfectionists will reply that anything worth doing is worth doing well. Which argument is right? The language of alternatives can shed some light on this issue.

Imagine you're hiring someone and you have imperfect information about the person's abilities and weaknesses. This is the point where anyone who has ever hired an employee shouts, "But you never have perfect information about a job candidate!" Exactly. The only choice we have is between less and more information.

After the first interview, you assess the candidate and find that you still have more questions. The perfectionist would interview the candidate again and again until no questions remain. But, of course, questions will always remain. Given that, do you hire her, reject her, or interview her again? The answer depends on the costs and the benefits. It's pretty easy to ascertain the cost of an extra interview. And the benefit of an additional interview may be zero simply because it's not possible to learn everything more about this person in an artificial job interview setting.

At this point, it makes the most sense to either hire or reject the applicant, accepting the imperfect nature of information—and accepting the risk of a bad outcome as the cost of doing business. On one level, your decision is between hiring the candidate or not. On another level, your decision is between getting out of business completely or remaining in business *even though* it is inevitable that some employees will disappoint you. (See Chapter 12 for more on the value of information.)

With this in mind, consider the decisions made by the Food and Drug Administration. Critics frequently complain that some of the medicines the FDA approves later show problems.

> One in five new drugs has serious side effects that do not show up until well after the medicine has received approval, according to a study that exposes what one researcher calls an alarming game of medical Russian roulette.[81]

The unstated implication is that the FDA could and should approve only safe drugs. How are drugs deemed safe? Well, only by long-term usage by many thousands of patients. But giving a large number of patients drugs for long-term usage before they are proven safe is "Russian roulette," to use the words of the critics. So we have a Catch-22, an infeasible alternative. The only feasible alternatives are never to use any new drug or to use new drugs that may have problems that will show up only after lots of experience. Which is better: the possibility of health or the guarantee of illness? Medicines provide the possibility of a better life. To prevent the risk associated with medicines requires preventing the possible benefit, too. We explore risk in more depth in Chapter 10.

Focus on the Inputs You Control

Happy people plan actions, they don't plan results.
— Dennis Wholey

We've cautioned against choosing infeasible alternatives, and now we have one more caution. It's also important to realize that what you're choosing is what you'll *do*, not necessarily what you'll *achieve*. What you achieve depends not just on your actions, but also on chance and other people's actions. In the language of economics, even though you want outputs, the one thing you control is your own inputs. Life is a series of inputs and outputs: we "put in" the inputs and "get out" the outputs. The alternatives we choose are largely inputs, while the outcomes (outputs) we get are partly determined by our chosen actions and partly by uncertain, probabilistic events. You may choose to live in Florida instead of Wyoming because you think you'll have a better life in Florida, but the actual life you get depends on many things outside your control—such as whether your potential future best friend independently settles in Florida or Wyoming, whether the economy is healthy, or whether a truck comes crashing through your living room window.

Apolo Anton Ohno thrilled Americans with his short-track skating at the 2002 Winter Olympics in Salt Lake City. Reporters who interviewed Ohno held great hope that he would win four gold medals. He won "only" one gold and a silver medal because he had a few disasters along the way. In his first race, he was knocked down and hit the pads heavily, causing one skate to gash his leg. In another race, he bumped a competing skater and was disqualified. In his last race, a teammate fell, causing the U.S. relay team to drop far behind and into last place. Ohno's speed and smart moves caught our attention, but his grace in defeat was what won him praise from supporters. Interestingly, he insisted that he never thought about winning medals. "I think that's what makes me a good skater," he said. "I'm just trying to give my best and walk off the ice with no regrets."[82]

An athlete thinking of winning the gold medal is thinking of the outcome he wants. Although thinking about outcomes helps guide his strategy and objectives, when he competes he doesn't have direct control over winning the event. The only thing he controls is his actions. He can hold back for the first four laps and plan to explode for the last few. He can pass on the inside or outside. He can wait for others to make mistakes. He can increase his effort to try to boost his raw speed. During an event, focusing on the final outcome, in this case a gold, silver, or bronze medal, is a distraction that takes his attention away from the things he can control. In other words, no one offers Ohno the alternative labeled "Gold Medal." He can't decide, therefore, to win the gold. The only things he can decide are how to control his body and mind before and during an event—and, his demeanor after the event, win or lose.

Your focus should be on the inputs you control. Since you have only a finite amount of attention and effort, focusing on the outputs leaves you less attention to focus on the inputs—which are what will get you the desired outputs. Can you see a similar logic in George W. Merck's 1950-era credo? "We try never to forget that medicine is for the people. It is not for the profits. The profits follow, and if we have remembered that, they have never failed to appear. The better we remembered it, the larger they have been."[83] Mr. Merck was arguing that if his pharmaceutical company, Merck & Co., would take good care of its patients, the profits would take care of themselves. While not always true—a new treatment for poor Africans will rarely repay the investment—the logic is similar to that employed by Ohno: Focus on the inputs you control, and the outputs you desire will follow.

The Lessons Learned

Some men see things as they are and ask why. Others dream things that never were and ask why not.
— George Bernard Shaw

If you define your situation according to a set of existing choices, then you are in the first category described by Shaw. You've accepted the status quo. If you create new, and better, choices, then you are in the second category—you've asked, "Why not?" All of the above stories show how we can create better alternatives in our lives. Ronnie Lott (see the story in Chapter 1) knew that he wanted both a healed finger and the ability to continue playing football. A little extra thinking convinced him that he didn't need a whole finger to achieve his goal of playing ball. So, Lott and his doctor created another alternative. The people running the university department knew that they needed another faculty member and took as given the number of office spaces available. If they had thought further, they would have realized that some modest incentives would have encouraged at least one member of the existing faculty to give up an office. They should have asked, "How can we hire another faculty member even though we have no free offices?" And, when vacationing in Phoenix, David thought he wanted a bigger, more comfortable, and inevitably more expensive hotel room. But when he started talking about what he didn't like about the room he had, he realized that it really wasn't the room at all; instead, it was the simple absence of soft pillows, something he could buy for a fraction of the additional cost of a nicer room. He and his wife asked, "Why not? Why can't we enjoy the comfort of a more expensive room with the economy of this room?"

Charley could have kept losing employees and hiring new people until he found the right office manager. Instead, he asked why the most recent hire was not satisfied and then figured out how to give both the employee and the company what they wanted. The Stanford wedding couple (see Chapter 1) should have considered ways to enjoy the rest of their reception. We're sure that there are even more creative possibilities, but a simple solution would have been to pay the $60 penalty and relax.

When we make a decision, we are actively selecting one of many alternatives. To select the best one, which is our goal, we should have a good list of choices. The first mistake people frequently make is to stop their search much too early and not explore other ideas. We have also discussed the value of considering otherwise distasteful options, as Ronnie Lott did when he had his fingertip amputated.

Decision-makers need to take two steps to be successful. The first is somewhat passive: consider the available alternatives. The second, and more active step is to create new, potentially better alternatives. Both steps are important.

The examples in this chapter show that a little extra thinking helped, or would have helped. That's partly because we've presented the stories with their solutions. As legendary GM executive Charles (Boss) Kettering, once said, "All problems are simple—once they're solved." Now, how can *you* use these stories to think through better solutions for your problems? Here are a few simple rules for thinking clearly.

Step #1: Think about what you want.
Step #2: Think of alternatives that give you what you want.
Step #3: Consider what you like and dislike about each existing alternative.
Step #4: Create hybrid alternatives, those that combine the best elements from the existing alternatives. "Cheat" the existing order by cherry-picking the best elements.
Step #5: Throw out all impossible alternatives.
Step #6: Pick the best alternative.

Clear thinking isn't just for businesspeople striving for profits. Here's an inspirational story showing clear thinking by someone in a horrible dilemma. A British couple, Angela and Gavin Moon, faced a difficult situation. Gavin was terminally ill and likely to die before their baby's due date. This thought tormented the couple; the idea that child and father would never see each other made them feel hollow and sad. The Moons developed a seemingly drastic, radical solution to this problem. Angela asked doctors at South Tyneside Hospital in northeast England to induce her baby two weeks early. Baby Imogen's father died of cancer three days later after holding her in his arms just once. "The three of us grasped onto each other. It was only one hug. But I will remember that moment for the rest of my life," Angela said. "He looked down at her and said: 'You're beautiful. I'm your Dad, remember me.'"[84]

Chapter 9

CONSCIOUSLY SELECT THE BEST ALTERNATIVE

A man is too apt to forget that in this world he cannot have everything. A choice is all that is left him.
— H. Mathews

Destiny is no matter of chance. It is a matter of choice. It is not a thing to be waited for, it is a thing to be achieved.
— William Jennings Bryan

Early Decisions are Important

When designing a building, the saying goes, all the really important mistakes are made on the first day. Efficiency expert Joseph Romm explains:

> Although up-front building and design costs may represent only a fraction of the building's life-cycle costs, when just one percent of a project's up-front costs are spent, up to 70 percent of its life-cycle costs may already be committed.[85]

All you have are wispy lines on drafting paper, but those lines commit the concrete, metal, wire, glass, and wood that will make the building. On the surface, you've just begun, but in reality you have committed more than half of the project. You never get another chance to make a good first start on a project.

The same thing happens in other situations and industries, even without building plans sketched on drafting paper. We all create expectations when we make small, or seemingly small, decisions early in the process, as the following example shows.

A large, successful pharmaceutical company was preparing for the launch of a major new cancer medicine. A year earlier, a company employee worked on the sales forecasting planning model. The forecaster was essentially a programmer, skilled at making forecasting models, but not skilled at pharmaceutical marketing. He plugged available information into the model so that he could check the mathematical calculations. Price was a glaring gap, so he set a ballpark price to enable his model to calculate reasonable results. A year later, when the price of this medicine was considered in earnest, can you guess what price was the starting point? That's right: the price the programmer had hurriedly put in the model a year earlier. Expectations had been created within management. The product team knew this, and they also knew they would need a good reason to stray from this price because the burden of proof would be on them. This is called "anchoring." The chronology of events extensively determines the final outcome due to human resistance to change. "The price is set at $10 in the forecast model. Why should we change it? What are the reasons? How will we explain the change?" Objective Insights helped this company work through this problem and, after lots of research and lots of insightful analysis, the company agreed to set the price at about double the original value. Our recommendation was compared to the original price by everyone on the team. "Why is yours better?" they asked. We took them through the data and analysis step by step until they, too, agreed that the higher price was better. This breakthrough cancer medicine was doing very well when this was written.

Early decisions are important because of all the downstream resources and actions they commit. We need to understand decisions and put the appropriate effort into making them because it is cheaper and easier to make the right decision than to change course and fix mistakes later.

A newly married woman is cooking a ham for dinner. Her husband watches her cut both ends off the ham before she puts it in the pan to cook. He asks her why she cut the ends off. "I don't know why. My mom always did this. I'll call her to ask why." So she calls her mom, who gives pretty much the same answer, "I don't know; my mom always did it." The woman was later able to reach her grandmother, who knew exactly why she always cut the ends off. "I always did it because my pans were too small." We all succumb to tradition, but we should make an effort to consciously select the best course of action and not just follow in our mother's footsteps blindly.

Do you think this woman's story has nothing to do with business decisions? Well, let us transport you to a profitable and well-known biotechnology company in 1999. A conversation is taking place between a company analyst and a consultant. Let's listen in.

Consultant: I've reviewed the forecast you created for the drug your company is thinking of in-licensing (licensing from another company). I've made a number of changes to it. By the way, will the business development (corporate licensing) people within your company rely on this forecast, or do they do their own forecasts?

Analyst: Oh, we do all the forecasts and they rely on them.

Consultant: Do you apply this level of effort to all in-licensing product forecasts? I mean, it doesn't seem as if much effort went into this. You are, after all, forecasting a product with the potential for multi-hundred million-dollar revenues.

Analyst: I put a few hours of work into this forecast. But it is only a business development product. It isn't one of our company's products; we put a lot more work into those. You've seen what we do for our products.

Consultant: But a multi-hundred million-dollar decision will be made based on this three-hour forecast. And regarding your products, you've already got them; they're already yours. You don't need to make big decisions.

Analyst: You're just trying to sell me more consulting.

The bottom line is that this company was going to make a multi-hundred million-dollar decision based largely on a forecast that had only three hours invested in it and still needed a lot of work to fix major flaws. And why? Because tradition said that the company wouldn't invest nearly as much in analyzing decisions involving another company's products. This was a problem because analysis supports decisions, and the decision to in-license a product is one of those early decisions in which the biggest mistakes can be made. Somehow, though, the decision-maker had categorized it as unimportant for the completely irrelevant reason that the product involved was not one of its own. There goes that ham.

Consequences

Unless principles or ethics are involved, decisions should be made exclusively according to their consequences and expediency. Consequentialism looks at the ends we hope to achieve and should be our only guidepost unless the means, or process, to these ends violates some ethics or principles we hold. Chapter 15, "Do the Right Thing," explores ethics and the tension between our processes and our results.

The former Soviet Union built and operated approximately 240 nuclear submarines, each capable of unleashing World War III. The Soviet Union is now gone and, with it, our immediate fear of a world war; however, we now have new things to worry about. Russia, the Soviet Union's replacement, has not devoted many resources to maintaining and dismantling its surplus nuclear submarines, and so they sit in the frigid Arctic water in the port city of Vladivostok, rusting and sinking into the sea.[86] These old Cold War weapons pose two threats to us today: radioactive spills causing environmental damage and the theft of radioactive fuel by terrorists. Assuming we've decided that it's all right for our government to spend tax money on environmental clean-up and on defense, should our government help the Russians clean up this mess at great expense? We could come up with many reasons to say no, citing irony and their own foolishness, but all that really matters now, given our assumption, are the consequences: will we be better off paying to avoid a disaster, or not? This is related to the Hatfields and McCoys story in which we determined that a good reason is not enough. Instead of following reasons, we should select the best alternative—the one with the best chance of securing the best consequences.

Decisions and Outcomes

A decision is the selection of an alternative from a set of possible alternatives. An action must be made and resources committed. Only later do you see the outcome of your decision and action.

There is a difference between a good decision and good outcome. Brian bought a house right after he started a new job as a consultant. He almost ran into trouble due to a dry spell of consulting work. Things turned out well, and he ended up selling the house for a $100,000 profit just a couple of years later because the real estate market appreciated wildly. Many people would say that, in buying the house, Brian made a good decision.

We're not so sure. A good decision is one that you would choose to make again and again, even though you occasionally get stuck with a bad outcome. Brian was fortunate, but would he buy a similar house under the same circumstances again? The answer to that question would help determine whether or not he made a good decision. Consider the following example.

A teacher in a third-grade class wants to select one of two children for a special privilege, such as cutting the end-of-year celebration cake. So she asks the two children to think of a number between one and ten, with the winning number being the one closest to the teacher's. Addie selects two and then Greer picks number one. The teacher announces that the number is one and that Greer has won.

Unless Greer knows in advance what number his teacher will select, Greer chose unwisely, but he got lucky. He would do better over time to select the best odds, that is, to pick the number with the highest probability of success. In this case, three is the best choice. The number one has a ten-percent chance of winning, two has already been taken, and three has an 80-percent chance because three wins if three through ten is the right number. Other, higher numbers have lower chances than three.

Granted, Greer would have to be quite an exceptional eight-year-old to have figured out these odds. But our point is this: a reasonable person who faced this "lottery" over and over should always select the number with the greatest chance of success. Those who choose otherwise will get lucky from time to time. This conclusion is important: **A good decision is the decision you'd make next time given the same information, not the decision that happened to give a good outcome this particular time.**

What you want is the good outcome. What you do to get the good outcome is choose among alternatives. Afterwards, you consider what happened and try to learn from the process. If you learned that you should always select the number one, we argue that you have learned the wrong lesson because we can prove mathematically that you will lose frequently. Given your state of information, choosing the number one is not a good strategy.

Using mathematics as our guide, we can formulate the best strategy for winning. If you are the first guesser, the best strategy is to select five or six. If you are the second guesser, you want to pick a number adjacent to the first guess, such that the number is on the side with the biggest remaining block. For example, if the first guesser guesses three, you should pick four, because four through 10 is a bigger block (seven numbers) than one through two (two numbers). If you play this game 100 times, this strategy will give you the best chance of winning, and, on average, you will get the best outcome. If you play this game only one time, this strategy will still give you the best chance of winning. With one turn, however, you either win or lose. To draw inferences about your strategy later based on whether you won after only one chance isn't statistically valid. The way you can test this is by asking yourself what you learned. "I learned to always pick the number one." Of course, this doesn't make any sense because we know the winning number won't always be one unless, for some strange reason, the teacher always picks one. In fact, the teacher will choose one only about ten percent of the time.

Consider the following gambling situation. You are playing poker and get a hand with the eight, nine, ten, jack, and queen of spades. Out of 2,598,960 possible poker hands,[87] only six hands will beat yours—straight flushes in diamonds, hearts, and clubs that are king or ace high. Three hands will tie yours—queen-high straight flushes in diamonds, hearts, and clubs—but we will ignore those for now. So out of 2.6 million possible hands, only six feasible hands can beat yours. You bet everything you have only to be shocked when another player puts down his hand with a royal flush (ace high) in diamonds. You made a great decision but had a bad outcome. If by some amazing chance you ended up with the same hand later that night or later in life, would you still bet everything? You should, because the odds are massively in your favor. With such a high straight flush, your probability of winning is 99.99977 percent.[88] Losing once was a fluke. A smart decision-maker would bet heavily on this hand again and again.

These examples may be new to some readers and familiar and obvious to others. We discuss them because in the more important decisions in life and business, many decision-makers make exactly the same mistake as Greer in the story above. Instead of losing in a child's game, they lose in an adult's game, where they have bet thousands, millions, or billions of dollars. Don't believe us? Have you ever noticed, for instance, how many people judge a decision purely by the outcome? A baseball team trades to get a big hitter who has had physical, legal, and attitude problems. An objective assessment would say that this is a risky decision. The player shines at the new venue and the team has its best record in years. Was this a good decision or not? Unless the team manager knew something no one else knew, this manager made a very risky decision and just happened to get lucky. Hoping to get lucky is not a good approach for the next ten trades. Managerial skill shows up in good decisions, which, over the long run, result in good outcomes, while one good outcome may be purely due to luck. Whom would you rather hire as team manager: someone who was lucky once or someone who can assess players and make intelligent decisions about risk over the long run?

Most of us aren't close enough to the action to know what kind of information the team manager had available to make that decision. We simply read the sports page and notice an article extolling the genius of this manager for trading that player. We frequently can't tell if they are good or lucky. In our own lives, however, we are much closer to the action. We often hear people say, "I'd rather be lucky than good." It's a clever saying, but the problem is that it misstates the choice. You can't choose to be lucky—that's why it's called luck. But you can choose to be good, or at least to be better than you are. Instead of being bad and hoping to get lucky, we'd prefer to be good and hope to get lucky.

I am a great believer in luck. The harder I work the more of it I seem to have. — Coleman Cox

What Did I Learn?

The way to avoid this pitfall is to ask yourself what you learned and then to question whether that lesson is reasonable, repeatable, and valuable. In the story above, Greer might say that he learned always to pick the number one. This is silly. Lessons should be more universal and based on principles, not arbitrary or mystical. If you ask yourself what you learned, you can more easily make the distinction between decisions and outcomes. If you made a good decision and happened to get an adverse outcome, as in the poker example, careful consideration may instruct you to make the same decision the next time you find yourself in a similar situation. Why? Because the principles don't change, while your luck might. If you made a bad decision but received a favorable outcome, what you should have learned is why you made a bad decision, so that you could decide differently the next time. (Yes. We realize this introspection is unlikely, but it is your choice.) Fortune will be on the side of those who put the effort into making good decisions and let luck take care of itself.

Still not convinced? Imagine that you own two uranium processing plants, and you believe that good decisions should be measured by the good outcomes they produce. The plants generate the same revenues, but one plant (Plant A) has 30 percent lower labor costs than the other (Plant B). Plant A certainly is enjoying a better outcome—higher profits, quarter after quarter. So it follows that Plant A's managers have made better decisions, right? How could anyone argue with this? For the last six years, Plant A's outcomes have been better than Plant B's by any objective measure. If you had a bonus pool to distribute, would you give more to the Plant A or Plant B managers and workers?

Before you hand out the bonuses, disaster strikes. Uranium processing Plant A suffers a horrible accident, killing four workers and nearly releasing massive amounts of toxic radiation into a nearby community. Lawsuits bury your company. How could this happen? Simple. Plant A workers skipped many safety procedures in their quest to reduce labor costs, increasing their risk of disaster from infinitesimal to perhaps one accident every 100 months. Each and every day they were able to speed their work by skipping burdensome and "unnecessary" safety procedures.

The Plant A managers were playing Russian roulette, yet you were rewarding them for their good outcomes during the last six years. Had you studied their *decisions* instead of their *outcomes*, you would have realized that they were making horrible tradeoffs to achieve their objectives. The question is: which processing plant made the best decisions? The best decisions are based on the cost of adhering to the safety procedures versus the expected cost—or risk—of skipping them. Managers who base their rewards purely on outcomes will unwittingly encourage risky behavior that focuses on the short term at the expense of the long term.

Is this example completely fictitious? Unfortunately, no. In 1999, workers at the JCO Co. uranium processing plant in Tokaimura, Japan didn't follow proper procedures and mixed too much uranium—16 kilograms instead of the approved 2.4—with nitric acid in a storage tank and started a fission reaction that went temporarily out of control. All 310,000 residents in the city were evacuated, 21 people were sickened, and three workers were hospitalized.[89][90] While this may have been an innocent accident, it probably was the result of a technique the JCO workers used to improve their efficiency. We're guessing that they didn't have to return their bonus checks.

Make Effort Proportional to Importance

Those who observe people making decisions will often notice an odd trait. The effort expended in the process of decision-making is frequently inversely related to the importance of the decision.

Imagine that you must purchase one of two cars, say a Honda Accord or a Toyota Camry. You may study *Road & Track*, *Car & Driver*, and *Consumer Reports* to see what the magazines say. You may talk to your neighbors and spend some time at the car dealerships considering transmissions, engines, and trim levels. Do you want a DX, LX, or EX model? Do you want special wheels? Should you borrow from your bank or directly through the dealership? How will this affect your insurance? When I (CLH) faced this decision, I chose the slightly sportier Accord over the slightly more durable and reliable Camry. Are the differences large? No. In the grand view of transportation, these cars are quite similar. Would our lives be much different with Camrys instead of Accords? We doubt it. However, this insight is lost to common behavior. Instead of spending *less* time and effort with less important but more complicated decisions, most of us spend significantly *more* time. This is because, in general, the difficulty of making a decision is greater when the alternatives are close in value; however, the importance of making a good decision is higher when the alternatives are clearly different. In other words, the decision-maker actually does something more than just choose between Tweedle Dee and Tweedle Dum. To choose between an Accord and Camry is hard because of all the details, yet the two are so close in features that this decision really isn't important. Do you want Tweedle Dee or Tweedle Dum? Both are fine cars, and you'd probably be very happy with either. An important decision would be whether to join the Peace Corp, join the Coast Guard, or work at a company in town. A wise decision-maker will realize that if alternatives are very close in value, it matters less which one he picks. He should save his energy for more important decisions—those with very different alternatives.

Options

Frequently, decisions appear to be huge steps that we take in life. Consider buying a house with a 30-year mortgage. You may say to yourself, "This is a huge decision because I will be stuck in this house and this neighborhood paying this mortgage until I am sixty years old!" Of course, the situation is not so frightful, as a number of escape routes are available to you. If necessary, you could sell the house a month later or you could rent it to another family. In extreme cases, you can get out of the mortgage by declaring bankruptcy and turning the house over to the mortgage holder.

When you buy the house, you aren't committing the 30 years and the hundreds of thousands of dollars you'll end up paying for the principal and interest; you are committing only a small fraction of this. If you sell the house in a month, you will pay just the transaction costs, things such as real estate commissions and taxes. You might be out $18,000, which is only a few percent of the total "decision" you were facing. **When you make a decision, you are committing only to the irrevocable part, not to the whole amount.** What you are really buying is not the entire house, but just the right, or the option, to keep living there and to have the same right next month. Every month you pay to renew the option to live in the house for one more month. These months can extend into decades if you want, but you can decide that later. That is part of the option you bought. We say that we "bought a house," but what we really bought is an option.

While we're discussing options, consider this question. Why do you have a spare tire in your car? You've probably never used it. You had to pay for the tire and wheel originally, it takes up space, and every time you accelerate, turn, or brake, your car is expending energy to move this bulky 45-pound object. Your life would arguably have been better had you never bought the spare tire in the first place. Of course, you know why you carry a spare tire. You want to protect yourself from being stuck with a flat tire in a bad part of town at night. Having a spare may mean getting home on time, or getting home at all. When you purchase a spare tire at a cost and carry it around for years at another cost, you are doing so to buy yourself an escape route. **In general, an option can be a right to some future opportunity, if things go well, or an escape route, if things don't go well**. It's not the metal and rubber you really want—it is the opportunities and escape routes the spare tire affords you.

When I was in college, a few friends and I (CLH) went skydiving. It was exhilarating. When you parachute, you have a main chute and a backup. You "pay" for the backup chute by lugging it around and paying for someone to check and pack it. But if the main chute malfunctions, the cost of the second chute will be insignificant compared to its value. The challenge is determining the value of an option, or escape route, beforehand. It all comes down to the costs you pay compared to the probability of needing it multiplied by the cost of not having it. If your life is worth $10 million, and one out of 100,000 parachutes fails (a 0.001 percent probability of failure), you should be willing to spend $100 ($10 million times 0.00001) for the spare chute each time you jump. Since the cost is actually much lower, the extra chute is a great bargain.

When we examine our lives, we can see that we're often buying options, even though we usually don't identify them as such. But if we start to notice options, we'll start using them more effectively and not blame ourselves so much when we don't exercise them. My wife and I (DRH) bought tickets to go with another couple to see the Gay Men's Chorus perform in San Francisco. At the last minute, a great business opportunity arose, and I decided not to go to San Francisco so that I could prepare for my cross-country trip and meeting. Our friend challenged my ability to plan. He was upset because the evening together would have been fun, but he was also upset because I "wasted" the ticket money. This event helped clarify in my own mind that the ticket price was an option. By buying the ticket in advance, I bought the right, but not the obligation, to attend the show. I bought the opportunity to go, but gave up that opportunity when a better one came along.

Choose the Best Alternative

This chapter is entitled "Consciously Select the Best Alternative." Sometimes people look at one alternative and, after judging it to be bad, immediately pick another. But this can be like jumping out of the frying pan into the fire. The goal is to pick the best alternative, not just to reject one. You should, for example, move your theater or machine shop to the best location, not simply get out of a bad one. Or, if someone offers you a job that looks better on net than your current job, it makes sense, given the high cost of moving, for you to beat the bushes and look for other jobs to compare against the one offered. You should make your situation as good as you can and not just improve on what you have.

Uncertainty and Risk

If a man will begin with certainties, he shall end in doubts, but if he will be content to begin with doubts, he shall end in certainties.
— Francis Bacon (1605) The Advancement of Learning

When making decisions, we have to deal with the added confusion of outcomes that might not be clear. Outcomes are unclear or uncertain because the world is full of events that are probabilistic, such as a coin toss, and because we rarely have perfect information. Most economists use the term "risk" to refer to a situation in which you know the probability of each of the possible outcomes; they reserve the term "uncertainty" for the more complicated situation, in which you know that certain outcomes are possible but you don't even know the probabilities. But this use of words defies common sense. "**Uncertainty**" should be used to refer to situations that are, well, uncertain. So that's how we use the word here. You are uncertain if you don't know the outcome beforehand. Even if you know the probabilities of certain outcomes, the specific outcome you'll end up with is uncertain. So, for example, there's a particular probability that you'll make it to the airport two hours before your flight and, let's say, a certain probability that you'll make it one hour and 50 minutes early. Either way, you make your flight. Let's say you literally don't care which outcome happens. Then you have uncertainty but no risk. How does risk enter? **You have risk when each of the outcomes has a different payoff, and especially when one or more of the possible outcomes is disadvantageous.** So, to go back to the airport example, if you have a 50-percent probability of getting to the airport one hour before your flight and a 50-percent probability of getting there an hour after your flight has left, you have risk. This brings us to decision analysis.

Decision Analysis by Dirty Harry

Decision analysis is the study of decision-making within uncertain and sometimes risky situations. A famous scene from Clint Eastwood's *Dirty Harry* gives a great example of such decision-making. After a gunfight, Dirty Harry has a criminal pinned to the ground and is pointing his gun straight at him. The criminal has one last chance to get his gun, but if he tries, Harry will shoot him. The question is whether Dirty Harry has any bullets left after the furious shoot-out. In a justly famous line, Dirty Harry tells the crook:

> Uh huh, I know what you're thinking. Did he fire six shots or only five? Well, to tell you the truth, I forgot myself now in all this excitement. But being as this is the 44 Magnum, the most powerful handgun in the world and it could blow your head clean off, you have to ask yourself one question: Do I feel lucky? Well, do you, punk?[91]

The criminal has a decision to make. He can surrender or he can grab his gun. If he surrenders, he will almost certainly serve years of jail time. If he grabs his gun, one of two things will happen, based on the number of bullets Dirty Harry has left: if no bullets are left, the crook will shoot Dirty Harry and escape, while if one bullet is left, the punk's head will be blown "clean off." Here is the decision laid out in a decision tree.

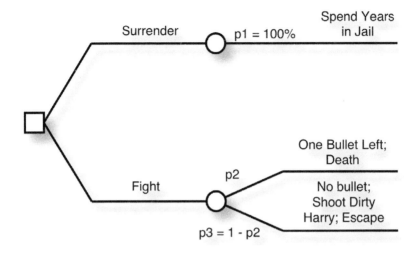

The punk needs to realize the overall structure of his decision, the probabilities of each event, and the value to him of each outcome. Someone who has vowed never to spend another night in jail may choose to fight even if he assigns a very low probability to the "no bullet" event. This "suicide by cop" approach may be acceptable to the decision-maker because he'd rather die than go back to jail. The uncertainty in this case is the issue of the remaining bullet. There is either one or no bullet remaining, and the crook has incomplete information.

Assume that the criminal assigns 50-percent probabilities to each bullet event. (Later in this chapter, we'll explain what you should do when you don't know the probabilities.) Now the criminal needs to consider what his life will be like with each outcome. On a scale from 0 to 100, he may assign death a score of 0, escaping 100, and jail 60. Multiplying the outcomes by their probabilities renders a score of 60 for the surrender branch and 50 for the fight branch, and so he surrenders. Note that we draw decision trees from left to right and then solve them from right to left. To draw this example, we first consider the alternatives, then uncertainties, then outcomes, followed by scores. The probability-adjusted score for each decision alternative is shown on the left. The arrow points to Surrender because Surrender is the best alternative.

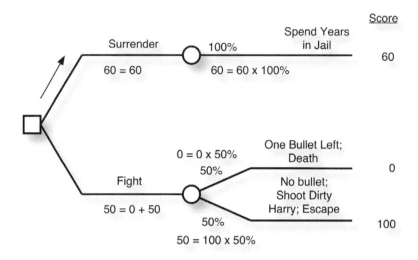

The risk in this case comes from the possibility of dying. In other words, there is some probability of a very bad outcome—death—if the criminal chooses to fight.

The Airplane Ticket Decision

Here's a decision we've often faced, and you might have also. We were deciding whether to purchase a ticket for a business trip, recognizing that the meeting had not yet been confirmed. At the time, the cheapest tickets were available through Travelocity.com, which had a strict change policy: if your travel plans changed at all, you must purchase a new ticket, without any carry-over credit. Of course, purchasing the ticket in advance meant a much lower price. The decision was to purchase now or to purchase only after the meeting was confirmed.

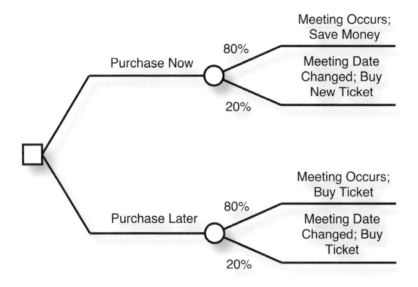

With a meeting probability, p1, of 80 percent, a ticket price today of $350, and a ticket price next week of $1,200, the Purchase Now alternative has an expected cost of $590. Note that $1,550 is the cost of both tickets ($350 plus $1,200).

$$\$590 = \$350 \bullet 80\% + \$1,550 \bullet 20\%$$

The Purchase Later alternative has an expected cost of $1,200 (a guaranteed cost of $1,200). In this case, the meeting will happen, but we just don't know when, and so we can see that by purchasing now we have some chance to acquire our ticket cheaper. By purchasing today, we expect to save $610 ($1,200 minus $590).

If the situation were different and the meeting either occurs when scheduled or is outright cancelled, the decision tree (see below) is a little different, but the result is the same: it is still better to purchase today. Purchase Now has an expected cost of $350 (a guaranteed cost of $350), while Don't Purchase has an expected cost of $960.

$$\$960 = \$1,200 \bullet 80\% + \$0 \bullet 20\%$$

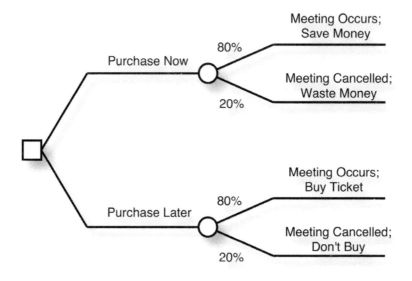

By purchasing today, we expect to save $610 ($960 minus $350). Someone may challenge us and ask us how we know the probability is 80 percent. Our response is simple. We've been doing this for years and our judgment tells us that four out of five times, our meetings are not cancelled. While this may be right, we may not persuade anyone other than ourselves with this rationale, and so we fall back on a stronger defense. We flip the problem around and ask what the probability would need to be to change our behavior and delay our ticket purchase. In this case, the probability of the meeting occurring would have to drop below 29 percent to convince us to delay our ticket purchase ($350 = $1,200 times 0.29). The $350 is the price of a ticket today and the $1,200 is the price of a ticket next week. We ask what probability, 29 percent, would make the two branches of the decision tree equal. In other words, if you think the probability of the meeting occurring is at least 29 percent, you are still better off buying the cheaper ticket today. This is an aspect of **sensitivity analysis**: How low or high does the probability need to be before we reach a different conclusion? You may believe that 80 percent is too high, but may be uncomfortable advocating a number as low as 29 percent. What this shows is that we are unlikely to be wrong in our conclusion to buy the ticket today.

To Be or Not to Be: Hamlet's Decision Tree

Decision analysis has been a part of your life and ours for a long time. It is around us every day—we just might not recognize it when we see it. Consider Shakespeare's *Hamlet*. We'd bet you've never thought of Hamlet's woes as a decision that lends itself to critical analysis using the tools we've described above. Can you see how Hamlet is really just making a decision similar to the airline ticket example? Here is the famous passage:

> To be, or not to be; that is the question:
> Whether 'tis nobler in the mind to suffer
> The slings and arrows of outrageous fortune,
> Or to take arms against a sea of troubles,
> And, by opposing, end them. To die, to sleep –
> No more, and by a sleep to say we end
> The heartache and the thousand natural shocks
> That flesh is heir to – 'tis a consummation
> Devoutly to be wished. To die, to sleep.
> To sleep, perchance to dream. Ay, there's the rub,
> For in that sleep of death what dreams may come
> When we have shuffled off this mortal coil
> Must give us pause. There's the respect
> That makes calamity of so long life,
> For who would bear the whips and scorns of time,
> Th'oppressor's wrong, the proud man's contumely,
> The pangs of disprized love, the law's delay,
> The insolence of office, and the spurns
> That patient merit of th'unworthy takes,
> When he himself might his quietus make
> With a bare bodkin? Who would these fardels bear,
> To grunt and sweat under a weary life,
> But that the dread of something after death,
> The undiscovered country from whose bourn
> No traveller returns, puzzles the will,
> And makes us rather bear those ills we have
> Than fly to others that we know not of?
> Thus conscience does make cowards of us all,
> And thus the native hue of resolution
> Is sicklied o'er with the pale cast of thought
> And enterprises of great pith and moment

With this regard their currents turn awry,
And lose the name of action.[92]

As Stanford professor Ronald Howard has noted, Hamlet is making a decision using just the approach we have been discussing. Hamlet chooses between living and dying—these are his decision alternatives. If he kills himself, he no longer has to deal with his problems—he can "take arms against a sea of troubles, and, by opposing, end them." If he remains alive, he must bear the ills he has. If he kills himself, he may end his troubles and sleep peacefully. But here is where risk becomes important, because if he sleeps, perhaps he may dream, and if he dreams, perhaps the dreams won't be good ones. We can't really know for sure, because no traveler returns from this undiscovered country. At the risk of being a tortured soul saddled with these unpleasant dreams, he determines that it is more prudent to face the devil he knows rather than the devil he doesn't, and consequently becomes a "coward" and loses the will to act. Read it again and you'll see how this scene matches the decision tree we have laid out below.

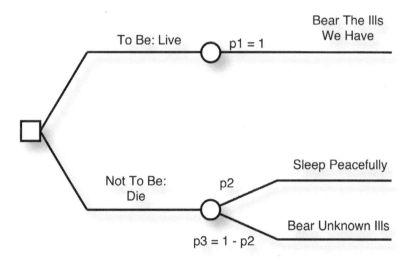

How Should You Assign Probabilities?

How should you assign probabilities? In the punk's case, he should try to remember as clearly as possible how many shots he heard from Dirty Harry's gun. But, more generally, given a complete lack of information, as in the case of someone who hasn't even seen the movie, the probabilities should be p2 = 50 percent and p3 = 50 percent. If you don't know anything about something, you should always assign equal probabilities. For example, if you are facing a multiple-choice question that you know nothing about, either answer will do. Probabilities can change as we get more information. Will it rain in Tasmania next Tuesday? We know nothing about Tasmania's weather, and so we should say there is a 50-percent chance. If we research the problem for five minutes, we may find that Tasmania is currently in summer, which is a dry season. We still don't know much about Tasmania's weather, but now we drop the probability to five percent. A lot of people will find fault with what we just presented. "If you don't know anything about Tasmania's weather, why are you making a weather forecast?" We are making a forecast because we are required to. Well, we aren't really required to in this case, but anyone making a decision must assess things about which he's not certain. To wait for complete certainty is to lie in your bed until old age steals your breath. If you snooze, you lose.

Scientists often have trouble with this. They work in a world where some things are known and others aren't. To move more things into the known category, scientists run experiments. Without the results of the experiments, they don't feel comfortable speculating. But we don't live in such a clean world. If you need to get to Sacramento, California from San Francisco, should you get there by driving across the Bay Bridge and then following Highway 80, or should you drive across the Golden Gate Bridge and go closer to Napa on Highway 37? It depends on the traffic and road conditions, among other things that we don't know for certain. Yet we make such decisions every day. Staying in San Francisco is not what you want to do; the only question is how best to get to Sacramento. A decision must be made, as must an assessment of the probabilities needed to make the decision.

The Lessons Learned

Here are some rules to follow to help make good decisions. The idea is to consciously select the best available alternative.

- When we make decisions or take actions, we commit resources. So carefully think through the downstream consequences of today's decision. A little upfront thinking has a huge payoff later.
- Assuming there are no ethical issues involved, the choice should be the one with the best consequences. We consider the ethical aspect of decisions in Chapter 15.
- Make decisions that logically have a good chance of a good outcome; don't plan on being lucky. On average you won't be, thus the word "luck."
- Make effort proportional to the importance of the decision.
- Realize that often we aren't locking ourselves into huge decisions, but are instead buying options. Consciously think of the decision as involving options and then buy the options if doing so makes sense.
- Many decisions involve choices where various outcomes have various probabilities of occurring. For such problems, build a decision tree and try to estimate the values of outcomes and probabilities.

Chapter 10

RISK IS PART OF GROWTH

Yes, risk-taking is inherently failure-prone. Otherwise, it would be called sure-thing-taking. — Tim McMahon

To get profit without risk, experience without danger, and reward without work is as impossible as it is to live without being born. — A. P. Gouthey

If at first you don't succeed, you're running about average. — M. H. Alderson

Peter Lynch, the famous Fidelity Magellan mutual fund manager, once told an audience the following story. One of his clients had just bought a stock for only $3 a share and asked Lynch, "How much can I lose?" Lynch paused, grinned mischievously, and looked around the room as a few people laughed and then the laughter spread in a wave. Of course, the investor could lose $3 a share—his entire investment.

I (CLH) once asked my father-in-law why he never invested in stocks. His reply: "The stock market is like gambling." I had to agree with him: the stock market *is* like gambling. In his mind, gambling was much too risky and so he stayed away completely. But many other things are like gambling, too. In fact, much of what we do in life involves tremendous risk. You study the situation, put down your bet, usually do just fine, sometimes hit the jackpot, and sometimes get totally hammered.

Although my father-in-law wanted to stay away from gambling, he accomplished many things that involved great risk. He got married and bought a house. He had five children, accepting the risk that they might not turn out to be wonderful. (They did, especially his second daughter.) Later in life, he left his engineering job and acquired a second mortgage on his house to buy a franchised Carvel ice cream store. He invested his time, energy, and money in a number of things that were as risky as the stock market. Perhaps he just wanted to keep one small part of his life, his moderate investments, away from any kind of gamble.

Professor Ronald Howard of Stanford University defines risk as the small probability of a really bad outcome. On the one hand, we have clearly risky endeavors: scuba diving, skydiving, auto racing, horseback riding, and Russian roulette, to name a few. On the other hand, we have events in which the outcome is guaranteed: if you hit yourself with a hammer, you'll hurt yourself; there is no risk involved. Strictly speaking, risk enters only when the outcome is unknown (there is some uncertainty) and the bad outcome is not very likely.[93] **Here, however, we are using a broader definition of risk: the chance of a bad outcome.** The "bad" label implies a value judgment of how that particular outcome affects you personally. The probability and the consequences of a bad outcome may be seen by all, but how they affect *your* life is subjective. Consider two people who each invest $1,000 in the same stock and plan to hold it for a year. Whatever the probability of loss, it is the same for each. The magnitude of the loss is the same for each. But the meaning of that loss, the harm caused to each, could differ dramatically. If one investor has a net worth of $10 million and the other has only the change from a fast-food lunch, then the potential $1,000 loss will be more devastating for the second person than for the first.

This simple insight, that risk depends on your situation, partially explains why certain people deal in illegal drugs and certain others, including us, do not.

The Drug Dealer's Risk

Manufacturing and distributing illegal drugs are commonly thought to be highly profitable; after all, who wouldn't want to sell products at 50 times their normal value? But if you could garner that kind of profit with no risk, then why not make methamphetamine in your garage or sell bags of dried marijuana buds to people in your neighborhood? You might answer that you hate drugs and their effects on people's lives, or you might answer that you're against breaking the law. But millions of people in this country either use or have used illegal drugs and don't object to breaking such victimless-crime laws. Why aren't they all dealers?

The answer is that dealing drugs is a very risky enterprise because of the possibility of death, jail, asset forfeiture, and the occasional need to go underground to hide from the law. Even if we all faced exactly the same probability of asset forfeiture, a 20-year old with assets of $1,000 may happily incur this risk to earn $20,000, while a 40-year old with $200,000 would look for safer ways to earn the money. They perceive the risk differently because of their different situations. One has a good chance of making $20,000 combined with a small chance of losing $1,000. The other has the same upside but a downside 200 times as large. They face the same probabilities but very different possible outcomes. The risk, in other words, is much higher for the wealthier person.

How about the need to go underground to avoid the police? One of my (CLH's) childhood friends actually lived at the creek near our houses as a young adult because he wasn't getting along with his parents and had nowhere else to go. He was already underground and selling drugs. But because I now have a career, house, investment portfolio, and family, going underground would be extremely burdensome. The cost to him was much less.

Dealing drugs can be profitable for those whose cost structure is very low as a result of their insulation from risks that would deter people like you (probably) and us (definitely). Notice, too, that this shows why dealers are foolish for staying in the business too long. Their success changes their risk profile and increases their costs until their risk-adjusted profits disappear. Their risk rises partly due to increased wealth and partly due to more time spent in the business, which aids those trying to track and catch them. On the surface, their business is still profitable, but once the risks are properly included, they are really operating at a loss and are fools to continue. One of my (CLH's) friends who has never sold drugs, wishes he had done so in college. He says he would have set a six-month time limit and sold drugs to his friends. This would have enabled him to earn a few thousand dollars, which was more than he earned in his summer jobs, and the risk would have been very low due to his situation and the finite duration. He didn't do so and would not do so today; it is just too risky for him now that he's successful. Drug dealing is a job for people at the bottom of the ladder, not the top. If you saw the movie "Blow," you might have had the same reaction I (DRH) had: early in his career, the dealer, played by Johnny Depp, scores big by shipping thousands of pounds of marijuana from California to Massachusetts via a Winnebago. With the money he made on that trip, he would have been set for life. Instead, he persisted and *got* life.

Your Risk Tolerance

Many people shudder when they think of risk because it conjures up negative images that compare to poison, disease, pain, war, and death. However, there are everyday risky situations where the negative outcomes are not that bad. Although a fire that destroys your uninsured house would be devastating, a $1,000 loss in the stock market would be minor for most readers. This latter loss is a risk most of us can easily absorb because, while we would miss the money, our lives would go on largely unchanged. Another way of saying this is that we all have a tolerance for risk, just as we have a tolerance for loud music and spicy food. Just as you may order food that contains salsa and chili peppers at a Mexican restaurant, once you know what your tolerance for risk is, you can choose appropriately.

Risk tolerance is roughly proportional to your wealth. IBM, Boeing, General Motors, Warren Buffet, and Bill Gates have a much higher tolerance for losses, and, therefore, risk, than we do. Ronald Howard has a way to estimate your risk tolerance factor and then use that number in all your decision analyses. This has the effect of neutralizing risk—just as discount rates neutralize time (see the Accounting for Risk section for a more complete explanation of how discount rates neutralize time)—to allow us to properly compare vastly different situations and decide wisely.

While we each have a tolerance to risk, as decision-makers, most of us are very risk-averse. According to the late Professor Aaron Wildavsky:

> [L]arge proportions of people care more about avoiding loss than they do about making gains. Therefore, they will go to considerable lengths to avoid losses, even in the face of high probabilities of making considerable gains.[94]

We *should* shy away from big risks, but for small risks, we should often just hold our noses and jump in. By staying away from all risk, we give up much of our chance to grow and profit since opportunity is usually disguised as either work or risk. We suggest choosing risks in situations small enough to absorb but big enough to matter. Also, by entering into a number of manageable situations, you can get the law of averages on your side. That's why people buy mutual funds. Although many stocks in the fund may lose value, many others will gain, and the overall result is to lower your risk through diversification. You are simply less exposed to the price fluctuations of any one stock and, therefore, you are less exposed to risk overall.

There is another very interesting and useful offshoot of risk tolerance. Once a venture is properly analyzed, you may realize that it is too risky for you or your company. A richer person or a larger company, however, has a higher risk tolerance value. A venture that is a good idea for one company may be a horrible idea for another. A company's size can give it an advantage, with a big company happily accepting huge and risky ventures, while a small company is attracted to smaller ventures that the big company wouldn't even consider.

Amazingly, when risk is shared it is lowered overall. Two companies that independently find a new opportunity too risky may find the same opportunity enticing when it is shared. This is another example of how wealth is created. Both parties value their half of the venture more than they value the whole thing. Wealth is created merely by rearranging the constituent parts, just as a bicycle or a clock is created by properly arranging its parts.

The Risk of Business Failure

Many businesses begin with a great idea, experienced management, and a good location, but still fail. Dun & Bradstreet analyzed 800,000 small businesses and reported that 70 percent were still in business after 8.5 years.[95] The U.S. Small Business Administration studied 12,185 businesses and found that 67 percent were still successful after four years.[96] These studies are certainly more hopeful than the often-quoted statistic that 90 percent of new businesses fail in the first five years. Still, failures are relatively common, and one way to explain this is that mathematics is working against companies.

If a chain has 100 links, it will hold only if all the links stay intact. If each link has a one-percent chance of failing, we can calculate the probability of failure, which is a sobering 63 percent in this case.[97]

Businesses are like chains; to succeed, everything needs to function adequately. Take a company with the best management, product, marketing, and financing. This might be a company with an intelligent, seasoned management team, all of whom formerly worked at other successful companies. Their scientists have developed and successfully tested a better therapy for a hard-to-treat cancer. Their marketing people are the best in the industry, and the company has $300 million in the bank. But the company has big distribution problems. What are the chances for success? Not good. Their distribution problems will likely kill them. The old adage applies here: a chain is only as strong as its weakest link.

If a business has ten critical functions, and each has a 90-percent chance of success, the business itself has only a 35-percent chance of success (0.90^{10} equals 0.35). If one function (e.g., distribution) has only a 50-percent chance of success, then the overall probability of success drops to 19 percent. Care to invest? To get a 90-percent chance of overall success, this company would need a 98.95-percent success rate for each function (0.9895^{10} equals 0.90). We admit that this is overly pessimistic in a sense, partly because companies can fix their mistakes as they go and partly because failure is a matter of degree; no company is perfect. However, the numbers are still sobering.

Now consider the much heralded "dot-com" Internet-based companies of the late 1990's. Their meteoric rise and subsequent fall earned many of them the "dot-bomb" moniker. Did they have any advantage over traditional "bricks and mortar" companies? They certainly did. With the advent of the Internet and the World Wide Web, the dot-com companies were clearly in the vanguard of easier shopping.

At the time, we were skeptical of Internet companies. Why? In addition to the hype, which usually scares us away, we intuitively followed the analysis above. Let's grant that Internet companies were much better than traditional companies in one function: easily and cheaply reaching the customer and taking their orders. They still needed to do the other functions that are required of a business, such as human relations, accounting, legal, financing, investor relations, shipping and receiving, management, and marketing. If their one good function has a 95-percent chance of success but nine other functions have a 70-percent chance, their overall probability of success is a measly four percent. The Internet bubble was a result of great expectations and a lack of clear thinking on the part of many investors.

Accounting for Risk

Teach yourself to work in uncertainty.
— Bernard Malamud

Have you purchased fire or flood insurance to protect yourself from costly damage to your house? How about for other expensive assets, such as your car or boat? Do you have health insurance and disability insurance to protect your most valuable asset—you? Most readers will answer "of course" to these questions because we all understand that we want to protect ourselves from risks that have the potential to devastate us financially. To protect ourselves from these risks, we buy insurance.

We don't buy insurance for everything, though. We don't insure our blue jeans against holes in the knees nor our cars for needing to refill their gas tanks. We don't insure our strawberry smoothie against spillage. No. We "self-insure," which means we don't purchase insurance for small stakes that we can tolerably absorb, and we insure through insurance companies for larger stakes. This makes sense. Insurance companies charge more for insurance than they pay out partly to cover their direct costs and profits and partly to cover their risk. A simple rule of thumb is that you will pay twice the expected loss for the insurance premium.[98] If you have a one-percent chance of a $100,000 loss, you have an expected loss of $1,000 (0.01 times $100,000) and should expect to pay $2,000 for the insurance to cover this event. If this weren't the case, insurance companies couldn't stay in business. This is understandable.

What doesn't make sense is this: many companies analyze risky situations using decision-making techniques that ignore risk! They use techniques that are either blind to risk or that dramatically understate it while ignoring their particular risk tolerance. By using these techniques, the financial analysts at these companies would recommend that you *not* buy fire insurance for your house—something that flies in the face of common sense.

Normal people buy insurance because they are highly sensitive to losses, and yet many companies act as if risk can be ignored. They talk a lot about risk and how they want to avoid it. The problem is that many people in industry use analytical techniques that are so blunt as to have almost no value in dealing with risk. We address three techniques to show the range of approaches: the *Heavy Discounting Net Present Value Approach*, the *Expected Net Present Value Approach*, and the *Risk-Averse Expected Net Present Value Approach*. **Please note that what follows is the only highly technical section of this book. Some readers may prefer to skip to Chapter 11.** Readers who want to understand this subject can read the following section and perhaps refer to the formulas in the Appendix.

Heavy Discounting Net Present Value Approach

The *Heavy Discounting Approach*, using a net present value calculation (NPV), begins with the realization that a dollar today is worth more than a dollar tomorrow. If we give you $80,000 to build an addition onto your house, you'd rather get it today than next year. Getting the money today will allow you to enjoy your addition for a full extra year. Also, if you don't really believe that we will deliver, getting the money today ensures that you will, in fact, get it. You won't have to worry for 365 days that we will skip town. This fear is due to risk, but let's ignore risk for the moment and discuss the time-value of money.

We account for the time-value of money by using a **discount rate** to discount future money flows, effectively reducing all future income and expenses to the level of a dollar (or yen or euro) today. For example, $80,000 today is worth $80,000, while, at an eight-percent discount rate, $80,000 next year is worth the same as $74,074 today. If you have a venture that has both expenses and revenues in the future, simply discount them all back to today to see the value more clearly and compare apples to apples. The problem arises when people take this straightforward technique and then try to shoehorn risk into the equation. Remember that one reason you prefer money today is the bird-in-the-hand argument, right? Tomorrow has many possible disasters and reasons that you won't get paid, which is another way of describing uncertainty and risk. Adherents to the *Heavy Discounting Approach* realize that risk is important, and so when they judge a particular venture to be riskier, they simply apply a bigger discount rate. Perhaps the base discount rate is eight percent to account for the time-value of money, and so they bump this discount rate all the way up to 30 percent to factor in risk.

This approach has a number of problems. First, what is an appropriate discount rate to account for the risk in a Mars landing program, or a cancer vaccination program, or a particular strategy in a high-stakes civil trial? There is no clear way to translate a given situation into a discount rate. Second, even if you could determine the "correct" discount rate, a discount rate simply discounts tomorrow's values to match today's. A higher discount rate will reduce *all* future cash flows, whether they are negative or positive, high-risk or low-risk. This approach doesn't discriminate among good and bad cash flows and just assumes that things further into the future are more risky and, therefore, need to be discounted more heavily. Revenues six years out will be discounted 30 percent more than revenues five years out, even through both are just as likely to occur. Lastly, this approach can handle only one outcome: success. There is no provision for other decision-tree branches with associated probabilities for the other possible outcomes: failure, mild success, moderate success, and stellar success. By ignoring the possibility of other outcomes, this approach does not help with realistic decision analysis and portfolio planning. One of the main goals of portfolio planning is to determine how many and what programs and products to develop today to have a manageable and profitable portfolio tomorrow. Assuming that all new products will succeed, when, in fact maybe only one out of ten will, can lead a company to develop only a couple of new products when it should develop dozens.

As you will find when you make the calculations, NPV results are very sensitive to the discount rate used. With a typical problem, the value of the project drops as the discount rate climbs, but only to a certain point, where the result starts increasing again. Picking a larger discount rate actually makes the result look better. This is exactly the opposite of what we, as analysts, would like.

Using net present value calculations with a large discount rate, as discussed above, is really a crude approximation for the next technique we will discuss, the *Expected Net Present Value Approach*.

Expected Net Present Value Approach

The *Expected Net Present Value* (ENPV) (or *Expected Value* (EV)) *Approach* attempts to rectify the problems described above by directly handling probabilities. For a bet at the roulette wheel, for instance, we can enter the probability of winning and calculate the expected, or probability-weighted outcome. This approach handles cases with probabilities of gains or losses, seemingly allowing us to measure and, therefore, deal with, risk. If we bet a dollar on black on the roulette wheel, we have a 47.4-percent (equal to 18 divided by 38, because there are 38 numbers, 18 of which are black) chance of making a dollar (getting two dollars back) and a 52.6-percent (20/38) chance of losing our dollar. The decision tree is as follows:

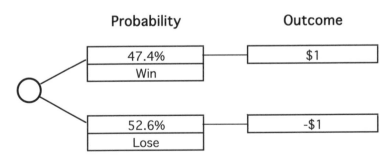

We can calculate the "expected" result from a bet on black as being 47.4 percent times $1.00 plus 52.6 percent times -$1.00, or -$0.052 each time we play. This is how gambling casinos pay for all those bright lights—each time we play, they expect to make a little money. Interestingly, the expected result is impossible because we either win or lose a dollar; it is impossible to end up with -$0.052. **The term "expected" is used here to mean a probability-weighted average or a long-term statistical result**. Even though fictitious, expected values are a great way of showing whether the odds are in our favor or not. With the roulette wheel, the odds favor the gambling house, not us.

We stated that the *NPV Approach* is a crude approximation of the *EV Approach*. What follows is a graph showing actual data for a medicine currently being tested in the clinic. If this medicine passes all its tests and the FDA decides to approve it for sale, it will reach the market and generate revenues. The probability of this event is very low. Unfortunately for the company developing this drug, the probability of spending money in the near term is 100 percent. In other words, initially, this company is guaranteed to spend money. Over time, the drug may fail, and only a number of years down the road will the company receive revenues if everything succeeds. We can show this in the following graph. Notice how the actual probabilities of success at each stage of development keep dropping until the year 2014, at which time the medicine has succeeded or failed. These are the actual probabilities for this particular drug.

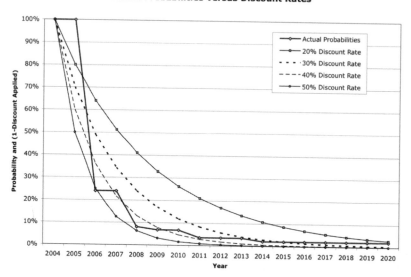

Actual Probabilities versus Discount Rates

Against the actual probabilities, we compared the results of different discount rates. Of the values tested, the 40-percent discount rate gives the best approximation, generally tracking the actual probabilities. However, as the table below shows, even the 40-percent discount rate has a mean absolute percentage error of 58 percent. Are you willing to settle for such a high error rate?

Approach	Mean Absolute Percentage Error
20-Percent Discount Rate	228%
30-Percent Discount Rate	69%
40-Percent Discount Rate	58%
50-Percent Discount Rate	71%
Actual Probabilities	0%

As you can see, the real probabilities are the best to use. This drives us to our conclusion: why use a crude approximation when the actual probabilities are both better and, for those with some industry knowledge, straightforward to derive? Also, the 40-percent discount rate seems "best" in this situation, but we can determine that only because we can compare it to the actual probabilities. For a different pharmaceutical, how would we know the best discount rate without looking at the actual probabilities, and once we did that, why not use the real probabilities? Note that we are oversimplifying when we say that the 40-percent value is the best. We don't have to use round values, of course, and optimization shows us that a discount rate of 36.2-percent is the winner for this example, but it still gives an error rate of 55 percent. For another pharmaceutical example that we tried, the best discount rate was 14.0-percent with an error of 32 percent. We could apply ourselves to resolving the rules that show when to use a 36.2-percent discount rate and when to use a 14.0-percent value, but why not just use the real values and eliminate this source of error?

The *EV Approach* is significantly better than the *NPV Approach* because it uses real probabilities. But would either of these approaches tell us to buy insurance? Interestingly, no. As we pointed out earlier, insurance companies set premiums so that the expected payout is, on average, 50-75 percent of the premium. This is how they stay in business. If you are buying insurance, you have a different perspective. You buy insurance not because you expect to be average, but because you fear that you will be extraordinary. Most people's houses don't burn down, so if you plan on being average, you will never buy insurance because, on average, insurance is a bad investment. You purchase fire insurance because you will be devastated if you are that unlucky person who suffers this disaster. Some may quibble with our terminology here. In their minds, they don't invest in insurance, but pay for insurance premiums to prevent a loss. We acknowledge this, but note that the results are exactly the same.

We can say more precisely why we all buy insurance. Most of us are more sensitive to losses than we are to gains. This is what it means to be risk-averse, and almost all of us share this viewpoint, whether we are a college student just starting out or the CEO of a $20 billion-a-year company. Consider the following lottery. You will flip a fair coin. If you win—by calling tails and getting tails, for example—you will win $10. If you lose, you will lose $5. A fair coin gives a 50-percent probability of winning. If you ever get to play this game repeatedly, as we did for a real-life test, your payout might look like this.

Win or Lose	Payout	Cumulative Payout
Win	$10	$10
Win	$10	$20
Win	$10	$30
Lose	-$5	$25
Win	$10	$35
Lose	-$5	$30
Lose	-$5	$25
Lose	-$5	$20
Win	$10	$30
Win	$10	$40

We played ten times and ended up with $40 more than when we started. If ever given the chance to play this game in *your* life, you should play all day and every day. If you play one thousand times, you could expect to be $2,500 richer because each play has an expected gain of $2.50 (50 percent times $10 minus 50 percent times $5). So far, so good. Now increase the stakes such that you either win $100,000 or lose $50,000. If you played this game one thousand times you could expect to be $25 million richer! Unfortunately, most of us would pass at a chance to play.

The prospect of getting four heads in a row and owing $200,000 is enough to deplete the liquid assets of many of our readers. While the odds are the same in both games, we choose not to play the second game because the stakes exceed our ability to absorb losses. Companies are in exactly the same boat, except that the amounts are typically larger. Perhaps a particular company would continue to play with $20 million wins and $10 million losses, but not with $50 million wins and $25 million loses. The point at which you walk away from this type of lottery is your **risk tolerance. Your risk tolerance factor is the higher of the two numbers, or the winning payout** — $20 million in this imaginary coin-toss lottery. We all have a risk tolerance; for some of us it is small and for others it is quite large. The *EV Approach*, however, assumes that you have a risk tolerance, but that it is infinitely large. The *EV Approach* assumes that you are risk-neutral and would happily enter into this bet with a coin toss determining a $1 billion gain or a $500 million loss, even though you'd probably rather walk in a pit of venomous snakes.

Risk-Averse Expected Net Present Value Approach

The *Risk-Averse Expected Net Present Value Approach* (or REV for short), our final method, puts together everything we have learned so far. The *Risk-Averse Expected Net Present Value* is also called the *Certain Equivalent*[99] or *Certainty Equivalent*[100] because it should be equivalent to what you would accept for certain today—in other words, cash. As before, a discount rate should be used to account for the time-value of money and probabilities should be used to calculate expected values in uncertain situations. On top of this, this approach also explicitly adds your risk tolerance so that you don't enter situations that exceed your comfort level.

Risk tolerance can be determined roughly through introspection. Think about playing the lottery above. At what point do you walk away? When I (CLH) was in graduate school, my risk tolerance was $5,000. Because I am significantly richer now, my risk tolerance is $50,000. That is, I would take a 50/50 bet whereby I'd either win $50,000 or lose $25,000. I (DRH) am more risk averse even though I am wealthier than Charley; my risk tolerance is $30,000. Most people underestimate their wealth (your future income and all your current assets) and, therefore, assign a measly risk tolerance. Hint: if you properly take into account all your possessions—your house, your car, your investments, your future earning potential—you'll find that you are much richer than you think.

Try a simple thought experiment to figure out how wealthy you are. What would someone have to pay you today to take away all your future earning potential? After agreeing to this, you could never earn another penny for as long as you lived, through a job, investments, gifts, inheritances, Social Security, pensions, IRA's, gambling, charity, insurance, speaking engagements, or that great American novel you hope to write next year. This number you calculate, along with your current net worth, is your total effective wealth. Even for poor people, this number is pretty high. With this estimate of your wealth in mind, take a minute and consider what your risk tolerance is using the imaginary coin-toss lottery described above. You don't have to come up with the perfect, correct number. Just being aware that you are risk-averse and have a tolerance for risk will allow you to make better decisions.

Your risk tolerance value can be one number, as we have discussed above. It describes how you look at risk. In real life, you are simply faced with possible outcomes, some positive and some negative. No one ever asks for your risk tolerance value, but you can take it and apply it to any possible loss or gain. Ronald Howard has developed a mathematical formula to help you judge all possible gains and losses using your risk tolerance as an input. (See the Appendix and the website for this book, www. MakingGreatDecisions.com, for a more complete explanation.) This formula can be used to convert monetary gains and losses into risk-adjusted values, which are called utils, short for utility. Utility is the term that economists use to measure how much you like or dislike something. Utils incorporate how you think about gains and losses. For instance, winning $1,000 might give you +0.1 utils, while losing $1,000 is worth –0.2 utils.

The best way to show the difference between a straight monetary result and the utility result is to use a graphical approach developed by Bill Picht, Jr. In the first graph, the X-axis shows the cumulative probability of each outcome, while the Y-axis shows the return. Consider the coin toss example with a possible win of $100,000 and a possible loss of $50,000. There is a 50-percent probability of a $50,000 loss (light gray area) and a 50-

percent probability of a $100,000 gain (dark gray area), for an overall expected value of $25,000 (0.5 times $100,000 minus 0.5 times $50,000). Note that the dark gray rectangle is bigger than the light gray rectangle. This tells us that the monetary result of the coin toss bet is positive and that this would be a good bet to enter.

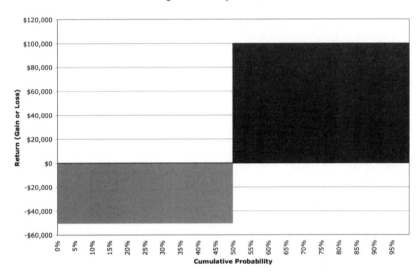

Straight Monetary Outcomes

When we adjust the results using my (CLH's) $50,000 risk tolerance factor and the utility formula in the Appendix, we essentially stretch, or expand, the light gray area, which now overwhelms the dark gray area. There is a 50-percent probability of a 1.72 util loss (light gray area), and a 50-percent probability of a 0.87 util gain (dark gray area) for an overall risk-averse expected value of –0.43 utils (0.5 times 0.87 minus 0.5 times 1.72). The utility result indicates that this is not a good bet to enter because the light gray rectangle is now bigger than the dark gray rectangle.

Risk-Averse Utility Outcomes

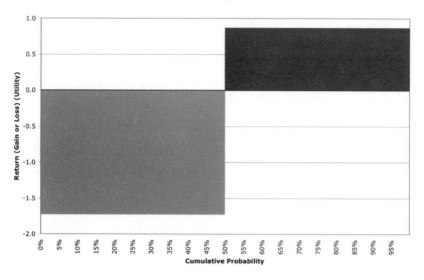

As an aside, this is an easy way to show probability results to senior management without needing to show much of the detail behind the calculations. With more complicated situations with correspondingly more decision tree branches, the graph becomes more interesting and useful, but the process is the same: is the light gray area bigger or smaller than the dark gray area? If the dark gray area is bigger, it's a good venture to enter. See the following graph for an example that results from a decision tree with five branches (five possible outcomes).

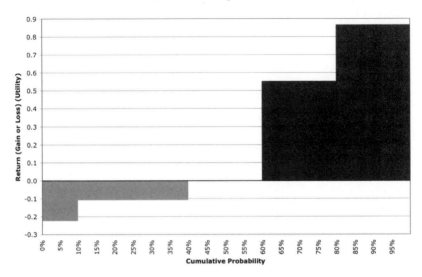

Buying Insurance

We started this discussion of risk by noticing that almost all people purchase insurance to protect themselves in risky situations. Let's consider fire insurance for your house. As we mentioned, you will never buy insurance if you follow the *NPV* or *EV Approaches* because, on the surface, insurance is a bad investment. On average, only 50-75 cents of every premium dollar you pay goes to pay for homeowner claims.[101] This means that the expected value from insurance purchases is negative; you plan on losing money (i.e., paying the premiums and not getting any claims paid) when you buy insurance.

Consider the following specific situation. You have a $300,000 house, and you face a one-percent probability of fire within the decade. Your risk tolerance is $50,000 and you believe that, even with insurance, if your house burns you will still suffer losses of $10,000. Should you pay $400 per year ($4,000 per decade, ignoring the time-value of money for simplicity) for fire insurance? To resolve this decision, you need to think about four things because there are four possible outcomes:

1. What will my life be like if I keep the $4,000, don't buy insurance, and never have a fire?
2. What will my life be like if I keep the $4,000, don't buy insurance, and have a fire?
3. What will my life be like if I spend the $4,000 on insurance and never have a fire?
4. What will my life be like if I spend the $4,000 on insurance and have a fire?

A good place to start is to rank the outcomes from best to worst. This is easy. Keeping the money and not having a fire is the best, followed by spending the money and not having a fire, spending the money and having a fire, and—dead last—not spending the money and having a fire. We assign a monetary return for each outcome and build a decision tree.

Outcome	Return at Ten Years
Keep the $4,000, no fire	$0
Spend the $4,000, no fire	-$4,000
Spend the $4,000, fire	-$14,000
Keep the $4,000, fire	-$300,000

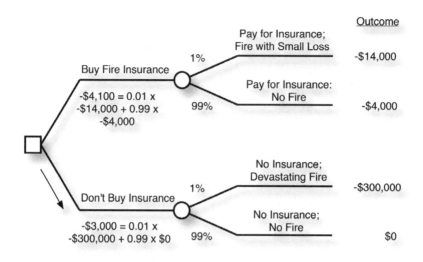

Now it is a simple matter to calculate the expected value of each alternative; these values are shown as the overall results on the left side of the decision tree.

- ❑ Buy the fire insurance = 99 percent times -$4,000 plus one percent times -$14,000 = -$4,100
- ❑ Don't buy fire insurance = 99 percent times $0 plus one percent times -$300,000 = -$3,000

Using the *EV Approach*, as we did here, we see what we already knew, that insurance is a bad investment ($1,100 worse than not buying it). Let's redo the analysis using the *REV Approach* and see why we buy insurance: we are happy spending a little money to protect ourselves from big losses. We will use our risk tolerance of $50,000 and convert the outcome results to utils with the aid of the formula in the Appendix.

Outcome	Return at Ten Years (Utils)
Keep the $4,000, no fire	0.00
Spend the $4,000, no fire	-0.083
Spend the $4,000, fire	-0.323
Keep the $4,000, fire	-402.43

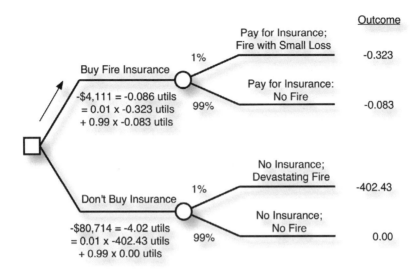

Again, it is a simple matter to calculate the expected value of each alternative.

- ❑ Buy the fire insurance = 99 percent times -0.083 plus one percent times –0.323 = -0.086 utils, which is equivalent to -$4,111 given our risk tolerance
- ❑ Don't buy fire insurance = 99 percent times 0.00 plus one percent times –402.43 = -4.02 utils, which is equivalent to -$80,714 given our risk tolerance.

In this example, buying insurance for a decade is equivalent to paying $4,111 in cash today. Notice the value of not buying insurance. By not buying insurance, you are entering a situation that is equal to losing $80,714 today. If you ignore your risk tolerance, you would never buy fire insurance. If you consider your risk tolerance, you realize that insurance is a great deal. Buying insurance is worth $76,604 to you (-$4,111 minus -$80,714). This is an incredible deal! Essentially, you make a certain profit today of $76,604 if you purchase insurance. Wow! Why is the value of the fire insurance so high? Because the insurance gets you out of the risky situation you got into when you bought your house in the first place. Imagine buying this $300,000 house and having it burn down two years into the 30-year mortgage. You would still owe most of the $300,000 but not have a house to live in. This is a loss that very few of us could easily absorb. Insurance gets you out of the risky situation you entered into when you bought your house.

Note that both you and the insurance company benefit from this transaction. How can this be? The insurance company sells insurance for 33 to 100 percent more than its expected payout, and you buy insurance that is worth over 19 times the amount you paid. The world is filled with examples like this, where both parties gain. A zero-sum situation requires one party to lose if another is to gain. But in many situations, including this one, both sides gain. This is how we can be so much richer than our ancestors—through mutually beneficial trades like this that build wealth over time.

Fail Earlier or Fail Later?

Consider a project to develop a new medicine. This drug will cost $40 million and take seven years to develop, have a five-percent probability of success, and bring in $400 million per year if it reaches the market. Should you care whether the bulk of the costs are early or late in the development process? Should you care whether failure is more likely early or late in the development process? The results are interesting. Of course you want your new pharmaceutical to succeed, but *if it fails* (remember, there is a 95-percent chance of failure), you want it to fail as quickly and cheaply as possible. We will use the *REV Approach* with a risk tolerance value of $200 million and a risk-free discount rate of eight percent to compare the results. For this example, we hold the overall values constant, just shift the costs from late in the development process to early and, likewise, shift the step with the highest probability of failure from early to late in the process. We are using an Objective Insights proprietary model to compute these results.

When most of the expenses are earlier, this drug is a loser and you shouldn't develop it. If the expenses are later in the process, this drug looks favorable to develop; however, the outlook is much better, almost 45 times as good, if failure is likely earlier, also.

New Medicine Situation - REV	Most Expenses Earlier	Most Expenses Later
Failure Likely Earlier	-$10,712,000	$8,408,000
Failure Likely Later	-$13,744,000	$188,000

This rule is applicable in all ventures. **If you are going to fail, you would like to know as quickly and cheaply as possible.** A man in Davis, California has been developing consumer-targeted flying cars for the last 35 years. Paul Moller is out $50 million and three wives, but he isn't empty-handed; he has 43 patents and a Moller M400 Skycar that he claims is ready for liftoff.[102] Still, he has a long way to go before everyone is buzzing around like the Jetsons. Perhaps he never will succeed. If he could know definitively that his flying car company would never "get off the ground," he could take his losses, lick his wounds, and then apply his efforts to his next good idea. In your own life, you should prefer ventures that show their stripes early and cheaply. Then you can get out and move on to something that *can* succeed wildly.

We've spent a lot of space comparing the three approaches discussed above. Let's see how the three compare in our drug-development example with the "early/late" conclusion in mind. As you've noticed, we don't advocate the *Heavy Discounting Approach*, and yet we still do use regular net present values in our work, so here we are using a regular, risk-free discount rate of eight percent for the net present value calculation.

New Medicine Situation	Net Present Value	Expected Value	REV
Failure Early, Expense Early	$2,435,200,000	$102,600,000	-$10,712,000
Failure Early, Expense Later	$2,443,600,000	$121,000,000	$8,408,000
Failure Later, Expense Early	$2,435,200,000	$100,900,000	-$13,744,000
Failure Later, Expense Later	$2,443,600,000	$115,100,000	$188,000

The *NPV Approach* shows a slight preference to the Expenses Later scenario and is not sensitive to when failure is most likely to occur, which is what we'd expect because net

185

present values assume success. The *EV Approach* shows a preference for later expenses and a slight preference for Failure Early. The *REV Approach* most closely reflects what we know to be true. It is very sensitive to the timing of both expenses and development stumbling blocks.

Some may worry that the *REV Approach* shows much lower numbers than they are accustomed to. "Do you mean that we will make only $188,000 after all this work, time, and money invested?" That's a good question. The REV result doesn't show you how much you will make; instead, it shows you *what the venture is worth today*. Stated differently, you should be willing to pay $188,000 in cash today to get the rights to this venture. $188,000 is a positive number, so the venture is worthwhile. A negative value indicates something that you want to get rid of and so should sell or terminate. Of course, the higher the positive number, the better. In short, you should want to enter into ventures that have positive REV results, and the higher the value, the more you should want to enter. If you want to see what you'll make if you succeed, look at the NPV result of $2.4 billion.

Objective Insights usually uses all three of these approaches, partly because our clients request them, and partly because they illuminate different sides of the problem. The *Expected Value* shows how a risk-neutral company would view the opportunity. The regular *Net Present Value* shows you how much money your company will make if it succeeds. The *Risk-Adverse Expected Net Present Value* shows how a risk-averse company views the situation. By weaving all three results into a whole, you can have a much clearer idea of which opportunities to pursue, which to avoid, and why.

We are realists and do not expect people to cease using the *Heavy Discounting Approach* overnight. Nonetheless, whatever reasons companies have to avoid employing the powerful techniques described here must be compared to the cost of making uninformed decisions. In our experience, the cost of a poorly analyzed decision is just too high.

Probabilities Are Subjective

One parting thought. We have presented all the probabilities in this book as objective, knowable quantities. It turns out that that's the exception, not the rule. When most of us think of probabilities, we think like statisticians eagerly calculating the odds of knowable, repeatable events. For instance, you can know the probability of being dealt a royal flush in poker. Now consider the following. What is the probability of war between the United States and North Korea in 2007? It is a unique situation with untold wild cards. Either it will happen or it won't. It isn't written in any book. We are living it today, from our perspective in 2004, as this section is being written and as the situation unfolds in front of us. To come up with a probability, we can start with statistics—looking at the frequency of past wars— but, because this situation is unique, we must move beyond statistics based on our information about the psychology, perspectives, and capabilities of the key players. One reasonable person may give a 20-percent probability while another assigns two percent. Who is right?

They both are right because probabilities are expectations of future events, and expectations are, by nature, subjective, being based on one's state of information. If I pull a foreign-looking coin out of my pocket, what probability would you assign to my flipping a head? The answer is fifty percent *if* the coin is fair. What if the coin isn't exactly clean, balanced, unblemished, and symmetrical? You have to *believe* that the coin is fair to assert 50 percent, and beliefs are based on information. If we flipped this particular coin 10,000 times and counted the number of heads and tails, then you might have more reason to assert a 50-percent probability, but you also, at that point, would have much better information. **Probabilities move from subjectivity towards objectivity as our information improves**. But it is only the trivial cases that have perfect information and can be called objective. Not only the majority of cases, but also the most interesting cases must be called subjective because they're based on our personal assessments of future events. With the North Korean example, by 2007 we will know whether or not there was a war, but today, all we have are our best predictions. If the war doesn't happen, which probability, 20 percent or two percent, was right? We can't tell based on one data point, and history won't give us enough data points to make a definitive assessment. The only probabilities that can be proven wrong with one data point are 0-percent, if the war happens, and 100-percent, if the war doesn't start.

The Lessons Learned

That which does not kill us makes us stronger.
— Friedrich Nietzsche

Risk is one of those things that in large doses can kill, while in smaller doses simply makes us stronger. Amazingly, the great majority of corporate analyses we have seen ignore risk either explicitly or by treating it in a clumsy way. If you use these blunt analytical techniques, you wouldn't even buy insurance for your house, but you know better than that. This chapter explored analytical techniques for measuring risk.

If you want to grow and prosper, you need to swallow the proper dose of risk "medicine," and your dose can be determined by evaluating your circumstance and assigning a risk tolerance number. Then you can use the *Risk-Adverse Expected Net Present Value Approach* to evaluate any venture to determine if it is too risky for you. If it is too risky, either walk away or find a way to reduce the risk. Risk can be reduced by delaying the expenditures, accelerating failure, or simply sharing it with others. Shared risk is lower risk.

Chapter 11

EXPLOIT INEQUALITY
Appreciating Non-Linearity, Balance, and Proportionality

When Jon Krakauer reached the summit of Mt. Everest in the early afternoon of May 10, 1996, he hadn't slept in fifty-seven hours and was reeling from the brain-altering effects of oxygen depletion. As he turned to begin his long, dangerous descent from 29,028 feet, twenty other climbers were still pushing doggedly toward the top. No one noticed that the sky had begun to fill with clouds. Six hours later and 3,000 feet lower, in 70-knot winds and blinding snow, Krakauer collapsed in his tent, freezing, hallucinating from exhaustion and hypoxia, but safe. The following morning he learned that six of his fellow climbers hadn't made it back to their camp and were in a desperate struggle for their lives. When the storm finally passed, five of them would be dead, and the sixth so horribly frostbitten that his right hand would have to be amputated.[103]

Mountain climbers spend $100,000 and a year preparing to climb 29,035-foot Mount Everest.[104] This is reasonable and prudent given the complexity and risk inherent in the climb. The statistics are chilling; since 1921, there have been 179 deaths during 1,924 successful ascents.[105] Even after they've reached the top, climbers have to descend while exhausted, oxygen-deprived and exposed to the wickedly dangerous weather. Little help is available, for their fellow climbers are tired and oxygen-deprived, too, and the summit is far outside the reach of helicopters or other mechanical transport.

There are 6,000-foot peaks near my (CLH's) house, far from Mount Everest, that the local outdoorsy newspaper reporters recommend to weekend hikers. To climb these peaks, you would need little more than good hiking shoes and a bottle of water. With a trail all the way to the top, you need only sturdy legs and enough daylight.

To spend $100,000 and a year preparing to climb the peaks near my house would be silly and wasteful for most climbers. To climb Mount Everest with only good hiking boots and a bottle of water would be suicidal. Balance and proportionality are needed. **The amount of effort applied to the problem should be proportional to the importance of the problem.** Big mountains and decisions justify big efforts, while small mountains and decisions justify only small efforts. This is where the biotechnology company with the printer problem in Chapter 1 failed. Its licensing decision was at least 100 times as important as its printer decision, and yet it spent more money and energy on the lowly printer decision.

While this insight directs us to strive for proportionality in balancing our decisions and analyses, it tells us only relatively what to spend. It does not tell us an absolute level to spend on analyzing any particular decision. Economic theory can help determine how much is the right amount.

Economic theory tells us to purchase something, anything, if the benefit of that item exceeds the cost, or, more precisely, if the marginal revenue exceeds the marginal cost.

Purchase something only if its marginal revenue is greater than its marginal cost.

For example, if something costs $100 but has a value to us of $200, we should buy it. We use the word "marginal" here because we are interested in purchasing the next "chunk"—one extra delivery truck, for example—and we want to measure the net effect of this purchase. Notice that this is another example of thinking on the margin, which we discuss in more detail in Chapter 2. In a nutshell, thinking on the margin means thinking about the next increment only. We also look at marginal purchases because the cost and value can change based on how many we have already purchased. Perhaps the cost of buying the first five delivery trucks is $30,000 each. The sixth, however, ends up costing us a whopping $230,000 because, with the sixth truck, we outgrow our current facility and need to move to a bigger one. Note that the cost of the sixth truck could be more or less than the cost of the five previous trucks; it depends entirely on the situation.

Just as with cost, marginal revenue varies as we move from one to six delivery trucks. If we are smart and choose our business wisely, our marginal revenue should decline as we purchase more trucks. In other words, if the trucks are all the same, we should go for the best business first. If the sixth truck gets us to a lucrative new customer, we have to ask ourselves why we didn't try to reach that customer back when we had only one truck. In general, if the things we are purchasing are very similar, marginal costs can go up or down with each purchase, while marginal revenues should decline. If the things are very different—as with employees, for example—both the marginal revenues and costs will vary on a case-by-case basis.

For each truck, if the marginal revenue exceeds the marginal cost, you should happily buy it. We illustrated the point with delivery trucks, but we could have used any good or service.

How do you decide what's important? How do you decide, for example, who your most important customers are and to which tasks you should apply your efforts? To those issues we now turn. Two of the powerful tools to help you decide are Pareto's Law and Factor 16.

Pareto's Law and Factor 16

Vilfredo Pareto, born in 1848, is widely known for his law of income distribution.[106] **Pareto's Law** has been popularized as the **80/20 Rule, saying that 20 percent of the inputs cause 80** percent of the outputs, or that 20 percent of the people create and enjoy 80 percent of the total income. Pareto noticed that many relationships in life are non-linear. A linear pattern occurs when there is a straight multiplicative relationship. For example, a linear hill is 10 feet high 100 feet from the base, 20 feet high at 200 feet, 30 feet high at 300 feet, and so on. We can calculate the height as the distance from the base times 0.1.

The most well known non-linear example is the straw that broke the camel's back. That last straw had a very different effect than all the straws that preceded it. Gradually heating paper provides another example. As the heat rises, the paper gets hot and perhaps discolors. Then, at 451 degrees Fahrenheit, the paper erupts into flames. The change in temperature from 440° to 460° produces a very different result than the change from 400° to 420°. Lastly, putting bricks in a canoe shows us that the last brick sinks the boat, while all the previous bricks simply made it ride lower in the water.

Here are some other examples of non-linearity:

❑ Six percent of Medicare beneficiaries cost the system 50 percent of its total costs.[107]
❑ In 1998, the top one percent of households held 38 percent of the total wealth.[108]
❑ In the fast-food industry, some customers account for a disproportionate share of sales. These so-called heavy users are only 20 percent of the customers, but they make about 60 percent of total restaurant visits.[109]
❑ Twenty percent of the world's people produce and consume 80 percent of its resources.[110]
❑ One percent of Americans grow food for the rest of us. 87 percent of the food comes from 18 percent of the farms.[111]
❑ Three-quarters of the world's food comes from only seven crop species.
❑ Less than one-half of one percent of the 31,734 music albums released in 2001 sold more than 500,000 copies each.[112] Total sales were 712 million and the top-selling CDs sold almost 15 million copies each.[113] On average, each CD sold only 22,437 copies.

❑   Economists who studied the movie industry in the late 1990s found that a mere 1.3 percent—just four of the 296 movies released—earned 80 percent of the box office revenues.[114]

A fledgling drug company was interested in entering the anti-angina drug market. To get an idea how to promote its new drug to doctors, this company looked at how doctors wrote prescriptions for products being currently used to treat the same disease. Objective Insights found 20.1 percent of the doctors writing 80.0 percent of the prescriptions and 79.9 percent writing the rest. If this company could reach the right 20 percent of doctors, it could tap into 80 percent of the market. This relationship is surprisingly common: another of our clients found that the top 20 percent of doctors accounted for 82 percent of the sales of their growth hormone product.

You might reply that the top 20 percent of the doctors are geographically dispersed and harder to reach because they are busy—and everyone else is trying to reach them, also. That is entirely true, and they may be two to three times as expensive to reach. This is enough to dissuade most management teams. "We can't spend that much to reach these doctors!" But the value of reaching these doctors is not two to three times the value of reaching the less prolific doctors; instead it is 16 times. If this isn't immediately obvious, consider it this way. Assume 100 doctors, 20 of whom prescribe 400 prescriptions each, for a total of 8,000 prescriptions. Therefore, under the 80/20 rule, the other 80 doctors must be prescribing a total of 2,000 prescriptions, which means that these other 80 doctors are prescribing only 25 prescriptions each. Four hundred divided by 25 is 16.

The "prolific" doctors are 16 times as valuable, but surely they are much less than 16 times as expensive to reach. Even if these physicians are twice as expensive to reach, their value is 16 fold, which means that reaching them is eight times as efficient as reaching the low prescribers.

This non-linear phenomenon is so widespread and powerful that we've decided to give it a name: *Factor 16*.

Factor 16: The individuals in the 20-percent group are 16 times as important as those in the 80-percent group.

80/20 Rule examples abound. IBM found that, on average, 80 percent of the run time of a software application is due to only 20 percent of the lines of code.[115] This realization helped them streamline the most important lines of code and speed up their applications by working on the lines of code that were 16 times as important. In another example, the top 15 percent of households paid 74 percent of all federal income taxes.[116] This means that the top households paid on average 16 times as much as the lower 85 percent of households. Wherever the *80/20 Rule* exists, we also see *Factor 16*.

Farm subsidies follow a similar non-linear pattern. A study of Iowa farmers shows that half of the subsidy money went to only 12 percent of the farmers. The most fortunate farmers, often large corporations, were 7.3 times as successful in garnering subsidies as their less fortunate neighbors.[117]

This uneven gain from a government program raises a more general issue. Is it possible that 20 percent of people in America gain about 80 percent of the benefits of all government programs—social security, farm subsidies, tariffs on steel, welfare, defense spending, etc.? Note that this would go against the perception that the benefits of these programs are spread evenly to buy support from voters. Is it also possible that 20 percent of Americans pay 80 percent of the cost of these programs? If income taxes were the only way of paying for government programs, this would be roughly right because, as noted above, the top 15 percent of income tax payers pay 74 percent of all income taxes. But, of course, other revenues—payroll taxes, corporate taxes, and excise taxes being the main ones—are used to pay for government programs. And, of course, there are often huge costs of government programs that don't show up in government revenue. A classic example was the Interstate Commerce Commission, which, by regulating prices for shipping by railroad and truck, imposed tens of billions of dollars of costs annually[118] even though the ICC's annual budget never exceeded $200 million (in 2005 dollars). The people who pay these non-budget costs are consumers who pay higher prices because of steel tariffs or farm subsidies, to take two examples. Now an even more interesting question: assuming that 20 percent of Americans get 80 percent of government benefits and that 20 percent of Americans pay 80 percent of the cost of government programs, how much overlap is there between the two 20-percent groups? Obviously, the biggest gainers from farm programs are likely to be the highest-income farmers, which also makes them the biggest payers of income taxes. But how general is this? We have no idea, but it could well be among the five most interesting and important questions in government policy.

Back to your decision-making. You are hiring an employee and five candidates progress far enough to be interviewed. They all have impressive degrees from prestigious universities. They all have experience in your industry. Are they all equally good candidates? Should you just pick one and move on? There is a high probability that, far from being equal, one candidate is sixteen times as good as the others. This makes sense intuitively. Many of us have worked in organizations where some of the people appeared to do no work at all, or even get in the way, while a few superstars were working heroes. When I (CLH) worked at NASA, one coworker had the job title "Computer." I'm not making this up, as Dave Barry says. She *was* a human computer, good at mathematical calculations long before we had the electronic computers that eventually superseded her. The government was reluctant to terminate her even though she had nothing to do, so she sat in her office all day and read magazines, talked to coworkers, and handed out home-baked cookies. In the seven years I worked there, I can't recall her doing one bit of productive work. Contrast this with a few NASA employees who were extremely productive designing new aircraft, conducting wind tunnel tests, developing aerodynamics software, and writing scientific papers. They easily produced 100 times more than the obsolete "Computer."

Factor 16 raises some interesting questions. If 20 percent of your employees produce 80 percent of the results, what would happen if you hired only the 20-percent types? Mathematically, as shown above, the 20-percent types are 16 times as productive as the 80-percent types. Of course, everyone tries to hire the best employees, so it will be difficult for you to assemble this top team when every other company wants them, too. Consider the following creative solution. You pay these employees four times the going rate. If engineers make $80,000 a year, you pay yours $320,000. If administrative assistants make $30,000 a year, you pay yours $120,000.

Of course, this is not as easy as it sounds. It is very challenging to find and hire the best employees, and paying your assistants $120,000 will not ensure their excellence, only their generous paychecks and a lot of competition from hungry applicants for each job opening. Competition for baseball players leads to good players, but only because their performance is easily measured. If you have 200 people outside your office on Monday morning hoping to fill your administrative assistant slot, can you really pick the best person? The performance of baseball players can be measured a lot more easily than that of middle managers and administrative assistants, and the cost of choosing unwisely is high, due to the personal, legal, and economic costs of firing employees. Lastly, there are some jobs where productivity just doesn't mean very much. For instance, a bridge toll collector can grab money only so fast. The speed of the paying drivers in their moving cars greatly limits the number of drivers who can cross the bridge within any period of time. We can think of many jobs that fall into this category: receptionists and ushers are just two more examples. Can one usher seat 16 times as many of the slow-walking elderly as another?

But that doesn't mean you shouldn't try. If you could make it work, your employee costs would go up by a factor of three (they would be four times as big as before) but your employee productivity would go up by a factor of 15 (16 times as much). Now that is a good investment. That is also a way to increase your company's profits by a healthy multiple. A more cautious and cheaper approach would be to pay ten or 20 percent more than other employers. Over time, your company would become known as a desirable place to work, leading to more job candidates and giving you the potential, if not the ability, to hire only the best employees. What we have done here is show the value of employing the best people and then propose a few ideas for capturing that value. We will leave it to creative employers to determine the most effective ways for actually finding and hiring the best people.

Profiting from Non-Linearity

By understanding non-linearity, we are well positioned to take advantage of opportunities to profit from it, as the following two examples show.

"Eighty percent of antibiotics are used for viral infections, where they are of no use." Martin Burnham should know. He is Senior Researcher at GlaxoSmithKline, one of the world's largest producers of antibiotics. Many people ask their doctor for help with an illness. Not wanting their patients to leave empty-handed, and without a quick and easy test to determine the cause of the illness, doctors frequently prescribe antibiotics. Even if we ignore the issue of resistance, in which the overuse and improper use of antibiotics cause bacteria to mutate and develop super-strains that are resistant to even our best antibiotics, this situation shows how we could be five times as effective. If we could "fix" this situation, so that antibiotics were prescribed only for bacterial infections, society would be five times as efficient in this area. Understanding non-linearity helps us appreciate the value of a good solution.

Instead of simply selling your company some carpet, Evergreen Lease rents your company carpet and is responsible for keeping it clean and in good condition. Every month, when the company's employees come to inspect "its" carpet, Evergreen may choose to replace certain highly worn pieces. They replace overnight the ten to 20 percent of the carpet that shows 80 to 90 percent of the wear. Notice the non-linearity of the wear. Not all the carpet wears out at the same rate. The pieces in front of bathrooms and major hallways go first. To replace the entire carpet each time would be expensive and wasteful, so Evergreen Lease has learned to cut expenses dramatically by realizing, and acting on, the non-linear nature of carpet wear.[119]

We got the following idea from Klutz Books,[120] and we'll share it with you here. We will pay you $1 million if you do this simple task and send in all the results. We're serious: We will pay you $1 million. Place one penny on the first circle below, two on the second, four on the third, eight on the fourth, doubling each time. Follow these rules to put pennies on all of the 27 circles below, then send the paper and all the pennies to us and we will pay you $1 million immediately.

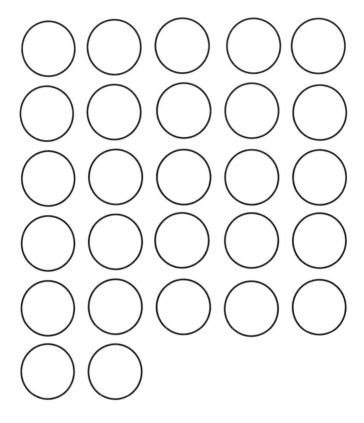

Why are we so generous? We're not. You will send us $1,342,177.27 in pennies (in one very strong, exceptionally large shipping box).[121] From this amount, we will happily return $1 million to you (via check, not pennies—we're not crazy), keeping the $342,000 and change for ourselves. How did we solve this problem? There are a number of different ways, but a spreadsheet is one easy way. If you prefer direct formulas, use this, where n equals the number of circles.

$$Total = (2^n - 1) \bullet 0.01$$

$$\$1,342,177.27 = (2^{27} - 1) \bullet 0.01$$

Circle	Amount on Circle	Cumulative Amount
1	$0.01	$0.01
2	$0.02	$0.03
3	$0.04	$0.07
4	$0.08	$0.15
5	$0.16	$0.31
6	$0.32	$0.63
7	$0.64	$1.27
8	$1.28	$2.55
9	$2.56	$5.11
10	$5.12	$10.23
11	$10.24	$20.47
12	$20.48	$40.95
13	$40.96	$81.91
14	$81.92	$163.83
15	$163.84	$327.67
16	$327.68	$655.35
17	$655.36	$1,310.71
18	$1,310.72	$2,621.43
19	$2,621.44	$5,242.87
20	$5,242.88	$10,485.75
21	$10,485.76	$20,971.51
22	$20,971.52	$41,943.03
23	$41,943.04	$83,886.07
24	$83,886.08	$167,772.15
25	$167,772.16	$335,544.31
26	$335,544.32	$671,088.63
27	$671,088.64	$1,342,177.27

On the 27th circle, you will have to stack 67,108,864 pennies. The total number of pennies on all the circles is 134,217,727, for a grand total of $1,342,177.27. From this booty we will be more than happy to pay each "winner" $1 million. Isn't it amazing how so few circles lead to so many pennies?

The next story has made the rounds over the years, but it beautifully illustrates the power of non-linearity. Here is how my (CLH's) father used to tell it. In a time of hunger, the Emperor of China wanted to repay a peasant who had saved the life of his child. The peasant could have any reward he chose, but the Emperor laughed when he heard the silly payment the foolish peasant selected: rice on a chessboard. The peasant wanted one grain of rice on the first square, doubling to two on the second, doubling to four on the third, and so on. After the Emperor agreed, his servants brought one bag of rice into his court and began tediously counting rice. Soon, he called for more and more bags of rice. Shortly, he realized that all the rice in China would not be enough. In fact, the Emperor now owed the peasant more than 300 times the total amount of rice in the world![122] And this from a chessboard with only 64 squares. The peasant understood the power of non-linearity, while the Emperor understood only too late. Those who think this lesson is merely about rice will miss the bigger message: to grow anything, often it is best to grow slowly. For instance, as we noted in Chapter 2, if you want to get rich, you can do so slowly through the power of savings and compound interest. A widely circulated quote that we've been unable to confirm is that Albert Einstein, when asked what was the most powerful force in the universe, replied "compound interest."

Surprising Growth Rates

With any organization—a church is a good example—that gains members at a steady rate, say two per week, it is easy to see how membership is growing and to predict future membership. Most of us are good at seeing growth patterns like this. However, other types of growth patterns are non-linear, and they can take us by surprise because they behave in ways that are hard to predict unless you understand the underlying mechanism.

A three-acre pond has a lily pad invasion during the warm summer months. Each day the number of lily pads doubles, and they cover the whole pond in 100 days. How much of the pond did they cover on the 99th day? Answer: half. And on the 98th day, they covered only one-quarter of the pond. By doubling every day, the lily pads start growing very slowly and then appear to accelerate. This is why the Emperor of China didn't predict how much rice he was committing. This same explosive growth can happen with other processes that multiply their membership, such as bacteria or the latest fad. This is also why most of us don't see it coming—the growth is deceptive.

Manufacturing Non-Linearity

Here's another example of non-linearity that produces surprising results. Let's say that you have a manufacturing process with ten steps. You concentrate on reducing waste and are able to shave 20 percent off each step. What are the overall savings? The intuitive answer is 20 percent. This is the correct answer for a lot of situations. For example, if there are ten people in your office, and each person's car payment goes down by 20 percent, the total car payment cost of the office also goes down by 20 percent. But here we are adding monthly car payments together: Total payment = A + B + C.

With a manufacturing process, if I do one step more efficiently, I need less input to create the same quantity of output. If I do every step more efficiently, to get the same quantity of outputs at the final step, I need much less input at the first step. The total amount of initial raw materials saved is not 20 percent, but a whopping 89 percent. In this case, the total answer is the result of multiplication, not addition. Total = A x B x C. For the environmentalists among us, this realization offers great hope for reducing our resource usage and waste. A simple example is the production of plywood.

Have you ever wondered how plywood is made? No? Well, here's how. Plywood sheets are made by cutting trees and debarking the logs, which are then cut into lengths. These logs are put on a lathe and peeled to produce veneer sheets. The sheets are then cut into sections. Workers cut out bad areas, such as knots or flaws, and fill them in with fresh veneer pieces. Sheets of veneer are placed in alternating layers and glued together with a huge, heated hydraulic press.[123] Now consider increasing the efficiency. If we were more efficient at each step of this process, fewer trees would need to be cut in the first place. What types of gains can we expect?

Starting with the consumer, if we find a way to build our houses with ten percent fewer plywood sheets, we can reduce by ten percent the number of pieces that need to be produced. If we can also press the glued layers together ten percent more efficiently, we can reduce by 19 percent the number of patched veneer sheets that are needed. If patching is also improved by ten percent, we need 27 percent fewer veneer sheets. If each step through debarking is improved by ten percent, we find that we can reduce the cutting of trees by 47 percent. In other words, by making small, but noticeable, improvements along the six steps of this process, we can still build our houses, yet cut only half as many trees. This reduces the environmental burden and saves a lot of money. But the point is that seemingly insignificant improvements build into a crescendo because they cascade into each other. Because the results of one step are used at the next, our savings multiply. With a ten-step process, we end up reducing the first step by 65 percent!

Our time spent on projects is not multiplicative, but our productivity can nonetheless be surprisingly non-linear. If I have 30 minutes to work each on Projects A and B, do I advance them both equally? Not necessarily. I work on Project A and move it ahead by 30 minutes. I work on Project B and move it ahead by three days. For Project B, I phone my client to set up a meeting, allowing us to meet three days earlier, moving the whole project three days ahead. Where is my value higher? In general, how should we allocate our time and which tasks should we work on?

How to Allocate Your Time

Dost thou love Life? then do not squander Time; for that's the Stuff Life is made of. — Benjamin Franklin

In Chapter 3, we explored the value of your time. Here, we look at a more focused problem: what, specifically, should you spend your time doing? Perhaps the deck needs restaining, thank-you notes need to be written, and you need to sell your old car. Which one should you work on first? We have found significant value in organizing our time so that we work on the most important problems first. Why? Because the value of our time applied to the most important problem may be one hundred times that of our time applied to the least important problem. Of course, whatever approach we use to steer ourselves to one project or another has to be easy and fast or it defeats the purpose of efficiency.

What follows is one approach to help productively allocate your time, which is your most valuable asset. Because we are busy, we try to spend ten minutes or less on this technique. We start by realizing that not all decisions and problems are created equal—some are much more important. But first, some ground rules. If your child has a broken leg, go to the hospital—decisions like that need no analysis. If you have already committed to a task, go ahead and do it. For instance, if you are due in court on

Tuesday morning, you need to follow through with your commitment. Last, if a task takes 20 minutes or less and seems important enough, just do it.

Think of the ten problems or tasks facing you right now. Write them down now and you'll get more out of this exercise. You can separate personal and business tasks. Here they are for our example:

- Decide what school to send my child to
- Place an ad in the newspaper to sell an old car
- Trim some tree branches in my yard
- Review all the insurance I have
- Get a flu shot
- Review, monitor, and update my investments
- Transfer a $600 account to another credit union that doesn't charge monthly fees
- Insulate my attic to save on heating and cooling bills
- Fix some boards in my deck
- Sell some unwanted stuff or donate it to charity.

Now consider the amount of time it will probably take to adequately perform each of these tasks. For instance, it will take me three hours to review my insurance coverage. Also consider the possible downside risk from ignoring the problem (I fall through a rotten board on my deck) or making the wrong choice, and the upside potential from solving the problem well (my investments grow). Assign a probability to each outcome. For example, if I spend three hours reviewing all my insurance, I believe there is a 50-percent probability that I can save $500. Spend approximately one minute thinking about each problem on your list, visualizing a decision tree like the one shown below.

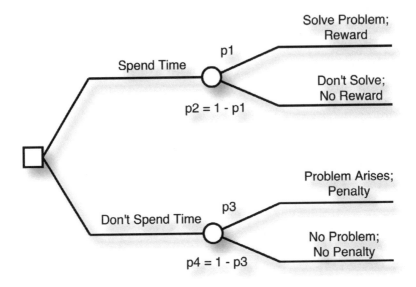

Not all tasks will have a decision tree with a complete set of branches. What follows is the decision tree for the "Review Insurance" task.

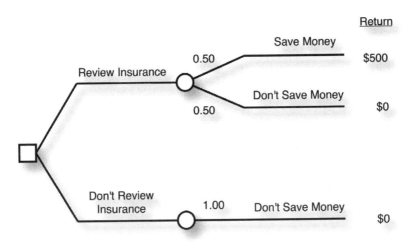

Then make a *Productivity Table* like the one shown below. Spreadsheets are great for this. Remember that the numbers that go into productivity tables are simply your best estimates. Divide the value of the problem (probability-weighted upside minus probability-weighted downside) by the time required. With the "Review Insurance" example, the probability-weighted upside is $250, or 0.5 times $500. The probability-weighted downside is $0, or 0.5 times $0. The total is $250 ($250 minus $0), which we divide by the three hours it will take to review the insurance. This leaves us with a value of $83.3 per hour ($250 divided by three). Notice that a great majority of the value comes from only one or a few of the projects.

Productivity Table

Personal Tasks	Estimated time needed (Hours)	Penalty if done poorly ($)	Probability of Penalty if Fail/Neglect	Reward if done well ($)	Probability of Reward if Finish	Weighted Return ($)	Value ($/Hour)
Best school for my son	6.0	$10,000	50%	$10,000	75%	$12,500	$2,083
Place ads for my old car	2.0	$100	100%	$2,000	90%	$1,900	$950
Yard tree trimming	12.0	$0	100%	$300	100%	$300	$25
Review insurance	3.0	$0	100%	$500	50%	$250	$83
Get a flu shot	0.5	$800	20%	$0	100%	$160	$320
Monitor and update investments	3.0	$5,000	50%	$10,000	50%	$7,500	$2,500
Transfer $600 account to new bank	0.2	$35	100%	$0	100%	$35	$175
Insulate attic	16.0	$500	100%	$0	100%	$500	$31
Fix deck boards	2.0	$500	50%	$100	100%	$350	$175
Sell unwanted stuff or give away	2.0	$0	100%	$100	100%	$100	$50

The top value, $2,500 per hour, comes from monitoring and updating my investments because it will only take three hours and offers a good chance of a better return than my current portfolio.

The lowest value, $25 per hour for tree trimming, is a piddling one percent of the highest value. The values of my time applied to these two tasks differ substantially, with the highest value being 100 times the lowest ($2,500 divided by $25). If I had been spending my time working on the less important problem and switched to the important problem, I could easily increase my productivity by a factor of 99. Of course this analysis uses ballpark estimates. A full analysis would use decision analysis techniques, which are more correct and thorough but also more time-consuming. The purpose of this exercise is to get a quick and top-level look at the value of the tasks you are facing, not to burden yourself with yet another task.

Fifteen Times as Much Money

Imagine that you have two retirement investments. You have $300,000 in a 401(k) through your employer and $20,000 in an individual retirement account (IRA). Your 401(k) statements come quarterly, and you tend to forget about this account. Your IRA statements come monthly, and you can monitor your progress via the Internet. How should you allocate your time between these accounts? We know someone in this situation. He puts 90 percent of his attention towards the IRA, when he *should* be putting over 90 percent of his attention towards his 401(k) because the 401(k) constitutes more than 90 percent of his portfolio. A given percentage improvement in the 401(k) account will put fifteen times as much money in his pocket as a similar improvement in the IRA. To increase his productivity by this huge factor, all he needs to do is to shift his attention from one account to the other. If he put these two tasks into a *Productivity Table*, he would clearly see the relative values.

Productivity Table

Personal Tasks	Estimated time needed (Hours)	Penalty if done poorly ($)	Probability of Penalty if Fail/Neglect	Reward if done well ($)	Probability of Reward if Finish	Weighted Return ($)	Value ($/Hour)
Monitor and update 401(k)	3.0	$5,000	50%	$10,000	50%	$7,500	$2,500
Monitor and update IRA	3.0	$333	50%	$667	50%	$500	$167

Mary's Friends

Mary has ten friends and she likes them all. So she tries to be equitable and spread her time equally among them. Is this the best approach for Mary? Based on the *80/20 Rule*, Mary probably gets 80 percent of her total friendship enjoyment from only two of her friends. Rather than trying for equality, Mary should consciously maximize the value of her time spent with friends. She can do this by spending more time with her two best friends and less with her other eight friends. And if her two best friends enjoy Mary's company more than that of their other friends, Mary will be helping those she cares about most. This is the best overall solution for everyone involved—producing the greatest good, so to speak.

The Lessons Learned

The challenges you face in life are like mountains; you struggle to get to the top. But is the mountain you are climbing Everest of some much smaller, unnamed peak? If it is Everest, you'd better be equipped with more than just hiking boots and drinking water. Balance and proportionality are needed so that we apply the right level of effort to each problem. Such insights are the essence of the *80/20 Rule* and *Factor 16*.

The *80/20 Rule* and *Factor 16* are incredibly powerful concepts that can help you be more effective in your life. The prospect of being 16 times as effective simply by astutely selecting the best customers, tasks, employees, and friends is mind-boggling. But it goes beyond that. You can deftly reduce expenses and increase revenues by knowing where to look, and the 20 percent that drives 80 percent of the result is the best place to start. After all, we want to treat mountains like mountains and not like molehills.

Chapter 12

KNOW THE VALUE OF INFORMATION

New knowledge is of little value if it doesn't change us, make us better individuals, and help us to be more productive, happy, and useful. — Hyrum W. Smith

In Chapter 11, we introduced the idea of using resources—goods and services—as long as the marginal revenue or marginal value exceeds the marginal cost. The same principle applies to information—information as a result of analysis and research that you perform; reports, magazines, and books that you buy; or experts that you hire. Because time is money, information costs us money whether we dig it up ourselves or purchase it. And if the marginal revenue of information exceeds its marginal cost, we should purchase it. But this approach can be impractical. There are many, many pieces of information that we could conceivably buy, and we would have to ascertain each of their costs and values. Sometimes, value is hard to quantify, even after a lot of work. We need a cheaper and easier way to determine what information to purchase. Decision analysis can help us solve this problem.

Information has a few components of value:

- ❑ The pleasure or entertainment value
- ❑ The long-term educational benefit
- ❑ The ability to change our behavior

For decision-making, knowledge should change us or our behavior. If I'm not going to sell my house or increase my home equity line of credit, its appraised price is of little interest to me unless I want to calculate my net worth. If I'm thinking of selling my house, its appraised price will help me set the asking price or cause me to time the sale. One value is a "nice to know," while the other directs my behavior. When I read about the world's record number of people stuffed in a Volkswagen Beetle at one time, I am entertained, but it doesn't change my life in the slightest.

For decision-making, the primary value of information arises when it changes our decisions.

Consider back pain. Doctors often think they should do something to alleviate a patient's back pain, and so they may administer X-rays and MRI (magnetic-resonance imaging) scans. There are four problems:

1. The tests cost money.
2. The tests expose the patient to further harm due to their methods of illuminating the details of the patient's insides.
3. The tests sometimes lead to unnecessary treatment for suspicious-looking, but otherwise harmless, abnormalities.
4. The resulting treatment is largely the same, regardless of the test results.

In other words, the tests rarely influence the proper choice of treatment; the treatment is usually the same whether or not the cause of the back pain is identified.[124] And, because the information the tests provide does not influence treatment, they have very little direct value.

A small pharmaceutical company was developing a nasally administered drug and needed to select a specialized delivery device that would allow patients to administer the exact amount of medicine. The search ended with a device that was accurate enough and advanced enough to allow the company to launch its product quickly. This device, however, was not the company's favorite. To ensure the success of this less-than-ideal device, the company wanted to conduct market research to get customer feedback and suggestions. For this, it would have paid $40,000 for primary market research. Objective Insights helped them think through this problem. The managers of the company realized that they had no choice—they had to choose this device to keep their current development timeline. They also realized that they would benefit from the market research, but because they didn't have any decisions to make for eight months, they could wait to conduct the research until after they had better information. In other words, they had already committed to this particular delivery system and their hands were tied for the moment. Why gather more information? After this meeting, the company president called to thank us for these insights and for saving his company $40,000. This leads us to another rule.

If possible, delay making a decision, or doing an expensive analysis, if better information is on its way.

Information sometimes affects our decisions and sometimes doesn't. If it does, it has value. Imagine you're buying a house that may have been built, of all things, over an old leaky gas station tank. The house is priced at $100,000—a great price—but if it was built over the toxic waste site, its value is exactly zero, for a $100,000 loss. If the site is clean, the house is worth $300,000, for a $200,000 gain. You would love to know which it is. If an additional piece of information about the site's status turns up, that information has real value because it may change your behavior. It would be more than just nice to know; it would make your life measurably better. Unfortunately, most information is imperfect. Companies spend millions of dollars on market research, and yet they must ask the same question over and over: is this information any good? What's wrong with it? Can I live with it? What does it tell me? I (CLH) have never seen a market research survey, even those that I conducted, that did not have gaps or flaws.

Decision analysis helps us calculate the value of perfect information and, therefore, the upper limit on the value of imperfect information. Once we establish the price for perfect information, we will always pay less for imperfect information because imperfect information is obviously worth less.

We can calculate the value of perfect information.

Take the house example and assume that you haven't bought it yet. What is the value of perfect information about whether or not the house is sitting on a toxic waste site? To calculate the value of perfect information, we need to know a little more. We need to know what probability you assign, before investing in any information, to the site actually being a toxic waste site. Let's say you estimate the probability at 0.3, or 30 percent, given the information you have available at the time.

To determine the value of perfect information, we look at how you would act if you knew this information *before* you had to decide whether to buy. Hint: The value is *not* $300,000, or the difference between the -$100,000 and $200,000 outcomes. And it is also not $100,000, or the cost to you of getting stuck with a worthless house. In this case, the value of perfect information is $30,000, or 30 percent times your potential loss of $100,000 if the house was built on a toxic site. The 30 percent comes from the probability you assigned to this event. With a higher probability, you would get a higher value of information. This value is due to your ability and willingness to change your behavior and, therefore, avoid buying a worthless house.

We saved you most of the mathematics by jumping right to the answer. But in general, to calculate the value of perfect information, you need to solve two decision trees. You first solve the regular, real-world decision tree whereby you make your decision and then get the piece of information you crave, as shown below. The overall expected value of this decision tree is $110,000 because you should select the "Purchase House" alternative. We get this by multiplying $200,000 by 70 percent and subtracting $100,000 times 30 percent. Note that the result of $110,000 would cause us to purchase the house because $110,000 is greater than $0 for the status quo alternative of "Don't Purchase." The arrow shows the best choice, which is "Purchase House."

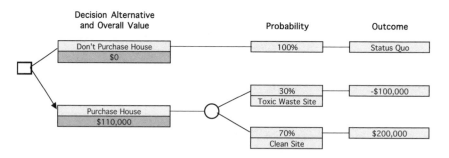

Next, you need to solve a rearranged, ideal-world decision tree (see below), in which you get the information you desire and then make your decision. This would be like knowing the winning lottery numbers *before* buying your ticket. The expected value of this decision tree is $140,000 (30 percent times $0—you don't purchase—plus 70 percent times $200,000—you do purchase). The difference in the values of the two trees is the value of perfect information—in this case, $30,000. Notice that the value of the second tree is higher because it is a better situation for you—you get to pick *after* you find out whether or not the house is on a toxic waste site. Again, the value comes from changing your behavior and selecting a different decision alternative by knowing the information beforehand.

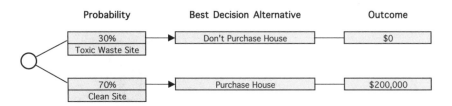

The value of imperfect information will always be less than the value of perfect information. Of course, buying this house is risky because we could lose $100,000. You may wonder, then, why we didn't use utility scores and the *Risk-Averse Expected Net Present Value Approach* to properly account for risk. Our answer is that we used the simpler *Expected Value Approach* so that we wouldn't get unnecessarily bogged down in details.

Techniques from decision analysis can help us calculate the value of perfect information, as we did above, but notice that we are already in the middle of an analysis. This is like correctly guessing how many jellybeans are in a jar after you have already counted half of them. Often, we need to know how much to spend on analysis *before* we get this far. This brings us to the *One-Percent Rule*, taught to us by Stanford's Ronald Howard. The *One-Percent Rule* helps us budget for analysis before we get too deeply into a project.

The One-Percent Rule

The One-Percent Rule: You should spend approximately one percent of the value of a decision analyzing the decision.

If you go to a week-long seminar that someone else is paying for and that will consume 50 hours of your life, spend half an hour (one percent) making sure the seminar is right for you. If you buy a $300,000 house, spend $3,000, or 150 hours at $20 per hour, making your selection. If the government is going to spend $100 million building a new sports arena, it should spend $1 million to determine if the arena is a good idea. If you are deciding between two brands of laundry detergent, and the difference in value between them cannot be more than $2, spend only two cents, or less than four seconds at $20 per hour, to make your purchase decision. Time's up. Throw that box in the shopping cart and move on with your life.

When you approach a decision, you frequently don't know all the details. This is where the *One-Percent Rule* is a useful rule of thumb: a first approximation for how much effort you should spend solving a problem that is just taking form.

The first step is to take the overall magnitude of the alternatives you are facing. If you are looking at houses in the $400,000 price range, plan on spending $4,000 of your time and money selecting the right house. If your non-work time is worth $40 per hour (The section entitled The Value of Your Time in Chapter 3 can help you determine this.), then spend 100 hours. In reality, most people spend much more time than this when buying a house and are generally wise to do so. This is why the *One-Percent Rule* is only a rule of thumb. Use the *One-Percent Rule* when approaching a new problem; then as you get better information, use the values of the specific case to calculate the benefit of spending more on analysis, as in the toxic-waste-site house example.

Here's a familiar challenge, recognizable to many with business experience. Say you are faced with two problems: a corporate printer problem worth $1 million and a product-licensing problem worth $100 million. You'll probably recognize this as a problem we discussed in Chapter 1. We know that we should spend 100 times as much studying the licensing problem as the printer problem. To help analyze these problems, you enlist the services of a reputable consulting firm, which sends you a proposal for solving each problem. The printer proposal is for $9,000 and the licensing proposal is for $150,000. Based on the *One-Percent Rule*, we realize that both proposals cost less than their one-percent value to us. However, we accept only the licensing proposal. Why? Based on our budget, or on other cash flow considerations, we don't have enough money to do all worthwhile projects. With a limited budget—or any cash flow problem regardless of cause—we should make only the best investments. We should not, however, accept this limitation without a challenge. It may be highly profitable for our company to initiate both projects. At this point, we need either to borrow money or convince the budget authorities within our company to modify our budget.

To summarize our rules:

❑ Make the analysis proportional to the problem.
❑ Follow the *One-Percent Rule* as a simple rule of thumb.
❑ Calculate the value of perfect information, if possible.
❑ Purchase information if the marginal benefit—the value—exceeds the marginal cost.
❑ With a constrained budget, do only the best projects.

The first rule is a rule that we should consider at all times. The second rule shows us how to approach problems that are taking shape. Rules three and four can be used when we are in the middle of an analysis to fine-tune what information we should buy. Rule five applies when we are constrained in what we can do.

The Data Trap

Many years ago my (CLH's) dad was a professor and a counselor at San Jose State University. He told me of students who would come in for a counseling session and confidently announce that they were going to change their major or leave school altogether. My dad would let them talk at length about such things as the job market, or their lack of intellectual satisfaction, or their poor grades, or their larger purpose in life, or whether they were in the right major. After some closer examination, my father often discovered that they had recently broken up with their girlfriend or boyfriend. The root of the problem was that they were broken-hearted and depressed and were considering changing anything about their life, but mostly they just wanted someone to talk to.

My father usually got to the root of the problem, but a less-experienced counselor may have spent a lot of time addressing the wrong problem. This is called **framing**, and it involves getting to the core of the problem and not falling into what we call the data trap. The key is to look where the student tripped, where his heart was broken, rather than where the student said he "fell." An upset student may initially conceal where he tripped, and may himself believe that the problem lies where he fell. A skilled problem-solver needs to dig deeper and not just take the situation as presented.

Often, if we are called upon to help others solve their problems, whether as a counselor, consultant, or friend, we will first get a detailed account of where they "fell" and how it hurts. We can and should commiserate with them, but to really help solve their problem, we must first ascertain whether they tripped elsewhere. Charley's father helped students see where they had tripped, where the problem started, so that they could move beyond merely feeling bad about where they fell. The following story further illuminates another aspect of the data trap.

A man was wandering around looking under a streetlight when another person walked up and asked what he was doing. He replied that he had lost his car keys and was looking for them. The stranger offered to help, and the two looked for fifteen minutes. Finally, the stranger gave up and asked the man where exactly he had lost his keys. "Over there," the man replied. "Well, then why have we been looking over here?!" asked the exasperated stranger. "Because it is too dark over there," was the reply.

The analyst's equivalent is what we call *The Data Trap*. **The Data Trap comes from doing analysis on a problem simply because data are easily available.** The result is that other, more important, problems go unsolved.

The question should be, is it worth trying to do, not, can it be done? — Allard Lowenstein

Not everything that can be counted counts, and not everything that counts can be counted. — Albert Einstein

The Right Amount of Information

Life is what happens to you while you are busy making other plans.
— John Lennon paraphrasing Alfred J. Marshall, famous early 20th century economist. Also credited to Betty Talmadge and William Gaddis.

A little bit of knowledge can be a dangerous thing.
— Unknown

What do these two quotes have in common? They both relate to how much knowledge you should acquire in life. That's right. You acquire knowledge as you acquire anything else in life; you pay a price for knowledge and you hope it helps you in some way. Too little is bad for obvious reasons and too much is bad, for other reasons, which we'll discuss. There is a sweet spot—the right amount.

When a decision must be made, a little bit of knowledge can be dangerous because it entices you to act with confidence when you are basically ignorant. Too much is wasteful and slows your progress. In the extreme, picture some organization that perpetually studies a problem and never gets further. The right amount allows you to handle decisions with confidence and dispatch. You won't ever feel that things are perfect—information will always be lacking and timelines will always be looming. The best you can hope for is that everything is equally lacking and there are no glaring gaps.

Information is good, right? So, can gathering too much knowledge be bad? You bet it can. You could literally spend the rest of your life studying, say, trashcans in any moderately sized city in America. The Monterey Peninsula in California, for instance, has perhaps 100,000 trashcans. If we could ask one thousand questions (what is in them, where were they made, where are they kept, how much they weigh, etc.) about each trash can, and each question took ten minutes to answer, we have a project that will take one billion minutes to complete. This is 8,333 person-years, or 208 full person-careers. So, we are guilty of gross understatement: you and 207 of your colleagues could spend the rest of your professional lives studying trashcans in Monterey. And why? Beats us. We never said anything about a mission, objective, goal, or purpose to this exercise. And that's the whole problem.

You should never embark on an information-gathering project without first establishing your objective. If you're designing a new garbage truck, for instance, perhaps you need only be concerned with the size and weight of a representative sample of trashcans. If you are an environmentalist studying refuse and recycling, perhaps you need only study the contents of representative samples to see what is recycled versus what could be recycled. If you are a biologist studying the growth of microorganisms, you can forget about how owners feel about their trashcans. If you are a criminal trying to steal the identity of Monterey's wealthy residents, you can forget checking the trashcans on the poor side of town. (Note to criminals: read Chapter 15 to see why you shouldn't be a crook.)

To answer these focused questions, we have reduced the problem from one requiring one billion minutes of work to one requiring, perhaps, four thousand minutes, or 1.7 person-weeks. By working on a meaningful and directed project instead of a silly and open-ended one, we have increased your efficiency by a factor of 250,000. What enabled us to make such gains? We did things in the right order: first define the question, second determine what you need in order to answer that question, and three, start working.

The Lessons Learned

Information is a precious resource and a decision-maker should make sure he or she has the right amount. Too much is wasteful, both in terms of money and time, as the trashcan's example showed. Too little is careless. Decision science shows us how to calculate the value of any piece of information capable of resolving a pressing issue, such as whether a house we are considering buying sits on polluted ground.

This chapter introduced the *One-Percent Rule*, which can help us set our information budget before we dive into a project. But there's more to it than that. The lessons of *The Data Trap* help us focus our energy on the right information. After all, we want the right amount of the right information. To do that, we need to understand and appreciate the value of information.

Another objective is to balance the information that feeds into a decision. If we have great information about one aspect of the problem and almost nothing on another aspect, we aren't equally happy and we should adjust our efforts. Nothing is perfect, but all information sources for a decision should be roughly equally imperfect.

Like everything else, information has costs and benefits. We need to gather the right amount of information to understand a situation and act clearly and quickly. Too little or too much information is bad. We can and should calculate the value of information because information's primary value results from its ability to change our behavior.

Chapter 13

THINK SIMPLE

Make everything as simple as possible, but not simpler.
— Albert Einstein

Frustration can arise when one person is helping another, and the helpful person thinks something is easy but it isn't. "Just open that lock. It's easy." "But I don't know the combination." If you know the combination, it *is* easy. If you don't know the combination, the problem is almost impossible. Computer manufacturers are infamous for this. "Oh, when that happens just hit Control ALT Delete or Control Command Escape." It's all in the word "just."

When I (CLH) was a senior in high school, I took the city bus to and from work each day during the summer. Decades had passed, and I hadn't even thought about taking the bus anywhere until my wife, Lisa, realized how convenient our neighborhood was for bus travel. We thought our kids would actually enjoy a bus trip, and so we rode from Campbell into Los Gatos for the day. Getting there was easy: we walked a block, waited at the bus stop, and hopped on when a Valley Transit Authority number 60 bus came. Much later in the day, getting home proved more difficult, because something that should have been easy wasn't. We needed to catch a 60 bus back home, and we waited and waited at a stop that listed three bus lines, including the 60, that were supposed to stop there. Many buses came and went, but not a single 60. As it started to get dark and our two young children tired, we finally talked to one of the bus drivers. Silly us. We didn't know that we had seen a handful of 60 buses come and go, but they were labeled with a different number because they change their numbers after they turn the corner, not 100 feet away. Worse, we had missed the last 60 of the day. The bus driver was nice enough to drive us half a mile to another bus stop so that we could wait 30 more minutes for yet another bus to take us home. But it was late and way past our kids' bedtime. It would have been easy for us to catch the 60 bus, had we known their little secret. They certainly didn't make their system simple to understand for us infrequent riders. Simple is good, and this chapter explores ways to help keep things that way.

Thresholds

Thresholds make it easier for people to judge what they think will happen in the future. Instead of finding out how high someone can jump, just see how high he needs to jump and then ascertain whether he can jump that high. Toward the end of a golf tournament, for instance, a golfer may feel pretty pessimistic about her chances of winning but not have more clarity than that. Using the power of thresholds will allow her to realize, that to win, she will need an eagle on each of the last three holes—which is possible, but highly unlikely. A company such as Apple Computer may say it needs to sell $100 million in December to reach its annual revenue targets; it is almost guaranteed to succeed. A performing arts group may realize that its new theater isn't big enough. Even if it sells every ticket for every show, it won't make enough money to recover its costs. Basketball fans born before 1945 may recall watching Red Auerbach, the legendary coach of the Boston Celtics, light up his cigar at the point in the game when his team was sure to win. Auerbach looked at the clock and score differential and computed a threshold.

We used thresholds in earlier chapters when we determined that we should look *at most* for 1.89 seconds to find the missing postcard stamps (The Missing Postcard Stamps, Chapter 3). In The Customer is *Always* Right? Section (Chapter 5), we looked at the breakeven threshold for the company that doubled the number of doses of its nasal inhaler. **Thresholds show us the most or the least we need to accomplish to be equally well off with two possible paths**. With the stamps example, the two paths are "look for the cheaper stamps" or not. With the nasal inhaler, we are comparing the path of the status quo (nothing changes) to the path of doubling the bottle size, holding the price constant, and trying to sell more units.

I (CLH) used thresholds at a small biotechnology company looking to out-license an HIV-AIDS medication to a large pharmaceutical company. A key assumption in the financial model was that the larger company would be more successful with this medicine due to its experienced management team, greater resources and much larger sales force. Instead of asking how much better the small company's management believed the large pharmaceutical company would perform, something they seemed uncomfortable doing, we set the threshold based on financial models. The answer? The larger company would need to sell five times as much product as the smaller company just to break even. The smaller company's management considered this outcome highly unlikely because of the nature of the HIV-AIDS market. People with HIV-AIDS in the U.S. are, in general, much more educated, organized, and aware of new therapies than people with other diseases. Strong promotion of a new medicine certainly helps boost everyone's awareness, but in this market, it would be difficult to keep a good medicine secret. So management concluded that, while the larger company would certainly be more successful with this drug, there was no way it could sell five times as much. The factor of five was the minimum possible to break even. Any factor lower than five would indicate that the smaller company would do better to keep its own product. It did, in fact, keep the product and was quite successful.

Or consider two true stories about using thresholds to decide whether to take a new job. I (CLH) talked to a former coworker shortly after his company had been acquired by a European company with U.S. headquarters in New Jersey. This person was "Mr. Los Altos, California." Cut him and he'd bleed Los Altos blood. He knew everyone and everything about Los Altos. I asked him if he was going to accept a position in New Jersey with the new company. He said he would for a salary of $200,000 a year, an amount we both knew was fantasy. His threshold was just too high.

I (DRH) faced a similar situation. When I was working with President Reagan's Council of Economic Advisers, the headhunting firm Korn Ferry approached me to find out my interest in becoming head of a think tank based in Kalamazoo, Michigan. The headhunter told me I had been recommended highly by an economist close to Alan Greenspan, so I sensed that I was on the short list for the job. Although I can live almost anywhere if the job is right, my wife, Rena, was decidedly less than thrilled about living in Kalamazoo. It made sense to me to express my concerns about location to the headhunter, and I did so at our second meeting. So he, sensibly, simply skipped over the normal process of making an offer and negotiating by asking, "How much would my client have to pay you to take this job." I had thought about this and had come up with a number that would allow us to fly out of Michigan regularly. After my reply, the headhunter said, "Well, just so you know, the client would never pay that much." My decision was made.

In late 2003, I (DRH) was involved with a ballot measure in Monterey, California. I was fighting on the side opposing this measure and the proponents had to get two thirds of the votes. At 8:10, ten minutes after the polls closed, a friend in Salinas who was closely tracking the count in the Salinas voter registrar's office, called and said that of the 66,000 votes counted so far, about 62% were Yes votes. I pulled out a scrap of paper and did some quick calculations. A minute later, I announced to a room of about 10 people that we had won. "Why are you so sure?," asked the host of the party. I started to show him my math and then decided that it would be more fun and more illuminating to show it to everyone. So he got an easel, a big pad, and a black marker from his closet and I laid it out.

Let x be the number of additional Yes votes they need and assume, highly unrealistically, that all votes yet to be counted are Yes votes. Then let's solve for x. We know that 66,000 votes have been counted and approximately 40,900 of them (62%) are Yes. For this ballot measure to win, 40,900 + x all divided by 66,000 + x must exceed 66.6%. Solving, x must exceed 9,000. And, realistically, there is no way that more than 90% of the uncounted votes would be Yes votes and so x must really exceed 10,000. And, preliminary indications were that there were fewer than 8,000 votes remaining to be counted.

Shortly after, Larry Parsons, the reporter for the *Salinas Californian*, whom I had come to respect for his even-handed reporting, called and asked if we were ready to declare a victory. "We absolutely are," I said, and I told him my reasoning. "Sitting here in our newsroom, we came up with a number like 10,000 too," he replied. By seeing how high the hurdle was for the Yes proponents, we could determine how likely their success was. When we determined that their success was almost impossible, we were able to declare victory. And, as expected, when the final vote totals were tabulated days later, we had won.

Breakeven Analysis

One of the most powerful techniques we have found for decision-makers is the breakeven analysis. The result of such an analysis is a threshold that a change of course must satisfy. For example, imagine you're selling 1,000 units a week at $100 per unit. If you drop the price to $90 per unit, how many units do you need to sell to break even, that is, do as well as you were doing before? In this case, when you find out that you need to sell only 1,167 units, you reduce the price because that seems easily achievable. For some products, the results are truly surprising. "We need to sell twice as many units if we reduce the price by a mere 20 percent? Just to break even?" For them, a price cut is a very bad idea. This simple analysis can provide persuasive results.

Top-Down Versus Bottom-Up

Bottom-up analyses and top-down analyses don't mix. A bottom-up analysis starts with fundamental assumptions and combines them to create an answer. For example, I (CLH) was forecasting a new product's revenues for a large pharmaceutical company. Based on the trend for this product, anticipated new competitors, and projected price increases, I came to a forecast of $68 million in the current year. This is a bottom-up forecast. You start with detailed assumptions and end with a conclusion.

With a top-down forecast, you start with an assumed result. In this case, my client didn't believe the $68 million and, instead, thought the number would be $66 million. This of course raises the issues of: (1) why they needed me if they already had a forecast they believed, (2) what they were basing the $66 million on, and (3) the client's rather conceited illusions of accuracy—the difference between $66 and $68 is less than three percent.

Anyway, I accepted their experience with this pharmaceutical market and tried to make this product's sales equal $66 million in the current year. So I reduced the whole trend for the product. To this they replied that they didn't want the subsequent years to drop, just the current year. So I dropped the trend in the current year, leaving two discontinuities, one from the current sales down to the reduced trend and one when the trend jumped back up again.

They didn't like this either, because discontinuities were obviously unbelievable. At this point, I surrendered and confessed that I saw no reasonable and tractable way of both making the month-to-month trend numbers smooth and reasonable, and dropping the trend to meet their $66 million target. After they agreed, I went back to my original trend producing $68 million in the current year.

The bottom-up and top-down approaches do not mix very well. Managers can ignore this to their peril, and analysts can ignore this if they want to make their problems exceptionally challenging. Complicated puzzles can be fun to solve, but life is already complicated enough. Simple is better.

Persuading Others

You can also use the approaches presented here to persuade someone to change his mind. For example, you may want to convince someone that the way he negotiates deals with customers is counterproductive and that there is a better, more productive way. Warning! Changing the mind of another human being may be very difficult, if not impossible. Human beings have very robust intellectual immune systems that are better designed to dispel new ideas than to evaluate them. Perhaps this is a result of evolutionary survival; perhaps it is just laziness or fear. After all, one new idea may shake us to our core and cause us to reevaluate many other deeply held ideas.

In the choice between changing one's mind and proving
there's no need to do so, most people get busy on the proof.
— John Kenneth Galbraith

You still want to persuade the other guy, and so you start feeding him information. You believe that the person you want to persuade needs enough information to push him over the critical threshold, thereby causing a change in his behavior. So you pile information on him, whether it is welcome or not. Only later do you find that no amount of information is enough. When trying to persuade others, the best tactic is first to find out what will persuade them. The impeachment of President Bill Clinton was highly controversial: some people believed that Clinton was a criminal, while others thought he was just facing an angry mob. Conversations we had with people often revolved around whether or not he had a sexual relationship with Monica Lewinsky, whether this relationship was appropriate or an abuse of power, and whether Clinton subsequently perjured himself. Many argued that, even if Clinton had committed these offenses, impeachment proceedings were not called for. Because they believed that these charges did not warrant impeachment, the facts about the relationship between Clinton and Lewinsky were irrelevant to them. For example, someone might say, "I don't care whether the president's sex scandal is true or not because it won't affect my opinion of the case." Consequently, trying to prove or disprove the sexual episode would be a waste of time with these people. Keep it simple by addressing only relevant issues.

Hopes, Dreams, and Wishes

In a workshop I (CLH) attended years ago, Jim Lee of the advertising agency Hamilton, Carver, & Lee lectured about hopes, dreams, and wishes. As he pointed out, they are good to have, but shouldn't sway your thinking. I may dream about making it in the National Basketball Association, but I should make my career decisions firmly planted in the reality of my age, size, and limited athletic ability. Me in the NBA? No way!

Companies, meanwhile, make this mistake all the time, and in the process, make their job significantly harder. For instance, they may say that forecasted revenues of $500 million are too low to satisfy management's desire to have another blockbuster product, and so they raise the forecast to $800 million. More work is required to craft a way to increase the forecast in a reasonable way. In the beginning, the new number is discussed with a nudge, nudge, wink, wink approach. Later, people forget where the fabricated number came from and start to believe it. Later still, life is made more difficult for those who have to explain why the product is under-performing. Management's job becomes harder as it tries to shift resources to account for the shortfall as the company's stock price dives. This would be like going to your doctor to get checked for heart disease and asking him to pronounce you healthy no matter how many clogged arteries he finds. Why go to your doctor? Why even *have* a doctor? If you want an objective opinion, go to a doctor. If you want to fool yourself, stay home and save your money.

Expert Direction

Paralysis by analysis is one possible negative result of analysis. The motivations behind this paralysis are sometimes evil and sometimes innocent, but the result is often the same. Do you know people who can't get to the point? You listen and listen, but you aren't sure where they are leading. Analysis can be like this, but it need not be. The art of analysis is to make the results as simple and direct as possible.

In 1982, Merck agreed to sell some of the Swedish company Astra AB's products in the United States. Merck also agreed that if revenues reached a critical threshold, Merck would form a third company, Astra Merck Inc., and later would allow Astra AB to purchase half. This was an important decision for Merck: it couldn't simply wait until the revenue threshold was hit before forming Astra Merck. If Merck expected the threshold to be hit, it needed an up-and-running company by the time that occurred. If it didn't form Astra Merck and the threshold was hit, Merck would have to scramble to meet its contractual obligations and to set up Astra Merck as a functioning company. So it needed to know well beforehand whether to form Astra Merck. If it formed the new company, and later the threshold was not hit, it would face the embarrassment and expense of having an unnecessary company.

I (CLH) did this analysis for Merck. I could have shown the company a lot of information, but chose to show them only what mattered: the probability of hitting the revenue threshold quarter by quarter until the end of the contractual period. Merck management was able to use this information to time the development of Astra Merck, for which Astra AB later paid $720 million for its half. Was Astra Merck successful? You bet—it had Prilosec, the best selling drug in the world just a few years ago.

This brings to mind a TV commercial. An elderly, crusty attendant at a gas station far out in the desert sees a car drive up. The driver asks how to get to town. The attendant surveys the car and then launches into lengthy and complicated directions to get the driver around the snow-capped mountains towering in the background. The next driver pulls up in a Jeep and asks the same question. The man looks at the Jeep and directs him up and over the mountain, saving the driver many miles of driving in the process. This expert evaluated the Jeep and found it sufficient to recommend the shorter, but more arduous, of the two routes.

Nothing gets to the point faster than direction from an expert. "Data" is defined as numerous bits of facts ("It is 30 miles to the next road."), while "information" is defined as organized facts ("It is an easy 120 miles around the mountain and a tough 20 miles over the mountain."). Neither, standing alone, is of much use for decision-making. What's needed is knowledge, which is what an expert may have learned over time ("Although it's a shorter route, a regular car will get stuck going over the mountain."). Even better, because it's more tailored, is direction, or customized advice, which is what an expert would recommend for someone in your particular situation ("Because you have a regular car, you'll do best by driving around the mountain."). Direction depends not only on outside conditions, but also on the individual's situation. Direction is what you would expect from a mentor with general experience and specific familiarity about your capabilities and objectives. Direction is powerful because it is so simple to understand and apply.

The Powerful Simplicity of Analogies

You've spent your life learning things and now you are faced with a new situation that confuses you. How should you proceed? Analogies can be powerful tools to help us think and act clearly. The philosopher Plotinus (204-270 A.D.) said, "All things are filled full of signs, and it is a wise man that can learn about one thing from another." This applies to analogies.

We used an analogy a few pages ago to question why you would seek the diagnosis of a physician and then ask him or her to tell you something else. We certainly don't do this when we visit doctors, so why should we do this with other specialists and outside experts? By applying what we have already learned (with doctors), we can be clear on what we want from a new expert (an outside auditor, advisor, or consultant).

Analogies make life simpler because we see the similarities across situations and realize that we don't have to learn everything from scratch. We used an analogy about a cornfield in the introduction of this book: from a distance, cornfields look like a jumbled mess, but, up close, you can see down the rows and realize that the corn was planted in a line. We used this to make our point about business and personal problems having the same characteristics. The key is to put yourself in the right position to see the intrinsic patterns.

The Lessons Learned

If you want to make your life unnecessarily difficult, that's your business. If you want advice about solving problems and thinking clearly, that's our business, and one of the lessons is to keep things simple.

Simple doesn't mean simple-minded. You have to be clever and persistent to simplify an issue to its core essence, but once you do, you'll realize it was worth the effort. What are some helpful hints along the way? Use thresholds to show what is required, and use analogies to apply what you already know to new situations. Other than that, we can recommend only, as Einstein says, that you think simple and try to make things as simple as possible, but no simpler.

Chapter 14

THINK ARBITRAGE

As we described in Chapter 1, Pat Parker made $20,000 shortly after World War II ended, which is equivalent to almost $160,000 in 2005 dollars. He did this as a seventeen-year-old simply by buying boats with lead keels, selling the lead for scrap, refitting iron keels, and then reselling the boats. Pat helped alleviate the lead shortage and bring the price of lead down. Pat found lead that was being used for low-valued uses and transferred it to people who wanted it for higher-valued uses. In this way, he helped himself and others, too. This is a fantastic example of arbitrage—buying something, in this case lead, at a low price and selling it to another at a higher price.

Look carefully and you'll start to see some arbitrage opportunities of your own. Every time you pursue these opportunities, you make money but exploit no one—you actually make all who deal with you better off. Think, for example, of going to Costco to buy a 20-ream box of paper for your printer at home. You get a good per-unit price, say $1.25 per ream, because you're buying so many units. The per-ream price at the local stationary store, though, is probably at least $3.00. So if a friend runs out of paper, wants it quickly, and doesn't want to bother going to the store, you would be doing your friend a favor by selling him a ream for $2.50. You'd both benefit. In fact, you would probably benefit your friend even if you sold him a ream for $5.00.

When we think of arbitrage opportunities, we should consider the value of something, like the lead keel of a boat, in terms of its value to us—its value in use—and its value to others—its value in trade. As we discussed in the section What Constitutes a Good Deal?, a good purchase is made when the object purchased is higher in value to us than it costs us. This considers its value in use. To consider value in trade, we need to assess the value other people place on a good or service. If we currently own it and they value it more than we do, we should sell it. This is what Pat did with his first lead keel. Arbitrage pretty much ignores our values and looks at two other people or two groups and asks, "Would person A value that object more than person B, its current owner?" If so, we should try to buy it from B and sell it to A. This is exactly what Pat did with all the subsequent lead keels. He bought them from people who valued them less than the people he later sold them to. Pat was the conduit for transferring the lead to higher valued uses and because he had to pay a price just high enough to buy the boats and charge a price just low enough to sell the lead and the retrofitted boats, he pocketed the bulk of the value differential. In this case, that was a lot of money.

The Old Ford Tempo

After I (CLH) accepted a job in California, my family moved from Pennsylvania and my new employer picked up the tab for all expenses, including moving my wife's old Ford Tempo with over 120,000 miles on the odometer. Because her car was worth only about $800 at the time, my employer paid more to move the car than any reasonable person would pay to buy it.

I was aware of this fact and felt somewhat guilty. But my only alternatives were to move it to California, at no cost to me, or to unload it quickly before I moved, just when we had numerous other things to worry about. Had I been able to negotiate a deal with my new company, I would have sold the car and taken a cut of the reduced moving expenses. This would have benefited both of us. As it was, I would have gotten no direct benefit from selling the car, so I took the easy route and let them move it 3,000 miles across the country. A deal could have benefited both parties, but sometimes deals are hard to arrange.

Boissevain Bottles

Because my (DRH's) father gave me a very small allowance, approximately 25 cents a week in the late 1950s, I would find ways to make money to supplement my income. One such activity was walking along the side of the highway on Saturday mornings in my rural Canadian town of Boissevain, Manitoba, picking up pop bottles that people had thrown out of their cars. The local grocery store was willing to pay one penny per bottle in cash. However, for every bottle, they would pay two cents in merchandise. But I wanted money, not merchandise. What to do? Before taking the bottles to the store, I would ask my mother which candy bars she wanted at the store, and then I would redeem the bottles for those candy bars. I would then sell her the candy bars at store prices. I doubled my money and my mother was better off by saving a trip to the store. Not as lucrative or clever as my friend Pat Parker's arbitrage, but, hey, give me a break; Pat was 17 and I was eight. Interestingly, when I've told this story to classes, they've sometimes reacted negatively to me, the son, having taken advantage of my mother. But that just shows the zero-sum mentality—someone must lose for someone else to win—that so many people instinctively carry with them when they consider exchange. My mother knew why I was getting candy bars for bottles; I didn't try to hide it, but presented the situation to her as a chance for us both to do better. But even had I not explained why I wanted to get her the candy bars, she still would have been better off by avoiding the hassle of shopping. Exchange benefits both parties.

Los Gatos Square Footage

After purchasing a house in a nice neighborhood of Los Gatos, California, some friends added a second story because they needed more room for their family. Through this process they discovered something interesting. The value of their home went up by twice the cost they incurred to remodel. This insight led them to the conclusion that it costs $250 to $300 per square foot to add onto a house in Los Gatos, but each resulting square foot is worth $500 to $600 on the housing market. So they sold their house and purchased another one, keeping an eye toward remodeling. They are hoping to complete their current house, sell it, and do the same for a third house before their twelve-year-old son graduates from high school.

This arbitrage opportunity is significant because if they add 1,000 square feet onto each house, they plan on making $250,000 per house, which, because of U.S. tax laws, will be completely tax-free. As an extra bonus, if the real estate market keeps appreciating, they make even more money. Even if the market declines some, their arbitrage profits can offset some market valuation losses. If their plan works as anticipated, they will be three-quarters of a million dollars richer by the time their son is in college.

Billy Beane Baseball

One of the most exciting, powerful, and famous uses of arbitrage is in professional baseball. Here's the puzzle in a nutshell, "How the heck do you compete with the Yankees?" Because they have the largest market, they have the greatest ability to pay players without losing money. This ability to pay the most should assure them of the best players, which explains their dominance. That's the end of the story, right? Wrong. If that's the whole story, then how did the Oakland A's, with the second smallest payroll in Major League Baseball, generate so many wins in 2000, enough to make the playoffs? And how did they do it again in 2001, 2002, and 2003? There's something missing in the above story.

What's missing is arbitrage. A few years ago, the Oakland A's general manager Billy Beane—what a wonderful name for someone in baseball—did some great thinking that led to some great decisions. He noticed that baseball scouts had a huge effect on who was hired and that they were using what seemed like pretty subjective criteria for their recommendations. "Does so and so look like a baseball player?", for example. They also recommended many high school players, about whom little could be known because of the paucity of data on high school players relative to the abundance of data on college players. But what data would you want to look at? Surely runs batted in and batting average, right?

Well, not quite. A baseball analyst named Bill James had found, based on reams of data, that the scarce resource in offense was avoiding outs. So someone who gets on base, whether through a hit or a walk, is doing a huge service to his team. Beane and his assistant, Harvard economics graduate Paul DePodesta, were familiar with James's work. By measuring on-base performance, they found a lot of diamonds in the rough, so to speak, that is, players who were being ignored by the other teams and whom, therefore, they could hire at pay that was well below the value he estimated for their performance. Then Beane would lock them into contracts and get a lot of wins. This is arbitrage: finding resources that the market is valuing too low, hiring them at this low value, and then using them in high-value uses.

What Billy Beane was doing was in the same spirit as what 17-year-old Pat Parker did with his lead keels. In Parker's case, all he needed to realize was that the keels were worth more as scrap lead than as keels. In Billy Beane's case, it was a little more complicated. He realized that baseball had not yet adjusted to the fact that high-risk prospects were getting paid millions where their counterparts 25 years earlier, before salaries had soared, were getting on average less than $100,000. So the economic return from investing in information had soared. But virtually the whole of Major League Baseball was stuck in the old ways of judging players. The information technology revolution dramatically lowered the cost of getting information and processing it. With a lower cost of getting information and a higher benefit of getting it, Beane did the rational thing: he got more information. Beane then used the information to find those undervalued resources and then to arbitrage them by keeping enough good ones for his own team to win and selling off enough good ones to keep the Oakland A's financially viable.

The above is an abbreviated version of one of the most outstanding economics books published in the last 10 years. It's not billed as an economics book: it's a baseball book. And even someone with zero background in economics can understand it totally. The book is *Moneyball* by Michael Lewis. Not coincidentally, Lewis has previously written about successful businesses. It took someone with his sophisticated eye to see what now appears to almost all of us as an obviously good strategy. And it took someone with Lewis's writing ability to write about the economics of baseball in such a seamless way that you think you're reading a mystery novel rather than an economics book. Interestingly, though, many baseball owners still don't get it. According to Michael Lewis, other baseball owners are picking up on Billy Beane's method, the Boston Red Sox and the Toronto Blue Jays, to name two. But as long as enough other owners don't get it, Billy Beane and like-minded general managers will keep picking $100 bills off the street.

Looking for Arbitrage

One sure way to make your company run well is to look for arbitrage opportunities. Arbitrage is the action of buying something from one person and then selling it to another person, essentially unchanged but at a higher price. Why would this have anything to do with how well your company is run? Because exchange benefits both parties. By uncovering opportunities for trade, you can simultaneously benefit two groups within your company. This is truly like finding a fifty-dollar bill on the street.

We've talked to people at large corporations who work under defined criteria for any internal investments they make. For example, if they design a new marketing program, senior management will accept it only if it pays for itself in the first year. In other words, senior management is demanding a 100-percent annual rate of return on marketing. Other people in the organization have different rules. They may have to generate only a 20-percent annual rate of return on a new manufacturing plant. Implicitly, the manufacturing person can borrow money from the company at a 20-percent annual interest rate, while the marketing person has to pay 100 percent. If you could borrow the $10 million that the manufacturing group gets and pay them a "generous" 30-percent annual interest rate, and then lend it to the marketing group at a "cheap" 90 percent, everyone would gain, especially you. The manufacturing and marketing groups each "make" an additional $1 million, and you make an additional $6 million. Even if you act simply as an unpaid middleman, you pay the manufacturing group 60 percent for the money it has already "borrowed" at 20 percent from management and charge the marketing group 60 percent to borrow this money. Each group gets half of the $8 million gain. So it isn't like finding a fifty-dollar bill in the street; it's like finding a suitcase full of money.

An even better way to do this would be to change the whole situation by allowing manufacturing and marketing to negotiate a direct exchange and find the right equilibrium. Or, the company could determine the standard rate from outside capital sources and then allow both marketing and manufacturing to borrow money at that rate. Both of these departments may have projects that will return profits far beyond a ten-percent annual return that normal investors might find attractive. This company should realize that, by adhering to such artificial and inconsistent standards, it is being wasteful.

Saving Costs

Money is where you find it. Sometimes you make money by increasing your sales, sometimes by reducing your costs. Reducing costs is an internal focus, similar to arbitrage, because it creates nothing new, but rearranges existing elements. Such cost savings can be substantial.

Dow Chemical held a contest to generate ideas to save costs. "In 1981, Dow Chemical's 2,400-worker Louisiana division started prospecting for overlooked savings. Engineer Ken Nelson set up a shop-floor-level contest for energy-saving proposals, which had to provide at least a 50 percent annual return on investment (ROI)."[125] Management got a number of good ideas, implemented them, and then repeated the contest. They were surprised to learn that the rate of return for the winning ideas kept getting higher with additional contests. The average payback time ranged from six months (200-percent annual return) to four months (300-percent annual return) over time. "By 1993, the whole suite of projects taken together was paying Dow's shareholders $110 million every year." Most other companies have similar savings waiting for enterprising miners. Is your company one of them?

Return on Investment Versus Payback Time

Investments pay you back over time. How do you think of this return when you evaluate investments? Some people think of investments in terms of the rate of return, usually an annual percentage, while others think in terms of payback time. For instance, if you invest $100 and start getting $100 every six months, your payback time is six months. Many people understand the two approaches but have never considered how the two relate. The results may surprise you.

Typically, energy-saving devices are chosen by engineers at the firm's operating level, using the rule-of-thumb procedure called "simple payback," which calculates how many years of savings it takes to repay the investment in better efficiency and start earning clear profits. Four-fifths of the American firms that even think about future savings (instead of just initial capital costs) use this method. Moreover, they do so with the expectation of extremely quick paybacks – a median 1.9 years. Most corporate officers are so immersed in discounted-cash flow measures of profitability that they don't know how to translate between their own financial language and the engineers' language of simple payback. They therefore may not realize that a 1.9-year simple payback is equivalent to a 71 percent real after-tax rate of return per year, or around six times the cost of additional capital.[126]

Seventy one-percent is an incredibly high hurdle rate. You almost certainly invest your own money in stocks, bonds, and mutual funds that are expected to grow at much lower rates. When new electric power plants are built, they are expected to recover their initial investment in twenty to thirty years—about ten times as long at the 1.9 years described above. "Our society, therefore, typically requires roughly tenfold higher returns for saving energy than for producing it."[127] This is where arbitrage opportunities come from: different perspectives, different states of information, and inconsistent requirements. Whenever you see arbitrage opportunities within a company, consider the exploitation of these opportunities as a gift for you and a lesson for the company's management.

If you want to calculate this yourself, the annual return on an investment (ROI) equals one divided by the number of years to pay back the investment (see the Appendix). For example, for an investment of $100 that returns $100 every six months, the payback time is six months and the annual ROI is 200 percent. For every year into the future, you will get $200 back from your $100 investment, as if you received 200-percent interest from a bank.

An Investment Your Leftovers Will Love

Depending on your investment opportunities, we would bet that you have some money invested in bonds or bond funds that yield well below ten percent per annum. Would you be interested in a risk-free investment that yields over twice this rate? Stated like that, the answer is pretty obvious. This investment opportunity, however, isn't so obvious.

If you have a refrigerator that is more than 10-15 years old, you can almost certainly save money by buying a new one. Purchasing a new one will cost you money in the short term; however, the lower operating costs, due to more efficient motors and compressors, will save you money over time. Not very interesting? Think of it this way: you can make a 22.5 percent pre-tax, risk-free return on your investment. A 22.5 percent risk-free return compares favorably with almost any investment. To calculate this, we assumed $140 in annual electricity savings, a $900 purchase price, and a marginal tax rate of 31 percent. You get a 15.6 percent return every year from the energy savings, which is the same as a 22.5 percent pre-tax investment return. Not only is this investment essentially risk-free, but you get a squeaky-clean place to keep your milk and leftover Thai food. And, your energy savings will help protect the environment.

Friedman's Secretary

Milton Friedman was fond of telling the reason he hired a black woman to be his secretary. He didn't set out to hire a black person—or, for that matter, a white person. What he wanted was the best secretary he could find at a given hourly rate. He found that other people's prejudice caused African-American women to be valued slightly lower in the job market than, for instance, equally productive white women. This enabled him to get a better value by selecting a black woman.[128] He was effectively taking advantage of an imbalance in the job market and shifting lower valued resources (black women) to higher valued uses (better jobs), which is the essence of arbitrage. By doing this, both Friedman and his secretary benefited, getting a better deal than they would have otherwise. Friedman was fond of this story because it teaches an important economic lesson, and it shows how he helped others and himself.

The Lessons Learned

Arbitrage is the action of buying something from one person and then selling it to another person, essentially unchanged but at a higher price. We have seen how exploiting arbitrage opportunities benefits society and you. Pat Parker, for instance, helped alleviate the lead shortage and bring the price of lead down—while making a small fortune for himself. Such opportunities are available if you look, too. By keeping an eye peeled for arbitrage opportunities, you may find ways to improve your company's profitability, because all parties involved benefit from such exchanges. If you've got an even better story than these, write to us at Hooper@ObjectiveInsights.com and DRHend @Mbay.net.

Chapter 15

DO THE RIGHT THING

Honesty is the first chapter in the book of wisdom.
— Thomas Jefferson

This above all: to thine own self be true, and it must follow, as the night the day, thou canst not then be false to any man.
— William Shakespeare

So far, we've discussed how to make the most profitable or most effective decisions. In this chapter, we consider how—and why—to be ethical. We suspect that some of you are already squirming in anticipation of a boring, holier-than-thou sermon about all the things you should feel guilty about. Relax. We're not about to lecture you. The study of ethics, far from being a downer, can show you how better to achieve the things you want in life in an uplifting and enlightened way. You need a code of ethics to survive and thrive. We aren't going to give a complete one here, but we will hit some of the highlights. We expect that at the end of this chapter, many of you will feel better about yourselves than you do now, and perhaps see the close connection between an ethical life and an effective one.

The Wedding Toast

Years ago at a wedding, the best man, Gary, stood up to toast the newlyweds. His message sounded as if he was still at the bachelor party. "There is a lot of give and take in a marriage," he said with a smile. "So take all you can get." Guests were flabbergasted at Gary's sense of humor. Fortunately, everyone lived through this uncomfortable moment and, many years later, the marriage is still intact.

If we want to live a rich, full life, shouldn't we follow Gary's advice to take all we can get? After all, isn't the goal to have more of the good stuff? But look at the context. Gary was giving advice to two people entering into marriage, which is an agreement. I may want to take all I can get, but if my wife thinks the same way, we won't get very far. To foster a long and happy relationship, we need to consider our spouse's needs and to limit our own "taking," so that he or she gets enough to want to stay married. We need to think of others.

We have all heard of companies having a "customer focus." What this means is that they think of their customers long enough to understand their needs and situations, which allows the companies to see opportunities, create value, and offer appealing services and products.

Consider young children. They value themselves more than others and focus almost entirely on their own needs. If companies behaved this way, they would never make products that others want to purchase and, therefore, would never generate profits. Only by focusing on the needs of others and caring about them at some level, do we further our own goals and objectives. A large part of the education of children, which happens primarily outside of school, is getting across to them that the way to further their own ends is to figure out how they can help others pursue their goals. This is an apparent contradiction in free-market economies: people selfishly promote their own ends by finding out what other people need and want and helping them get these things. In other words, people frequently don't do what they want, but what others want them to do. And the reason they do what others want is that those others are willing to put their money where their wants are, and pay for having those things done. Economist and philosopher Adam Smith is justly famous for identifying the fact that our self-interested behavior causes us to promote the good of others, and for labeling this connection "the invisible hand."

Doing good for others is not the same as self-sacrifice or self-denial. This whole process, in fact, starts with the self, starts that is, with you and an assessment of your values and objectives. Only then do you turn your focus to the external world and ask yourself how you can get what you want. There are really only three ways to do so (aside from receiving gifts and begging): create it yourself, steal it, or trade with others for it. As we shall see shortly, there are tight limits on your ability to do the first two, leaving trade as your main way of getting what you want.

Consider creating it yourself. This is the Robinson Crusoe approach. When I cut brush, blackberries, and oak branches on my property for aesthetics and fire safety, I am converting my time and energy into something that I value more—a better yard. I am directly creating value.

How about stealing? If I steal, I engage in a negative-sum game. Nothing is created; belongings merely changes hands, usually reducing wealth in the process due to the time taken to steal, transaction costs, protection costs, and the personal nature of value. For instance, you may love your car, but after I steal it and send it to a chop shop, it is worth less than the value you assigned. Theft reduces society's total wealth.

The third way to get what you want is through trade. More than 99 percent of the things we enjoy in life are obtained through trade with others, not through personal creation or theft. This is by far the most important path for value creation. Right this minute you're reading a book. The book you're reading came from two authors (us), a publisher, a printer, and a retailer. The chair you're probably sitting in was provided to you by loggers, woodworkers, accountants, truck drivers, and retailers. The electricity for your lamp is being provided by the countless people who build and maintain the electricity grid and run power plants. You are sitting by yourself but you are relying on the services of literally thousands of people, most of whom you will never meet or even know of.

In civilized society, he stands at all times in need of the cooperation and assistance of great multitudes, while his whole life is scarce sufficient to gain the friendship of a few persons. — Adam Smith[129]

Adam Smith described how, even though we might have only a few real friends in life, we rely on countless others in order to perform our jobs and, ultimately, to live our lives. We are not islands. We are members of a big, gregarious web-like community, each of us dealing with others on a voluntary basis. The term "voluntary" is key here. The people we exchange with can say "no" to us at any time, perhaps because they have found someone else more favorable to deal with. Would you rather marry an obnoxious slob or a charming, clean, hard-working person? Would you rather work with someone who yells at coworkers in meetings or someone who tactfully explains her position? Do you willingly hang around "friends" who laugh at your new glasses and humiliate you when they beat you at tennis?

In the competition for friends, spouses, customers, and coworkers, we realize that others have choices, and if we don't give them what they want, they may choose someone else. This is neither cruel nor unfair. In fact, it's usually very fair. We certainly don't want to give up our right to choose and we doubt you do either. The end result is people choosing whom they want to be with. What that means is that others will judge you, and judge you largely by your behavior, which is a sufficient reason for thinking about how you should behave.

Your Own Constitution

The study of ethics is really a study of your personal code of conduct. Ethics often conflicts with what is expedient. If you were an ethical gunslinger in the Wild West you might say, "Well, I guess I won't take over this gold-mining town because I'll have to kill some innocent people." The purely expedient person does whatever is necessary to take the town. Killing innocent men, women, and children is just one more task to be checked off his list on the way to achieving his goals. The ethical person's behavior is limited, while the expedient person's isn't. The purely expedient person says that the ends justify the means, and this focus on the ends leads to the conclusion that *any* means are justified to achieve the desired ends. "We can increase our cotton production if we simply hold these workers as slaves." "We can cure cancer forever if we just torture and kill 100 innocent kids as part of this experiment." The ethical person says that while the ends are good, they never justify using certain means.

Emma Goldman, a famous American anarchist and feminist, was so hated and feared that she was deported to the Soviet Union in 1919, two years after the Russian revolution. She expected to find like-minded people in the revolutionary USSR. She didn't. In 1924, she wrote a book entitled *My Disillusionment in Russia* explaining why. Based on her observations, Goldman was one of the first to predict the demise of the Soviet Union. What was its fatal flaw? The Soviets were willing to use *any* means, however violent, to achieve their ends. "The end justifies all means," they said. She replied, "There is no greater fallacy than the belief that aims and purposes are one thing while methods and tactics are another."[130] Lenin committed precisely that fallacy. Goldman went on:

> No revolution can ever succeed as a factor of liberation unless the means used to further it be identical in spirit and tendency with the purposes of the ends to be achieved. Today is the parent of tomorrow. The present casts its shadow far into the future. That is the law of life, individual and social.[131]

This can be shown best through the following famous Russian story.[132]

Anarchist: Comrade Lenin, we are all of course
    revolutionaries here, but you are just going too far.
    Even anarchists are being imprisoned.
Vladimir Lenin: Don't you realize comrade, that one must
    break eggs in order to make an omelet?
Anarchist: Yes, I see your broken eggs everywhere. But
    Comrade Lenin, *where* is the omelet?

This book has an entire chapter extolling the benefits of expanding the alternatives available to you. So you might think that the expedient person, by freely using any means and, therefore, having more alternatives available to him, would be more successful. If I have five alternatives and you have my five plus five others, you should be more successful than I, right? Not necessarily. In the case of ethics, a powerful force works against this. The problem arises when the expedient person works for, works with, works around, or employs others. The problem arises, in short, in over 99 percent of real-life situations.

Consider what would happen if you took up cannibalism. At first, you would expand your eating options, but then your friends, coworkers, and neighbors would shy away from you, fearful that you would mistake them for a snack.

Or think back to your last visit to a doctor. Aren't you thankful for the things he or she *didn't* do, such as laugh at your

245

paunch or make jokes about your chances of a painful death? A doctor who limits his behavior is a better doctor. You get a lot more value from an airline pilot who actually flies you to Des Moines, so that you can visit your family, than from one who, on a whim, takes you to Las Cruces. A train that stays on the tracks is most valuable. A car that starts every time and runs smoothly without belching smoke is the car we want. What someone or something *doesn't do* is often more important than what he/she/it does. For example, to become a team player, you have to appropriately limit your behavior to fit into and support the team.

While governor of California in the 1970s, Jerry Brown was noted for his Zen-like statements, such as "less is more." While, in general, we'd like to have more and not less, sometimes less really is more. Consider a case where your lawyer is working for you. When the option of over-billing you arises, you want your lawyer to say, "Nah, I guess I shouldn't." You'd like even more for him to say to himself, "It's wrong to overbill." In short, you *want* your lawyer's behavior to be limited. Less is more.

To avoid getting directly ripped off, you also want to ensure that your lawyer has your best interests at heart. Your lawyer is working as your agent. There are at least two ways for your agent not to do his job. The first is by being primarily interested in his gain and only secondarily interested in yours. The other way the agent can fail to do his job is even worse: that is to actively work against your interests. Two of the biggest fires during the summer of 2002 were set by paid forest workers! Leonard Gregg stands accused of starting the largest fire in Arizona's history in hopes that he would be hired to put it out. The fire destroyed 468,000 acres and cost $32 million to contain, none of which has gone into the pockets of the incarcerated Gregg.[133] Forest Service employee Terry Lynn Barton is accused of setting Colorado's largest wildfire, which burned 137,000 acres and destroyed 133 homes during its onslaught.[134] With employees like these, who needs competitors, enemies, and terrorists?

This is the classic agent-principal relationship. The principal wants to be assured that the agent is really working for the principal, not for himself and not for someone else. For example, you want your doctor to perform surgery when it benefits you, not him. Some companies realize this and state their code of ethics in prominent places. For example, "American

Century has a Code of Ethics designed to ensure that the interests of fund shareholders come before the interests of the people who manage the funds."[135]

Now ask yourself this: Whom do you *trust* as an agent, a *trustworthy* person or an *untrustworthy* person? Duh. You can't trust someone who isn't trustworthy. We have worked with a lot of people over the years. Flakes are hard to work with because they may or may not deliver. Liars and cheats are almost impossible to work with. When we get in such situations, we sever the relationship and leave as soon as we can. The effort is simply not worth it. **Herein lies the ultimate problem for the unethical person: he may be able to enrich himself in any given situation, but doing so steadily limits his opportunities, because the circle of people who trust him gets smaller and smaller**. The conclusion: Either you limit your behavior yourself or others will limit it for you.

Does this rule apply only to individuals? No. The same forces are acting on organizations, corporations, and governments. Look around the world and you'll notice something quite striking: the countries that are the most successful have governments with *limited* abilities to act. An unlimited government is a totalitarian dictatorship, able to do anything at any time. Care to live under a dictator like Adolf Hitler, Joseph Stalin, Fidel Castro, or Saddam Hussein? Of course not; people often risk their lives to get away from countries run by such people.

Consider the United States Government. It is directly and clearly limited by the Constitution. The Constitution describes what the federal government may do in general terms, but it specifically describes how these powers are *limited*. To describe what a government may do isn't very interesting or unique, because in any number of oppressive countries around the world, the government can do anything it wants. What made the U.S. Constitution radical was the awareness that limited governments are better governments. It is this very limitation on its power that enabled U.S. society to become one of the most successful societies the world has ever known. This irony is, sadly, lost on most people. Otherwise, they would understand that the limits on government mainly limit its power to create mischief and thus prevent it from operating as if it, not we, were of primary importance. This is another example of the agent-principal issue. Most governments, including, unfortunately, governments in the United States, act as though they are the principals, and the citizens are merely the agents whose ultimate purpose is to support a strong government. The U.S. Constitution says that, no, the citizen is the principal and the government is the agent used to promote, in the famous words of Thomas Jefferson, the life, liberty, and pursuit of happiness of all citizens.

Your code of ethics is your personal constitution. Even if you don't write it in fancy calligraphy on parchment or advertise it to others, both you and they can usually see generally what it contains. And by knowing how you will operate and how you will treat others, they can decide whether to trust you and to invest in short-term and long-term relationships and commitments, whether marriage, friendship, or business enterprises.

Being on Top for Once

I (CLH) worked with John at a large corporation where we were analyst-level employees. John and I noted and discussed myopic and disrespectful behaviors of some of the managers at this corporation. One manager asked us, as the experts, to evaluate a new forecasting system he was considering purchasing. We thoroughly reviewed it and came back in a week with a clear answer: it was a mediocre system that only slightly addressed our problems and did a poor job of solving them. In short, it was a total waste of time and money. Upon hearing this, the manager informed us, in a Dilbertesque response, that he had already secured the approval of senior management to acquire the system, and now it was our job, as the "experts," to make it work. John and I were bitter about being manipulated and misled.

Years later, John and I had become the managers. I was shocked to see John harass a new employee. John apparently felt the new employee needed to go through a hazing process. John seemed oblivious to the irony. I made a mental note of it. John's personal constitution said that it's all right to abuse those below you when you get a chance.

If you ever want to see what someone is really like, observe how that person treats those lower down in the pecking order. A decent person will treat everyone with respect. A deceitful or weak person will treat well only those he thinks need to be impressed. This is not only sorrowful, but also shortsighted. We've seen a secretary advance into management and manage her former boss. We've also seen how powerful the "common" employee can be. If you want to talk to the person with knowledge, connections, and power, talk to a secretary.

The Case for Honesty

Sometimes on business trips, I (CLH) get the pleasure of staying with my brother Stan. When, after these visits, my wife, Lisa, asks me what we did, I remember hiking, listening to music, drumming, talking, eating, and playing with his computer. If I had actually been somewhere else and lied about it, I would still need to produce a "memory" of the evening. So my job would be twice as hard because I would have twice as much to remember: the real evening and the artificial evening. In fact, my job would be more than twice as hard because I would need to construct this artificial evening in the first place. Then I would need to know when to relate the real evening (to my confidant) or the artificial one (to the person I am lying to). Mathematics falls apart here, but we estimate that the liar works four times as hard.

Always tell the truth; then you don't have to remember anything. — Mark Twain

Exposing His Scheme

The next difficulty with lying and cheating is the message it conveys to family members, loved ones, friends, and co-workers. They see and hear how you treat others and get the hint that, "I will cheat them. Watch out because you may be next." Remember the story about the dishonest mortgage application in Chapter 1? The behavior of Charley's associate made Charley scrutinize the associate's other actions. It wasn't that the associate was necessarily doing anything else wrong, but the incident served as a wakeup call.

An analyst gave a coworker, Bill, meaningless work for his first few weeks on the job. Then suddenly, after never have lunched with Bill, the analyst invited Bill to lunch three days in a row. Bill suspected something. On the third day, the analyst confided to him that the boss's cousin's work status had been elevated from temporary to permanent. From the analyst's perspective, this was disturbing, so he suggested that Bill give the cousin a lot of meaningless work to "make life hard for him." Bill immediately realized that this was exactly what the analyst had been doing to him. The analyst exposed himself to Bill for what he really was: a deceptive and disrespectful coworker.

The Eventual, Awkward Truth

A good name, like good will, is got by many actions and lost by one. — Lord Jeffery

Another problem with unethical behavior is that the truth may become known at any time, resulting in painful outcomes. Evidence of Tanya Harding's involvement in the attack on Nancy Kerrigan before the 1994 Winter Olympics destroyed Harding's career and reputation. George O'Leary, the coach of the Notre Dame football team, resigned in December 2001 after a newspaper's "hometown boy does good" story uncovered his falsified credentials.[136] This story seems to play with certain regularity. "U.S. Olympic Committee president Sandra Baldwin resigned Friday, a day after she admitted lying about her academic credentials."[137] Baldwin had inaccurately claimed that she graduated from the University of Colorado in 1962 and earned a doctorate from Arizona State University in 1967.

We will readily admit that there are unethical and dishonest people who succeed for years or decades. The relevant question is: do you want to try to be one of them?

Keep in mind that choosing the "dark side" will not necessarily make you rich and powerful. Consider the Robert Hanssen spy case of 2001. He is now in prison without the possibility of parole. For what? For the $1.4 million he received from the Soviet Union.[138] Many of the readers of this book will make more than this during their careers, and will actually get to enjoy it, without ever having to stoop to selling national secrets and risk spending the rest of their lives in prison. When you factor in the risks, most spies sell their services for much too little.

All that you have is your soul. — Tracy Chapman

It is hard to study human beings and not appreciate the value of the soul. It is probably our most significant asset, and most people who "sell it," sell it cheap.[139] Without your soul, you drift through life with little direction, and your self-esteem suffers. If you *do* decide to sell your soul, at least do it for a high price. Remember that great line from Sir Thomas More, in Sir Robert

Bolt's *A Man for All Seasons*, when his "friend," Richard Rich, who has just become the attorney general of Wales, perjures himself to get More into trouble? More says, "Why, Richard, it profits a man nothing to give his soul for the whole world. But for *Wales*?"

Recall More's other great line when he explains to his daughter, Meg, why he refuses to take an oath that he doesn't believe:

> When a man takes an oath, Meg, he's holding his own
> self in his hands. Like water. And if he opens his fingers
> then—he needn't hope to find himself again.

The lure of unethical behavior is strong, but it is largely a siren call attracting those who don't really understand how life works. The purchase price of unethical behavior is low, but it is the maintenance costs that will kill you. Dishonest people "cleverly" sacrifice the war to try to win some battles; they seek painless, yet unethical ways to make money in the short-term, but this impedes their long-term growth and success.

I hope that my enemies are dishonest; they deserve it.
— Charley Hooper

Honesty in Business?

In many people's minds, American business has the huckster image of fly-by-night salesmen, used car lemon dealers, insider-trading CEOs, and vinyl siding scams. While this certainly happens, the great majority of transactions and relationships are, if not perfect, perfectly acceptable.

The huckster image persists, partly because hucksters persist, but also because the image is so strong, having been bolstered by years of fictional movie and television crooks. Consider P.T. Barnum, a man famous for the line, "There's a sucker born every minute." Here's the problem: he never said it. Not only that, but that famous statement went against everything Barnum stood for.

The truth is that Barnum made an important financial discovery early in his career. He noticed that nearly all his deceptive schemes "ended in disaster," reducing him to a low income of only $4 per week. His fortune, however, came almost wholly from his legitimate enterprises. "Barnum's great discovery," writes John Mueller, "was not so much that such behavior is immoral but that from a business standpoint it is *stupid*."

Barnum argued that honesty is sound business, and his argument was virtually identical to the one we make here. As Barnum put it, "no man can be dishonest without soon being found out and when his lack of principle is discovered, nearly every avenue to success is closed against him forever." "As a mere matter of selfishness," he concluded, "honesty is the best policy."[140]

As hard as this may be for many to believe, P.T. Barnum actually deserves credit, not for knowing the birth rate of suckers, but for discovering that it is easier to make money honestly than dishonestly. Barnum went so far as to write, "Poor fool! Not to know that the most difficult thing in life is to make money dishonestly!"[141] To take advantage of P.T. Barnum's experience, we suggest two techniques. One comes from the pharmaceutical powerhouse Merck & Co., named as America's Most Admired Corporation seven years in a row by *Fortune* magazine. Merck had an informal policy for avoiding ethical mishaps while I (CLH) worked there. "Ask yourself how you would feel to see your latest policy or behavior on the front page of the *New York Times*. If you don't feel proud knowing this, don't do it." Try this yourself and you'll see how much more clearly you think about questionable practices.

The second technique is to live by higher standards than the times require. We see the "current standards" approach over and over with behavior today. "It doesn't matter if I dump my used motor oil into the storm drain. Everyone does it." "It's okay if I drive drunk. I've done it for years, and my friends would think I'm wacko calling a taxi." Over time, some standards rise, so the safest bet is to live by higher standards than the times require.

An ethical person ought to do more than he's required to do and less than he's allowed to do. — Michael Josephson

Sometimes, people you're thinking of doing business with will give you, gratis, information that tells you all you need to know about their honesty or lack of same. You don't necessarily have to be eagle-eyed and looking for this information; you simply have to pay attention, not minimize, and not throw away information. The way I (DRH) put it is that I don't necessarily hold the information in my brain's volatile RAM, but I try to keep it in my stable ROM. But the person's behavior in the story I'm about to tell was so striking that I kept it in both memories.

In the fall of 1996, a former student whom I (DRH) had taught at the Naval Postgraduate School called me and told me he would be visiting his in-laws in Monterey and wanted to discuss a business proposition. I found it intriguing and had enjoyed his participation in my class; so I bit. He picked me up in his mother-in-law's brand-new Saab, and we stopped at a juice bar so that he could get a strawberry juice shake. While pulling his papers out of the Saab's trunk, he spilled the juice all over the light beige lining of the Saab's back seat. He did his best to clean up the stain, but what was left was very obvious. "Well," he said lightly but with no hint that he didn't mean it, "I'll just have to point it out to my mother-in-law and remind her not to leave lipstick in the back seat where the sun can melt it."

Instantly, I knew that I wanted no business dealings with this man, except in a situation where he paid me in advance. I stuck around for the presentation and found it reasonably interesting and thoughtful. Ironically, the presentation touched somewhat on business ethics.

Then the double whammy. While driving me home, he told me that his wife had once seen O.J. Simpson batter Nicole Brown Simpson in the parking lot of a retail establishment where she had worked. There was a chance, he said, that she would be called to the stand in the civil trial. She had not wanted to get involved in the criminal trial earlier, he said, because she wanted to avoid the limelight. All this was said matter-of-factly, with no hint of disapproval of his wife's actions. So, here was a guy who thought it quite all right to withhold information relevant to a grisly murder case. I looked forward to getting home and out of that strawberry-stained Saab. Of course, I had no business dealings with him.

When Is Dishonesty Acceptable?

Unbeknownst to him, General George S. Patton was given command of a military force consisting of fabricated "stage prop" planes, tanks, and artillery during World War II. He wasn't the only one misled. U.S. interceptions of Japanese transmissions helped the U.S. government learn that Adolf Hitler was fooled. The fooled Hitler had informed the Japanese ambassador to Germany, who had cabled Japan. As a result, the U.S. military knew the Germans were expecting an Allied invasion from the Straights of Dover, which was reasonable because that was also the narrowest section of the English Channel. As we know now, the Allied invasion actually powered into Normandy, further south.[142]

Did this kind of deception work? It certainly did. War is the single-minded pursuit of the submission of an adversary. A long-term relationship is secondary and deception can certainly help you win a war. If you are on the right side of a just war, dishonesty *should* be one of your weapons. (If you're on the wrong side of a war, please surrender now. ☺)

> *In wartime, truth is so precious that she should always be attended by a bodyguard of lies.*
> — Winston Churchill[143]

However, it is safe to say that for almost everyone reading this, life is not war. Your life is a web of relationships, including those with your family, friends, coworkers, and neighbors. You have settled on a place to live and people to live with. There's a Chinese saying: "You can do everything with swords except sit on them." Think of lies and deception as weapons, like swords. And lies, like swords, are good for everything except building fruitful long-term relationships with those close to you.

Here's our version of the Chinese saying: "You can do everything with dishonesty except live with it."

When is dishonesty acceptable, if ever? As we've already discussed, given all the terrible things people do in war, lying to the enemy seems rather insignificant. You should be careful lying to your own citizens, however, because you will have to live with them afterwards. If you are being robbed or blackmailed by thugs, you are, for all intents and purposes, at war with the criminals and should adopt the rules of war. That means, for example, not admitting that you are hiding $500 if you reasonably think you can get away with it. This is not to say that being dishonest will help you. The thugs might see right through your deception.

The main other time we can see the acceptability of dishonesty is when dealing with bureaucracies. Bureaucracies are frequently so hard to deal with that you may need to lie to them to comply with what you know they really want. The bureaucracy's objectives are clear, but their particular request may be peculiar. Here's a true story. A friend of mine (DRH) now hesitates to give blood to the Red Cross because every time she goes there, she must fill out a form. One of the questions on the form is, "Have you had sexual contact in the last five years with someone from Africa?" She and her husband met in South Africa and yes, she still sleeps with her husband. I'm virtually positive that this woman is faithful to her husband of 20+ years and he to her. But by answering "yes," she then must go into detail on another part of the form. It's humiliating and time-consuming. And the reason the Red Cross wants to know is that it doesn't want tainted blood. She would be better off, and so would the Red Cross, if she lied and said, "No." In such situations, it may be acceptable to lie so that you comply with the spirit, if not the letter, of the rules. Normally we would not condone this, but bureaucracies are difficult to reason with. If their objectives are obvious and we are meeting their needs, we may be creative in how we do it. Corporations sometimes have cumbersome bureaucracies, and non-profits also, but governments are the worst offenders.

Of course, whenever you are dishonest, you may open yourself to legal liabilities. With the bureaucracy example above, this would be highly ironic; you *tried* to give them what they wanted.

Are these the only cases in which we think it's all right to lie to bureaucracies? No. We think that someone who lied to Hitler to save the lives of innocent Jews, homosexuals, or Gypsies is heroic. That's dishonesty that has nothing to do with "complying with the spirit of the law," but has everything to do with achieving a good outcome. Of course, the U.S. government is not the Nazi government. So where do you draw the line? We have thoughts on that, but they will take us too far afield. Suffice it to say that it's important for you to develop your own code of ethics, and a good exercise is to actually write it down. One or two pages should do it.

There. That's it. We didn't preach much, but we did offer a lot of reasons why an ethical life is also an effective one. Jefferson said that honesty is the first chapter in the book of wisdom. We accept his counsel, but in this book, we made it the fifteenth chapter, believing that we needed first to discuss how to make good decisions and then temper those good decisions with good ethics. We hope that, regardless of the order, you can agree with Jefferson and the other successful people referenced here about the close connection between an ethical life and an effective one.

OUR FINAL THOUGHTS

A little clear thinking goes a long way. Thinking can help all of us, in our business and in our life, clarify our problems and decide with confidence. Thinking also helps us see that, while we want good outcomes, we don't want to compromise our own principles and ethics to get there. Here are the main insights of *Making Great Decisions in Business and Life*:

- ⇨ Use powerful techniques to help think clearly (Chapter 2)
- ⇨ Think about what is really valuable to you (Chapter 3)
- ⇨ For something to change, something else must have changed. Ask what changed. (Chapter 4)
- ⇨ Know what you want before you choose (Chapter 5)
- ⇨ Watch out for biases—and we all have them (Chapter 6)
- ⇨ Realize what's important (Chapter 7)
- ⇨ Think about what is available to you, and then create better alternatives (Chapter 8)
- ⇨ Consciously choose the best alternative (Chapter 9)
- ⇨ Accept risk and learn how to take account of it (Chapter 10)
- ⇨ Exploit life's inequalities, and in doing so, learn to appreciate non-linearity, balance, and proportionality (Chapter 11)
- ⇨ Get the right amount of information for any situation by first determining the value of information (Chapter 12)
- ⇨ Think simple (Chapter 13)
- ⇨ Discover arbitrage opportunities that help yourself and others, too (Chapter 14)
- ⇨ Do the right thing (Chapter 15)

Although thinking is important, it should, of course, lead to action, so we end this book and leave the rest to you, our readers, who will continue to write some of the most successful and interesting chapters in the history of mankind through thoughtful action.

The teenaged son of a friend of mine (DRH) was sitting around with his friends talking about how nice it would be to get a job at one of the golf courses in Pebble Beach. They talked about the jobs as if they were unattainable. Then one of the friends spoke up and said that, as a matter of fact, he had just gotten such a job. "Really?" said one of the others admiringly, "How did you do it?" "Oh, I just went down there and applied."

Failures are divided into two classes — those who thought and never did, and those who did and never thought.
— John Charles Salak

APPENDIX

Definitions, Formulas, and Variables:

Discount Rate (d) = The rate to discount (reduce) future values to account for the time-value of money, frequently as seen in the cost of capital (e.g. a loan's interest rate). Discounted future values are put on an equal footing with values received or spent today.

Number of Years to Pay Back Investment (n) = The number of years required for your venture to return an amount equal to the initial investment. At this point, you are even because you have received exactly what you invested.

Probability (P). Probabilities express the likelihood of a future event. Something that is impossible has a 0 percent probability while something that is certain has a 100 percent probability. Probabilities are usually expressed as percentages and the sum of all the probabilities for a decision branch must add to 100 percent. A 25 percent probability equals 0.25.

Return (R). Return is the payoff at the end of a bet, lottery, or venture. It is negative if a loss and positive if a gain.

Risk tolerance (T). Your risk tolerance is your sensitivity to risky bets. An individual's risk tolerance can be determined through the approach outlined in Chapter 10. Risk tolerance can be assumed to have a number of different shapes, including linear and logarithmic. We are using logarithmic here.

Annual Return on Investment (ROI) = $\dfrac{1}{n}$

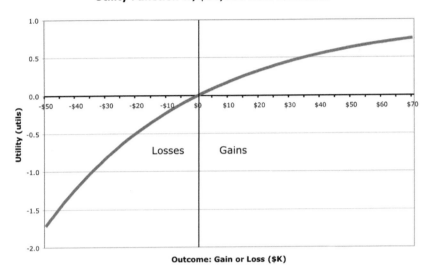

Utility Function w/$50,000 Risk Tolerance

Utility of a Return (**U**) = $1 - e^{(-\frac{R}{T})}$

The utility of a return is how the gain or loss feels to you. It is similar to a heat index that explains why the dry heat of Arizona may not feel as bad as the humid heat of New Orleans. The utility of a return is calculated using risk tolerance and it is measured in utils. Notice how the utility curve has a steeper slope on the losses side than on the gains side. For equivalent gains and losses, the negative utility of a loss will be greater than the positive utility of a gain. This is what it means to be risk averse.

Net Present Value (**NPV**) = $\sum_{i=1}^{t} \frac{R_i}{(1+d)^i}$

Expected Net Present Value (**ENPV**) = *Expected Value* (**EV**) = $\sum_{i=1}^{n} NPV_i \bullet P_i$

Expected Utility (**EU**) = $\sum_{i=1}^{n} U_i \bullet P_i$

Risk-Averse Expected Net Present Value **(REV)**
$$= -\ln(1 - EU) \bullet T$$

Certain Equivalent **(CE)** = **REV** $= -\ln(1 - EU) \bullet T$

About the Authors

David R. Henderson is associate professor of economics at the Naval Postgraduate School in Monterey, California and a research fellow with the Hoover Institution at Stanford University. He earned his Ph.D. at UCLA under noted economists Armen Alchian, Harold Demsetz, Jack Hirshleifer, Ben Klein, and Sam Peltzman. He also was on the faculty at the University of Rochester and Santa Clara University. Before moving to the Naval Postgraduate School, he was a senior economist with President Reagan's Council of Economic Advisers. Henderson edited the first, and still the only, reader-friendly economics encyclopedia, *The Fortune Encyclopedia of Economics*. It is now on the web at http://www.econlib.org/library/CEE.html as *The Concise Encyclopedia of Economics*. The second edition of *The Concise Encyclopedia* will be published by Liberty Fund in late 2006. His most recent book is *The Joy of Freedom: An Economist's Odyssey* (Financial Times/Prentice Hall, 2002). Henderson has written more than 60 articles and book reviews for *Fortune*, the *Wall Street Journal*, and *Reason* and dozens of short articles for *Barron's*, *National Review*, the *Los Angeles Times*, the *New York Times*, the *Public Interest*, the *Chicago Tribune*, the *San Francisco Chronicle*, the *Washington Times*, and the *Christian Science Monitor*. From 1997 to 2000, he was the monthly economics columnist for the *Red Herring*, an information technology magazine. He has testified on tax policy before the House Ways and Means Committee, on draft registration before the Senate Armed Services Committee, and on the Clinton health plan before the Senate Committee on Labor and Human Resources. He also has taught economics to federal judges for George Mason University's Law and Economics Center. He has appeared on C-SPAN, CNN, the Jim Lehrer Newshour, and the O'Reilly Factor. For more information, see www.David RHenderson.com. His e-mail address is DRHend@Mbay.net.

Charles L. Hooper is president and co-founder of Objective Insights, a consulting company that provides financial and marketing analysis for the pharmaceutical and biotechnology industries. Objective Insights has successfully completed more than 170 projects for 40 clients in the pharmaceutical, biotechnology, diagnostic, vaccine, and medical-device fields. Hooper is also a visiting fellow with the Hoover Institution at

Stanford University. He earned a Computer Science Engineering degree at Santa Clara University and a Masters in Engineering-Economic Systems (now renamed Management Science and Engineering) at Stanford University, where he studied under decision theorist Ronald A. Howard and economists James L. Sweeney and David G. Luenberger. Prior to founding Objective Insights, Hooper was with Syntex Labs, Merck & Co., and NASA/Ames Research Center. For more information, see www.CharlesLHooper.com and www.ObjectiveInsights.com. His e-mail address is Hooper@ObjectiveInsights.com.

Acknowledgements

We thank Dave Bashford, Brett Gaspers, Doug Hooper, Lisa Hooper, François Melese, Barry Nalebuff, William Picht, Jr., George Rosenkranz, Roberto Rosenkranz, and Dean Williams for their helpful comments. Rena Henderson once again did a great job of editing. Peter Dougherty of Princeton University Press, though unable to convince his peers to publish, was a strong believer in the project and gave us great comments. David's previous agent, Henning Gutmann, though no longer in the business, gave good suggestions and moral support.

We also thank some of the major publishers who loved the book even thought they wouldn't publish it. They argued that we weren't famous enough to make the book a sure success, but, more important to us, they liked the book and asked us to remind them when it came out because they were sure to buy a copy for their own libraries. Their desire to buy the book was a strong signal for us that we were on the right track.

Ken Euske and Doug Brook, the former Dean and current Dean, respectively, of the Graduate School of Business and Public Policy at the Naval Postgraduate School, allowed David to go on leave without pay so he could write the book. The Navy School's Provost, Richard Elster, supported this decision.

Finally, Charley thanks David Henderson, Thornton Hooper, Ron Howard, Gene Longinetti, and Jim Sweeney for their enlightened minds and accessible teaching styles. David acknowledges William Haga for his wise counsel over the years.

End Notes

[1] Ronnie Lott with Jill Lieber, *Total Impact*, Doubleday, 1991, p. 117-123.

[2] "Wellness made easy," *University of California Wellness Letter*, School of Public Health, University of California, Berkeley, vol 16, issue 6, March 2000, p. 8.

[3] For more on this, see "William Stanley Jevons" and "Carl Menger" in David R. Henderson, ed., *The Concise Encyclopedia of Economics*, pp. 796-798 (http://www.econlib.org/library/CEE.html) and to dig even deeper, see Mark Blaug, *Economic Theory in Retrospect*, 3rd edition, Cambridge: Cambridge University Press, 1978, Chapter 8, esp. pp. 320-324.

[4] Richard M. Steers, *Introduction to Organizational Behavior*, Second Edition, Scott, Foresman and Company, Glenview, IL, 1984, p. 139-144.

[5] Although psychologist Nathaniel Branden would argue that thinking clearly about how to save yourself from drowning would add to your self-esteem while people's compliments of you add only to your pseudo self esteem.

[6] David Kelley's essay, "*I Don't Have to*" at http://www.objectivistcenter.org/articles/dkelley_i-dont-have-to.asp

[7] "One Hundred Years Ago…," *The Union*, Grass Valley-Nevada City, California, 2 March 2002, p. A9.

[8] "One Hundred Years Ago…," *The Union*, Grass Valley-Nevada City, California, 7 June 2003, p. C7.

[9] James C. Simmons, *Diversion*, August 1988.

[10] Professor J. Rufus Fears, University of Oklahoma, *A History of Freedom* series of taped lectures, The Great Courses, The Teaching Company, lecture 26, 2001.

[11] Professor J. Rufus Fears, University of Oklahoma, *A History of Freedom* series of taped lectures, The Great Courses, The Teaching Company, lecture 26, 2001.

[12] Professor J. Rufus Fears, University of Oklahoma, *A History of Freedom* series of taped lectures, The Great Courses, The Teaching Company, lecture 26, 2001.

[13] One reader of a draft of this book thought we were making up this story. We assure you that it's true. It was told to me (David) by a fairly well-known economist. I promised not to mention his name because doing so would help many economist readers figure out who the famous economist with the headache was.

[14] Carl Menger (1840-1921) developed his "subjective theory of value," "Goods acquire their value, he showed, not because of the amount of labor used in producing them, but because of their ability to satisfy people's wants." See David R. Henderson, editor, *The Fortune Encyclopedia of Economics*, 1993, Warner Books, p. 815.

[15] "Design Defects of The Ford Pinto Gas Tank"   http://www.fordpinto.com/blowup.htm

[16] "Design Defects of The Ford Pinto Gas Tank"   http://www.fordpinto.com/blowup.htm

[17] "Record $4.9 billion award against GM for dangerous fuel tanks," CNN, 9 July 1999. http://www.cnn.com/US/9907/09/gm.verdict/

[18] Economists have long struggled with assigning a value to an average person's life. For reference, the White House Office of Management and Budget uses a figure of $4 million. Source: Balancing Act: Lives vs. Regulation, *Wall Street Journal*, 30 May 2003, p A4. As expected, the job market shows that risky jobs pay more than safer jobs. We can use these wage premiums for risk, along with the size of the fatality risk they compensate for, to estimate the value of a "statistical life." The answer turns out to be between $3 million and $10 million for Americans. Source: W. Kip Viscusi, "Job Safety," *The*

Fortune Encyclopedia of Economics, David R. Henderson editor, 1993, Warner Books, p. 490. (Updated for more recent data.)

[19] For further inquiry and background reading, we refer you to three papers:
Ronald A. Howard, "On Making Life and Death Decisions," *The Principles and Applications of Decision Analysis*, 1989, Strategic Decisions Group, p. 481.
Daniel L. Owen, "The Design of Hazardous Products," *The Principles and Applications of Decision Analysis*, 1989, Strategic Decisions Group, p 521.
Ronald A. Howard, "On Fates Comparable to Death," *The Principles and Applications of Decision Analysis*, 1989, Strategic Decisions Group, p 545.

[20] John Stossel, *"Give Me a Break: How I Exposed Hucksters, Cheats, and Scam Artists and Became the Scourge of the Liberal Media..."* HarperCollins, 2004, p. 95.

[21] For further inquiry and background reading, we refer you to three papers:
Ronald A. Howard, "On Making Life and Death Decisions," *The Principles and Applications of Decision Analysis*, 1989, Strategic Decisions Group, p. 481.
Daniel L. Owen, "The Design of Hazardous Products," *The Principles and Applications of Decision Analysis*, 1989, Strategic Decisions Group, p 521.
Ronald A. Howard, "On Fates Comparable to Death," *The Principles and Applications of Decision Analysis*, 1989, Strategic Decisions Group, p 545.

[22] Insurance Institute for Highway Safety, 1998,
http://www.hwysafety.org/news_releases/1998/pr021098.htm

[23] Yahoo! Maps states that it takes 8 hours to drive the 522 miles from Sacramento to San Diego. Southwest Airlines reports that flights to San Diego take about 1.5 hours and cost $113 each way as this book was being written. Given 30 minutes at the airport before each flight, the total time for flying is 4 hours and the total time for driving is 16 hours. If driving costs $0.10 per mile out-of-pocket, then we have a $120 difference between flying and driving.

[24] David R. Henderson, "Perspectives On Gas Prices: State to Blame for Gas Price Rise" San Francisco Chronicle, 23 July 1999.

[25] David R. Henderson, "Perspectives On Gas Prices: State to Blame for Gas Price Rise" San Francisco Chronicle, 23 July 1999.

[26] "Report on Gasoline Pricing in California," Attorney General Bill Lockyer, Staff Report, May 2000, pg 10-12.

[27] David R. Henderson, "Perspectives On Gas Prices: State to Blame for Gas Price Rise" San Francisco Chronicle, 23 July 1999.

[28] Mark Twain, "How I Edited an Agricultural Paper," *Mark Twain's Best*, Scholastic Book Services, 1970, p. 1.

[29] "Analyzing Customers, Best Buy Decides Not All Are Welcome," *The Wall Street Journal*, 8 November 2004, p. A1.

[30] "Shortages of Some Antibiotics Raise Concerns," *Wall Street Journal*, 2 February 2000.

[31] "Hospitals Say Drug Shortages Are Increasing," *Wall Street Journal*, 6 March 2001, p. A3.

[32] Assumes a 10 percent cost of goods sold, 10 three-month prescription refills for the life of therapy, and a 10 percent cost of capital and no dating (spoilage) problems. $10 per bottle cost times 0.8% monthly cost of capital (10% annual cost of capital) gives $0.08. ($100 retail price minus $10 per bottle cost) times 30 refills divided by 2, because the stockout could happen anytime with the therapy, gives $1,350.

[33] "Case Study," *Wall Street Journal*, 29 October 2002, p. B9.

[34] "Company Job Cuts at a Glance," The Associated Press, 22 March 2001.

[35] Many Say Layoffs Hurt Companies More Than They Help, *Wall Street Journal*, 21 February 2001, p. A2.

[36] Many Say Layoffs Hurt Companies More Than They Help, *Wall Street Journal*, 21 February 2001, p. A2.

[37] Frederick P. Brooks, Jr., *The Mythical Man-Month*, Addison-Wesley, Reading, MA, 1995, p. 16-19.

[38] Golden Gate Bridge Web site: http://www.goldengatebridge.org/research/GGBTraffToll.html - TollHistory

[39] Golden Gate Transit. http://www.goldengatetransit.org/researchlibrary/history.html

[40] "Mother Caught Speeding to Son's School," The Associated Press, *The Union*, 19 January 2004.

[41] Thomas T. Nagle and Reed K. Holden, *The Strategy and Tactics of Pricing*, Prentice Hall, 1995, p. 139.

[42] "At Ford Motor, High Volume Takes Backseat to Profits," *The Wall Street Journal*, 7 May 2004, p. A1.

[43] Yahoo! Finance website accessed on 3 December 2004.

[44] Yahoo! Finance website accessed on 3 December 2004.

[45] Thomas T. Nagle and Reed K. Holden, *The Strategy and Tactics of Pricing*, Prentice Hall, 1995, p. 208.

[46] "U.S. Sets Terms for Dialogue With Iran," George Gedda, The Associated Press, 30 December 2003.

[47] "Earthquake rocks Iran city," The Associated Press, printed in *The Union*, 27 December 2003, pg A7.

[48] Thanks to Stanford professor Samuel Chiu for this example.

[49] According to "Entering a new age of gender medicine," *Consumer Reports On Health*, Consumers Union, December 2003, p. 1, "…most of the prescription drugs withdrawn from the market in the recent four-year period caused more adverse affects (mostly heart-related) in women than in men. Chances are they never would have been approved had researchers closely examined data from women."

[50] "Where women's care fall short," and "What's a man to do?" *Consumer Reports On Health*, Consumers Union, December 2003, p. 5-9.

[51] John Berlau, "Leaders and Success: Ebony's John H. Johnson," *Investors' Business Daily*, March 26, 1998, p. A1, referenced in Dwight Lee and Richard McKenzie, *Getting Rich in America: 8 Simple Rules for Building a Fortune and a Satisfying Life*, New York: HarperBusiness, 1999, p. 184.

[52] For more on this, see http://www.maa.org/devlin/devlin_archives.html.

[53] See http://tchester.org/sgm/lists/lion_attacks_ca.html for a list of mountain lion attacks on people in California since 1890.

[54] See http://www.dogbitelaw.com/PAGES/statistics.html for more information on dog attacks in the United States. There are about two deaths per year in California from dog attacks.

[55] See http://www.dogbitelaw.com/PAGES/statistics.html and http://www.dfg.ca.gov/lion/ and http://www.dfg.ca.gov/lion/outdoor.lion.html.

[56] "Getting it 'Dead Wrong.' So, how fouled up are the nation's spy agencies? Oy." *U.S. News and World Report*, 11 April 2005, p. 32.

[57] "Top 200 prescription drugs by therapeutic category," *Med Ad News*, West Trenton, NJ, May 2002, p. 52.

[58] Peter L. Bernstein, *Against the Gods, The Remarkable Story of Risk*, John Wiley & Sons, New York, NY, 1996, p. 270.

[59] "Risky Business," *Wall Street Journal*, 24 October 2001, p. A1.

[60] *Wall Street Journal*, 15 March 2001, p. A11.

[61] Paul Hawken, Amory Lovins, and L. Hunter Lovins, *Natural Capitalism*, Little, Brown and Company, Boston, MA, 1999, p. 90.

[62] "To Win the Loyalty Of Your Employees, Try a Softer Touch," *Wall Street Journal*, 26 January 2000, p. B1.

[63] October 25, 1992 game with the final score Cowboys 28 and Raiders 13.

[64] David R. Henderson, *The Joy of Freedom: An Economist's Odyssey*, Prentice Hall, 2002, p. 37.

[65] Thanks to Stanford professor Ross Shachter for this example.

[66] "Hospice's Patients Beat the Odds, So Medicare Decides to Crack Down," *Wall Street Journal*, 5 June 2000, p. A1.

[67] "Hospice's Patients Beat the Odds, So Medicare Decides to Crack Down," *Wall Street Journal*, 5 June 2000, p. A1.

[68] "Hospice's Patients Beat the Odds, So Medicare Decides to Crack Down," *Wall Street Journal*, 5 June 2000, p. A1.

[69] "Early TIPS Corps Did More Harm Than Good in Hunt for Subversives," *Wall Street Journal*, 2 October 2002.

[70] See "Freedom And Education Versus 'Public' Schools," David R. Henderson, *The Joy of Freedom: An Economist's Odyssey*, Prentice Hall, 2002, p. 293.

[71] Lance Armstrong with Sally Jenkins, *It's Not About the Bike: My Journey Back to Life*, Berkley Books, New York, 2000, pgs 4, 57, and 87.

[72] Roger Fisher, William Ury, and Bruce Patton, *Getting to Yes: Negotiating Agreement Without Giving In*, Penguin, 1991.

[73] Adam Smith, *The Wealth of Nations*, The University of Chicago Press, 1976, originally published in 1776, p. 8-9.

[74] David R. Henderson, "The Case for Sweatshops," *Weekly Standard*, 7 February 2000, http://www-hoover.stanford.edu/pubaffairs/we/current/henderson_0200.html.

[75] Glenn Garvin, "View from the Garment Factory: We Need These Jobs," *Miami Herald*, 30 November 1997, p.1F.

[76] Ivan G. Osorio, "How the Anti-Sweatshop Movement Hurts the People It Claims to Help," *IPA Review*, Vol. 53, Issue 4, December 2001, p. 16. On the web at: http://www.ipa.org.au/files/Review53-4 How the antisweatshop movment hurts.pdf

[77] Paul Krugman, "In Praise of Cheap Labor," *Slate*, 20 March 1997, http://web.mit.edu/krugman/www/smokey.html

[78] Larry Rohter, "Hondurans in 'Sweatshops' See Opportunity," *New York Times*, 18 July 1996, p. A1.

[79] Nicholas D. Kristof, "Let Them Sweat," *New York Times*, 25 June 2002.

[80] Nicholas D. Kristof, *New York Times*, 14 January 2004.

[81] "Questions raised on medication's safety," The Associated Press, *The Union*, 1 May 2002, p. A1.

[82] "Ohno can still go down in history," The Associated Press. *The Union*, 23 February 2002.

[83] *Values & Visions, A Merck Century*, a book published by Merck & Co. in 1991 to celebrate its centennial, p. 32. Also, Remarks by Raymond V. Gilmartin, Committee for Economic Development, 16 October 2000 (see http://www.merck.com/newsroom/executive_speeches/101600.html)

[84] Reuters from the *London Times*, 24 April 2000.

[85] Paul Hawken, Amory Lovins, and L. Hunter Lovins, *Natural Capitalism*, Little, Brown and Company, Boston, MA, 1999, p. 111.

[86] "Russia's Floating Nuclear Graveyard, " *Discover Magazine*, July 2002, p. 10.

[87] You can have one of 52 possible cards for your first card, one of 51 possible cards for your second card, and so on. (You can't have two seven of diamonds, so the second number is 51 and not 52.) So for a five card hand, there are 52 x 51 x 50 x 49 x 48 = 311,875,200 possible hands if the order of the cards matters, which it doesn't. There are 5 x 4 x 3 x 2 x 1 = 120 ways to order a five card hand, so we divide 311,875,200 by 120 to get 2,598,960.

[88] 99.99977 percent equals 1 - 6 / 2,598,960.

[89] "Restrictions Eased Near Site of Japanese Nuclear Accident," CNN.com, 1 October 1999, http://www.cnn.com/ASIANOW/east/9910/01/japan.nuclear.01/

[90] "Twenty-One Hurt in Japanese Nuclear Accident," http://members.lycos.co.uk/digitalnews/page17.html

[91] http://www.clinteastwood.net/welcome.html

[92] Stanley Wells and Gary Taylor, *William Shakespeare, The Complete Works*, Clarendon Press, Oxford. Hamlet, Act 3, Scene 1.

[93] Actually, that isn't strictly speaking enough, at least to economists. Economists reserve the word "risk" for a situation where there's a known probability of each outcome and use the word "uncertainty" for a situation in which there are various probabilities of various outcomes but the probabilities are unknown.

[94] Aaron Wildavsky, "Riskless Society," *The Fortune Encyclopedia of Economics*, David R. Henderson editor, Warner Books, 1993, p. 431.

[95] *San Jose Mercury News*, March 1995, based on an analysis by Dun & Bradstreet of 800,000 small businesses.

[96] Brian Headd, economist for U.S. Small Business Administration. Quoted in *USA Today*, 18 February 2003.

[97] Here's how we got this. With a 1 percent risk for each of the 100 links, the probability that each link works is 0.99. So the probability that all the links hold is 0.99^{100}, or 0.37. Therefore, the probability that the chain breaks is 1 minus the probability that it holds, or 1 - 0.37, which is 0.63 or 63 percent.

[98] This rule of thumb is approximate. In 2001 and 2002, State Farm Mutual Automobile Insurance Company collected about $1.26 in premiums for every $1.00 they paid in claims. But State Farm also said that 2002 was a horrible year and warned of future rate increases. Source: 2002 Annual Report to State Farm Mutual Policyholders.

[99] Ronald A. Howard uses this term.

[100] Most economists use this term.

[101] "How to Ensure You Can Insure Your Home," *USA Today*, 7 June 2002, p. 3B. According to Insurance Information Institute estimate based on 1999 data.

[102] "It's a Great Idea if It Gets Off the Ground." *Wall Street Journal Startup Journal*, Peter Waldman. 2002.

[103] Jon Krakauer, *Into Thin Air*, Villard, 1997.

[104] In 1999, Mount Everest was found to be 29,035 feet high. Sources: "Climbing Everest, 48-year-old Nevada County woman makes attempt", *The Union*, 1 May 2003, p. C1 and "Learning about Mount Everest." See www.mnteverest.net and http://www.everestnews.com.

[105] To date, there have been 1,924 ascents of Mount Everest (more than 1,300 different climbers), and 179 people have died. The overall fatality rate is thus about 9% (fatality

rate is defined as successful summits compared to fatalities). Source: MountEverest.net. Website accessed on 9 January 2005.

[106] *The Fortune Encyclopedia of Economics*, David R. Henderson editor, 1993, Warner Books, p. 824 and http://cepa.newschool.edu/het/profiles/pareto.htm

[107] *Medicare Chart Book*, 2nd Edition, Fall 2001, The Henry J. Kaiser Family Foundation.

[108] "The Wealth Divide: An Interview with Edward Wolff," *Multinational Monitor*, May 2003, Vol. 24, No. 5.

[109] "Hamburger Joints Call Them 'Heavy Users' — But Not to Their Faces," *Wall Street Journal*, 12 January 2000, p. A1.

[110] Paul Hawken, Amory Lovins, and L. Hunter Lovins, *Natural Capitalism*, Little, Brown and Company, Boston, MA, 1999, p. 158 and The World Bank Group - http://www.worldbank.org/depweb/english/modules/economics/gnp/

[111] Paul Hawken, Amory Lovins, and L. Hunter Lovins, *Natural Capitalism*, Little, Brown and Company, Boston, MA, 1999, p. 191.

[112] "Almost Famous." *U.S. News and World Report*, 7 October 2002, p. 73.

[113] 2002 Music Industry Report Through Sales, 22 December 2002.

[114] Richard Koch, *The 80/20 Principle*, 1998, A Currency Book by Doubleday, p. 17.

[115] "In 1963, IBM discovered that about 80 percent of a computer's time is spent executing about 20 percent of the operating code. The company immediately rewrote its operating software to make the most-used 20 percent very accessible and user friendly, thus making IBM computers more efficient and faster than competitor's machines for the majority of applications." Richard Koch, *The 80/20 Principle*, 1998, A Currency Book by Doubleday, p 9.

[116] Computed from David Campbell and Michael Parisi, "Individual Income Tax Returns, 2000," Internal Revenue Service, Table 2, http://www.irs.gov/pub/irs-soi/00indtr.pdf

[117] "Iowa Agricultural Subsidies Aided Rich, Helped Family Farms Little, Study Says," *Wall Street Journal*, 14 January 2000, p A16.

[118] See Thomas Gale Moore, "Trucking Deregulation," in David R. Henderson, ed., *The Concise Encyclopedia of Economics*, http://www.econlib.org/library/Enc/TruckingDeregulation.html

[119] Paul Hawken, Amory Lovins, and L. Hunter Lovins, *Natural Capitalism*, Little, Brown and Company, Boston, MA, 1999, p. 140.

[120] John Cassidy, *Earthsearch*, A Kid's Geography Museum in a Book, Klutz, 1994, Palo Alto, CA, p. 84-85.

[121] The equivalent of 1,342,177.27 dollars is 134,217,727 pennies, which we estimate would weigh 840,000 pounds and would take about 18 trucks to transport. Please don't ship them to our house.

[122] Actually 323 times current annual worldwide production, assuming 200,000 grains per kilogram and 571 million metric tons produced annually (1997-1998) and half that amount produced during the time of the story. U.C. Davis Cooperative Rice Project. http://agronomy.ucdavis.edu/uccerice/STATS/faqs.htm

[123] Stephen Biesty, *Incredible Everything*, DK Publishing, 1997. p. 6.

[124] "Back Pain: Does anything work?" *Consumer Reports On Health*, Consumers Union, May 2000, p. 3.

[125] Paul Hawken, Amory Lovins, and L. Hunter Lovins, *Natural Capitalism*, Little, Brown and Company, Boston, MA, 1999, p. 245.

[126] Paul Hawken, Amory Lovins, and L. Hunter Lovins, *Natural Capitalism*, Little, Brown and Company, Boston, MA, 1999, p. 267.

[127] Paul Hawken, Amory Lovins, and L. Hunter Lovins, *Natural Capitalism*, Little, Brown and Company, Boston, MA, 1999, p. 268.

[128] Milton Friedman, presentation at Stanford University attended by Charles L. Hooper, circa 1989.

[129] Adam Smith, *The Wealth of Nations*, The University of Chicago Press, 1976, originally published in 1776.

[130] Emma Goldman , *My Further Disillusionment in Russia*, Doubleday, Page & Company, Garden City, NY, 1924.

[131] Professor Dennis Dalton of Barnard College/Columbia University. *Freedom: the Philosophy of Liberation*. Lecture Five. "Emma Goldman & the Anarchist Idea of Freedom." The Teaching Company. 1994.

[132] Professor Dennis Dalton of Barnard College/Columbia University. *Freedom: the Philosophy of Liberation*. Lecture Five. "Emma Goldman & the Anarchist Idea of Freedom." The Teaching Company. 1994.

[133] "No Bail for Arizona's Fire Suspect," CNN.com, 3 July 2002. (http://www.cnn.com/2002/LAW/07/03/arizona.wildfire.indictment/index.html).

[134] "Woman Indicted for Starting Colo Wildfire, *"The Washington Times*, 19 June 2002 (http://www.washtimes.com/upi-breaking/19062002-023551-5328r.htm).

[135] American Century prospectus, 1 May 2000, p. 8.

[136] "New Notre Dame Coach O'Leary Quits," AP, 14 December 2001 and University of Notre Dame Public Relations and Information, 17 December 2001 (http://www.nd.edu/~prinfo/news/2001/12-14.html).

[137] "USOC Head Resigns," The Associated Press, *The Union*, 25 May 2002, p. B4.

[138] "Hanssen Pleads Guilty to Spying for Moscow," CNN, 8 July 2001.

[139] This is one of the central ideas in Ayn Rand's book *The Fountainhead*.

[140] Review of *The Life of P.T. Barnum: Written By Himself*, Urbana: University of Illinois Press by John Mueller, *Reason Magazine*, March 2001.

[141] P.T. Barnum, *Art of Money Getting*, Applewood Books, Bedford, Massachusetts, 1999, originally published in 1880, p. 88.

[142] "Deception is Part of the Art of War. But Shhhhhh!" *Wall Street Journal*, 28 February 2002.

[143] *U.S. News & World Report*, January 27-February 3, 2003, p. 57.

Index

Index

Index

Index

Index

Index

Index

Index

Index

Index

Index